DATE DUE

Winning Without War

OTHER BOOKS BY AMITAI ETZIONI

Social Change: Sources, Patterns, and Consequences (editor)
(1964).

The Hard Way to Peace: A New Strategy (1962).

A Comparative Analysis of Complex Organizations (1961).

A Diary of a Commando Soldier (1952).

WINNING WITHOUT WAR

AMITAI ETZIONI

DOUBLEDAY & COMPANY, INC.
GARDEN CITY, NEW YORK
1964

Library of Congress Catalog Card No. 64-14279
Copyright © 1964 by Amitai Etzioni
All Rights Reserved
Printed in the United States of America
First Edition

For
Oren

ACKNOWLEDGMENTS

This volume was greatly helped by discussion with members of the Department of State, the Department of Defense, and the political sections of several American embassies in Latin America. A small grant by the Littauer Foundation enabled me to conduct interviewing in Washington. Jane McFadden and Robert McGeehan assisted me in preparing the material for this volume as well as in editorial matters. Donald G. Brennan and Philip Shellhaas commented on parts of the manuscript.

I benefited from comments of the participants of the Airlie House conference on Soviet Attitudes on Disarmament and Arms Control (July 1963), following a presentation of the main ideas dealt with in this book. The initiation of this volume was stimulated by discussions of the problems of war and peace at the 1962 summer institute of the American Academy of Arts and Sciences, of which I was a core-member.

INTRODUCTION

Since 1947, the United States has been adhering to a defensive strategy to counter expanding Communism. As world conditions have changed, the United States has modified its response. In some cases the adaptations have been fairly limited; in others, quite extensive; *but the over-all strategy has remained the same.* It is the central thesis of this book that the various piecemeal and segmental adjustments that have already been made *now point to a new over-all* approach. Only when the new approach, implicit in these measures, is faced squarely and explicitly will the full value of past innovations be realized, and the need for complementary ones be clear.

Americans correctly pride themselves on their pragmatic, common-sense approach, on avoiding all-embracing master plans. They tend to see new measures as improvements of old policy. But this orientation exacts an ever higher price as history moves farther away from the general pattern that prevailed in 1947. To face the 1960s and '70s effectively requires a new look—not only at the new trees, but at the new forest which has sprung up around them.

The working out of a Western strategy has been a prolonged endeavor. A defensive posture gradually evolved, in 1946 and 1947, after many rounds of reappraisal and long deliberations in the White House and State Department. It then had to be approved by Congress, explained to the American people, and accepted by the United States' allies. Then followed years of trial and error in working out details, producing the necessary hardware, and generally implementing the strategy. The Russians could not have been less cooperative; they tossed out challenges that kept the West in constant readiness over a protracted period of time. The large investments in the defensive position assumed since 1947, the great commitment to justify it to the American people, and the expectations generated among friends and foes alike, have entrenched the American position. To shift now to a new strategy is expensive and complex; it is likely to be avoided as long as possible. Strategies are not changed like jackets with the changing of the weather.

But the weather has changed to a degree that even the wisest and most farsighted policy-maker could hardly have foreseen in 1947. At that time the Soviet Union had suffered much devastation and was attempting to recover from a war during which it lost almost twenty million people. Its major industrial sectors were all but ruined under enemy occupation. America's economic capacity, on the other hand, was fully intact; its military establishment, although significantly reduced after the war, was undamaged; and it was the only country in possession of atomic weapons. With Germany and Japan defeated, Britain's resources all but exhausted, and France greatly weakened by years of occupation and internal dissension, the United States was the only world power.

Half a generation later, the Soviet Union is a highly developed industrial state with an economic growth rivaling, if not excelling, that of the United States; it is fully equipped with nuclear weapons and is a global power comparable to the United States. Meanwhile France has regained much of its power and is increasingly pursuing its own foreign policy, while the Soviets, for their part, are confronted with a China determined to follow an independent course. The underdeveloped countries, many of which were colonies in 1947, are now proud new nations acquiring weight in the global power scales. The days when two super-powers, each directing its own bloc, could overshadow the rest of the world are coming to a close.

At the same time, the social and economic transformation in the less developed countries is progressing at an ever-faster pace; no one can be sure which country will make tomorrow's headlines—Indonesia, Yemen, British Guiana—but it is clear that somewhere, somehow, the *status quo* will be disturbed.

Finally, the technology of weapons has been radically altered; in 1947 there was probably a total of not more than four atomic weapons in the world, while in 1963 the United States alone had about forty thousand nuclear weapons. In short, few military, political, or economic factors have remained the same in the seventeen years that have passed since the foundations of the present American strategy were laid.

Assessing tomorrow's events in yesterday's context is a quite common and especially detrimental practice. Once a context has been established, it is to be sure both psychologically economical and politically expedient to make new adjustments, in the old framework. But as the roads keep changing and the corrections on the old map accumulate, the chart becomes blurred. Frequent mishaps, based on misreading, warn us of more extensive troubles to come unless a fresh view is taken. It is then that drawing up a new map cannot sensibly be delayed much longer.

The American people have become increasingly dissatisfied with the global stalemate that has developed and United States strategy of containment and deterrence. Unable to bring freedom to people on the other side of the containment wall, maintaining its positions tenuously and at increasing cost, constantly facing the possibility of a major nuclear showdown, the United States is now searching for a strategy that has a higher yield and lower cost, that advances freedom more and risks survival less. Several steps have been taken that point to a way out of the present stalemate; others are more counterproductive than productive. Surely there are no easy solutions, and any change of strategy must be gradual; but there does seem to be a more effective way of advancing freedom and social justice and of maintaining peace than the line the United States is presently following. This book attempts to explore this other way.

The United States can observe and react more successfully to the constantly changing international situation if the trend of present events is examined and the range of new possibilities assessed; if, in short, our strategy is oriented toward the future rather than bound to the past. What do the next years harbor? What steps need to be taken now? Since it is becoming more and more apparent that the United States cannot mold the future in its own image, we must ask in what direction other states and groupings of states are moving. This is not to imply that history is predetermined, that some nations advance with the incoming tide while others recede in its ebb; but studying the contours of the waves—rather than vainly trying to redirect the tides—will allow the United States to select and follow more closely the course it wishes to navigate. The forces at work have never been more potent and fateful; the stakes have never been higher.

The overriding importance of the strategic context in which specific measures are evaluated should be emphasized, particularly in view of the American tendency to regard measures as complete in themselves. Psychologists have demonstrated that objects appear close or remote, light or dark, depending upon the context in which they are viewed—a baseball among basketballs seems small, among golf balls, large. The same holds true for international events. Some observers, for example, favor summit conferences on the ground that if the statesmen can be kept talking, they won't start fighting. Others firmly oppose such conferences on the grounds that they lower the guard of democratic societies and generate false hopes. Both sides should realize that the value of a summit conference depends on the context in which it occurs; it might be used to lull an opponent while preparing a surprise attack; it might serve to confirm agreements reached in carefully prepared, lower-level negotiations; or, if the sides are deadlocked, it might have little effect. Summit conferences, like any other specific tool of foreign policy, can be adequately appraised only if their context is delineated.

Several important new policies introduced by the Kennedy and by the Johnson Administrations can be effectively implemented only if they are more consistently employed, if other supporting measures are introduced, and if the wider context is more explicitly taken into account and presented to the voting public.

History is filled with examples of countries as great as the United States that, being wedded to past policies, were unable to cut themselves loose from outworn perspectives when confronted with new situations. Constantly trying to interpret new developments in old terms, they lost touch with reality and were left behind. The ancient Greeks, for instance, adhering to their small city-states, went under when faced by the rising super-power Macedonia. Today the accelerated change of societies, economies, technologies, and, above all, of international relations, makes the need for broad reappraisal more essential than ever. Accordingly, this volume is not an essay on what we want and how we might get it—an approach that all too often assumes that we can shape history largely as we desire if only we are wise enough or wishful enough. It is rather a study of international trends, American responses to them, the directions they indicate, and, most especially, the new context that must be comprehended before the West can develop an effective strategy for the sixties and seventies.

CONTENTS

CONTENTS

Chapter I

THE GLOBAL STALEMATE

In 1947 *Foreign Affairs* published an article stating many of the principles American foreign policy was to follow in the years to come. And little wonder, since it was an article by George Kennan, then director of the State Department Policy Planning Unit. In 1964 the West is still basically engaged in "a policy of firm containment, designed to confront the Russians with unalterable counter-force at every point where they show signs of encroaching upon the interests of a peaceful and stable world." The intention is still firmly to maintain the peace without feeding pieces of countries to the hungry bears, or without, on the other hand, having to hunt the bears down with an all-out posse. The aim is still to contain Communist expansion, in order, as Kennan put it, "to promote tendencies which must eventually find their outlet in either the break-up or the gradual mellowing of Soviet power."

There is a fairly explicit behavioral theory at the foundation of this foreign policy; it seeks to buy time for Russia to outgrow the immature behavior believed typical of societies with pre-industrial poverty and messianic ambition. It expects, through repeated frustration, to extinguish the undesirable drive for expansion. But as this approach was applied, it became increasingly evident that the instruments built for expansion and to counter expansion were dangerous; and the passive policy of containment has become unpopular among the American people. Already during the Korean hostilities General MacArthur argued that the United States should go beyond the North Korean border line and bomb the Chinese

"Manchurian sanctuary." His outspoken criticism led to his removal as U.N. commander; but his feelings were shared by quite a few Americans. In 1956 American dissatisfaction was again evident when the United States took no action to assist the Hungarian uprising, despite a long propaganda campaign beforehand encouraging "satellite" countries to revolt against Moscow's domination. More recently, such figures as Nelson Rockefeller and Richard Nixon have publicly stated that U.S. policy is stagnant, defensive, and devoid of positive results. It has been labeled a no-win policy in conservative Republican and Democratic circles, and in some liberal ones. Intended to frustrate the Russians, containment has frustrated Americans as well.

A review of international developments since 1947 suggests the gradual emergence of another approach, more balanced psychologically, and more promising politically. This approach seeks to provide constructive outlets for expansionist drives rather than trying to suppress them; to differentiate between acceptable behavior that is condoned or rewarded, and unacceptable actions, which it seeks to discourage and extinguish.

THE PERIOD OF DUOPOLY

The major changes in American foreign policy toward the Soviet bloc since 1947 have been changes of instruments and tactics, not of strategic goals. U.S. basic policy remained the stabilization, through a combination of containment and deterrence, of a division of the world between the two superpowers. The West in effect agreed not to challenge the Eastern sphere of influence, and posted notice that it would not tolerate penetration of its sphere. And it defined peaceful coexistence as acceptance of the existing division of the spheres of influence.

Even before the end of the war the line of demarcation be-

gan to be laid down; the Yalta Conference set an early precedent for the later pattern. Although Churchill and Stalin and
surely Roosevelt understood different things when they spoke
of "spheres of influence," a line was drawn through Europe,
with a Western and an Eastern side and no third area in between. The United States did not challenge the Soviet heartland (for instance, by bombing Moscow in the days of U.S.
atomic monopoly, as Bertrand Russell suggested in 1948),
nor did it free countries in the Communist orbit (as Mac-
Arthur favored). On the other hand, the countries and people
on the Western side of the containment line were granted
U.S. protection, whatever their military value. Allowing Communist encroachment in any place this side of the line was
and is viewed as encouraging it in other places.

In a succession of local crises the United States consistently endeavored to restore the state of affairs that existed
the day before the particular conflict broke out. Thus in
Greece in 1947 the United States fought a Communist take-
over, but did not extend the conflict into neighboring Yugoslavia and Bulgaria, which provided bases and supplies for the
Greek Communists; in Korea, it protected South Korea but
did not free North Korea, restoring the border at the 38th
Parallel. It defended two small islands a few miles off the
shore of the Chinese mainland, presumably this side of the
containment line, but it did not allow Chiang Kai-shek to try
to invade the mainland on the other side of the line. In West
Berlin it held the line again and again, without interfering in
East Berlin.

American reactions to more recent challenges in South
Vietnam and Cuba have the same character: if the Communists lay down their weapons in South Vietnam, on this
side of the containment line, the United States seems quite
willing to keep its hands off North Vietnam, on the other side
of the line; conversely, the presence of Russian ground troops
in Cuba does not so much threaten American security as it

undermines its postwar strategy.[1] The Communist bloc, according to this strategy, must be contained in the area it controlled when the strategy was formulated thirteen years ago.

The Korean War, in which this defensive strategy of restoring the *status quo* lost the support of large segments of the American public, is often viewed as the end of the policy of containment, and the election of Eisenhower to the presidency in 1952 as the advent of a new approach. Eisenhower and his Secretary of State, John Foster Dulles, did indeed expect to deter Communist aggression rather than counter it. Instead of holding the containment line with conventional troops, they hoped to preserve it by the threat of massive nuclear retaliation. While the threat was expected to stop Communist expansion, Dulles warned that if such expansion nevertheless occurred, the United States would no longer be committed to the stabilization line but would consider itself free to respond by pursuing the aggressor into his own territory, to "roll back" Communism, and liberate the people under its yoke. Clearly if this strategy of liberation had really been introduced, it would have been a basic change in Western foreign policy. Rather than seeking to defend an existing division of spheres of influence, the West would have sought to reduce and eventually to eliminate the Communist sphere, opening the door to the much-heralded American Century.

But when it came to a showdown, the Eisenhower Administration—despite many statements to the contrary—followed the containment line, as Truman's had before it and Kennedy's did after it. The decisive test came in Indochina in 1954, after the concept of rollback had been declared with great fanfare and its dynamic virtues widely publicized. The Communists in Indochina were largely indigenous forces; the flow of provisions from the Communist bloc was small and

---

[1] Strategy throughout this volume refers to a specific, systematic pattern of policy. The strategies discussed here are those of foreign policy, unless explicitly designated as military, economic, or some other kind of strategy.

difficult to document. The Communists benefited largely from the unenlightened colonial rule of the French in the area. Unwilling to employ the conventional troops necessary to suppress the Communist uprising, reluctant to be involved in a land-bound, Korea-type war, which he had just denounced, Eisenhower faced a choice between a nuclear strike (widely opposed by Western allies and world public opinion) and withdrawing. Since by 1954 the Russians had exploded nuclear devices and had a growing stockpile of atomic weapons, the prospect of a nuclear bombardment seemed not only morally and politically, but also militarily, less than attractive. So Eisenhower accepted a new containment line; far from trying to roll back the Communists beyond the old line, he settled for less than he had had before. Indochina was one of the very few places in the past fifteen years where the West was rolled back, where it had to agree to redraw the line separating the two spheres of influence in favor of the East. No wonder that after Indochina, containment, although still unpopular, was more entrenched than ever.

The Western response to the uprising in Hungary in 1956 and to the Hungarians' call for Western assistance further demonstrated that the West respected the Communist side of the containment line as much as it expected the Communists to respect its side. Not only was no Western help forthcoming, but Eisenhower assured Khrushchev that none would be. Before Western food parcels were sent through the Red Cross to Hungary, the United States sought the U.S.S.R.'s permission to do so. Thus the Republicans' term in office did not alter the basic strategy, though statements about it were modified for a while.

The development of the deterrence system, sometimes regarded as a basic strategy change, was actually a new set of means to implement the old line. Originally, deterrence was to be one-sided; Eisenhower planned to threaten nuclear bombardment rather than to deploy troops. But even during the short period that this seemed effective, it was completely tied to the containment line and intended to prevent transgressions of it. The development of Soviet nuclear weapons and means of delivery in the early and mid-fifties turned one-sided deterrence into a two-sided threat or "balance of terror." In a sense, this development did provide a new strategic goal: the West's aim was no longer simply holding the line but the prevention of all-out war. The net effect of mutual deterrence was to add a nuclear stalemate to the territorial one. It was and is expected to protect the two rival powers from a showdown, while they continue to spar along and around the containment line. Deterrence provides a nuclear "roof" on the interbloc conflict that prevents the sides from "jumping" each other as the frustrating tug-of-war continues. Politically the goal is still the same: to buy time until the Soviet bloc disintegrates or mellows, meanwhile protecting the Western spheres of influence and not challenging the Eastern ones. Since over the years the military forces intended for containment were used for deterrence, and vice versa, the two strategic goals were largely fused, and I refer to the combined effort as a strategy of duopoly—one that seeks neither monopoly of one power nor the free competition of many powers, but the freezing of the existing division of spheres of influence between two super-powers, each protecting its own viability without directly challenging that of the other.

THE RECORD OF DUOPOLY

Half a generation after its beginning, one cannot fail to be impressed by the tactical record of this approach. Although, as duopoly was implemented, the Communists were consolidating their positions in China and Czechoslovakia, since then by and large the line has been held. Years of Communist efforts yielded no more than a minor expansion, in Indochina, into countries on the line, and one country—probably only temporarily—behind the line, Cuba. In the same years the Communist bloc lost Yugoslavia. All other presumed Communist "victories," such as left-wing revolutions in Egypt and Iraq, or the increase in the neutralist tendencies of countries like Brazil and Cambodia, have not expanded the Communist bloc. In a long series of challenges on and behind the line, the West consistently administered its containment policy. NATO and the Marshall Plan helped restore Western European strength; aid to Greece, Turkey, and Iran in 1947 helped to hold those countries in the Western sphere of influence; and the 1948 airlift to West Berlin signaled the Western resolve to hold the line there. When the Communists seemed to leapfrog the line, the West successfully countered their efforts—in Guatemala in 1954, in Lebanon in 1958, and in the Congo in 1962. In numerous other places the presence of American forces indicated a commitment that had containing effects. Western military and economic aid to rim countries, such as Pakistan, India, Turkey, Thailand, and Japan, paid off in terms of the tactical goals of the prevailing strategy: the line was held for the most part; the Communist bloc has barely expanded in the last fifteen years. At the same time, the nuclear stalemate has maintained a precarious balance, and despite the growing dangers, mutual deterrence has so far fulfilled its function of preventing a nuclear war. Many observers even credit it with preventing wars of the World War II type: as the danger of being dragged into a nuclear conflict looms large, both super-powers respond cautiously to challenges that in earlier, less perilous periods might well have raised the flag of war. In short, the tactical record of duopoly is nothing short of remarkable.

EFFECTS ON THE SOVIETS: DOMESTIC AFFAIRS

But the question remains: how effective has duopoly been in attaining its strategic goals? Kennan's theory was roughly that the Soviet desire to consolidate and justify the totalitarian regime at home required depicting and to a degree creating a hostile international environment. Expansionism served that goal. By consistently and continuously frustrating that drive, the United States sought to "promote tendencies which must eventually find their outlet in either the break-up or the gradual mellowing of Soviet power."[2]

Containment offered what seemed to be a well-hedged bet: if the Soviet regime was weakening—because of economic deficiencies, alienation generated by the terrorist regime, disappointment with lack of ideological purity—containment would serve the West as a holding operation until the process was completed, and would contribute to it by preventing the consolidating effects of expansionist victories ("We are the wave of the future"). If the Soviet society was changing—because of the economic success that allows mass production of consumer goods, industrialization that leads to pluralism, ideological impurity which brings tolerance—then containment would serve as a holding operation for the West until the process advanced enough to modify the expansionist drive that presumably would no longer be necessary after domestic liberalization. At this stage, the time would be ripe to shift to a state of genuine peaceful coexistence with a power that would be much more similar to the West—quite unlike Stalin's police state. Then, both psychological and military disarmament could take place.

Since these hypotheses were formed, the study of international Communism and Soviet behavior has become a major discipline, and many volumes have been written on the sources of Soviet conduct and its dynamics. This is not the place to evaluate the findings and conclusions of this extensive scholarship, nor is it necessary for the more limited purposes at hand. The crucial point is that whatever position one takes on the development of Soviet society and foreign policy, containment seems, at least now, an inadequate response.

2 "The Sources of Soviet Conduct," *Foreign Affairs*, July 1947, p. 582.

Few experts on Soviet affairs still expect Soviet society to disintegrate from within. The economic, political, technological, and military achievements of the U.S.S.R. over the last fifteen years have more or less ruled this out. Nor does there seem to be much disagreement that some "mellowing" has taken place in domestic affairs since Stalin's death. There has been a decline in police terror and forced-labor camps, some increase in freedom of expression, and a rise in the standard of living. The major point of disagreement seems to be over how *permanent* these changes are and how far they will advance. On the one side there are experts who see a close relationship between a mature industrial society, pluralism, and political liberties, and who expect the U.S.S.R. to continue to "liberalize":

> Accompanying this process of industrialization, there has been a transformation of the Russian social structure. . . . The rapid and thorough modernization of the Soviet Union produced an elite of administrators, military officers, managers, technicians, scientists, artists—educated, skilled, proud of its accomplishments, and intensely patriotic. With the death of Stalin, the demands of this elite for a predictable and safe social and political order, and for the material amenities of life, made themselves felt with increasing effect. The reforms of the Khrushchev era—the mitigation of the terror, the lowering of the risks of social and political life, the industrial decentralization, the emphasis on consumption, the loosening of controls—are all aspects not of a tactical maneuver, but of significant changes in the Soviet system.[3]

On the other side, there are those who believe that whatever changes have taken place could be reversed by Khrushchev himself, or by a Stalinist successor; that dictatorships

[3] Gabriel A. Almond, *The American People and Foreign Policy* (New York: Praeger, 1960), p. xvi.

do not voluntarily relinquish their totalitarian control; and that a regime that undertakes mass production of consumer goods is reinforced and not undermined by the rise in the standard of living.

There appear to be three major limitations that govern loosening of Stalinist controls in the Khrushchev era. First, the areas of permitted controversy are apparently determined from above, in the end probably by Khrushchev. The discussions are begun, and sometimes brought to an end, by a signal from the top level of the system. Second, the licensed controversies deal with partial aspects of the system—with how to overcome the apathy of the peasants, or how to make Soviet literature more interesting to its readers—not with its basic goals and central methods. . . . Finally, the permitted topics of discussion touch very lightly or not at all on Soviet foreign policy. . . . The Soviet public and even the party are not encouraged to go beyond a general attitude of trusting Khrushchev. They are not expected to discuss concrete events and issues of world politics in any terms except those set by the Party's monopoly of information and indoctrination. This tactic was frequently applied by Stalin, but Khrushchev has, I believe, surpassed his teacher in this field.[4]

Professor Philip E. Mosely refers to these changes as those of "style" and suggests that the first real test of the change has yet to come. To this another expert on Soviet affairs has added: "This de-Stalinization is not the result of irresistible pressures of social forces nor of irreversible imperatives of continued industrialization. It depends on more subjective factors, since even so crucial a decision can be willfully reversed at any time by the political leadership. . . ."[5]

[4] Philip E. Mosely, "Soviet Foreign Policy since the 22nd Party Congress," *Modern Age*, Fall 1962.
[5] Herbert Kitvo, "The Dynamics of DeStalinization," APSA, Washington, D.C., September 5, 1962.

Between these two poles one can find a variety of middle positions estimating the significance and, particularly, the degree of permanence of the changes that have taken place in Soviet society.

Without judging the validity of these positions, one can safely state that in any case containment is no longer an appropriate strategic posture. This statement does not rest on a claim that Western foreign policy did not change the U.S.S.R. "enough" over the last fifteen years. No serious advocate of containment has suggested that the West could determine internal Soviet developments. But it was assumed that the behavior of the West would have some effect on these processes, and that its power could be used to promote tendencies desirable to the West and conducive to peace. The question therefore is whether containment and, more generally, duopoly provide the best guidance to whatever limited effect the West can have on domestic developments in the U.S.S.R. Those who view the changes that have already taken place in Soviet society as significant and unlikely to be reversed must now explore the question: *when will the post-containment period start, and what provisions have to be made for it?*

Containment, according to one interpretation, was actively to encourage internal changes in the U.S.S.R.; according to another, passively to hold the West's position and buy time, in any event *until* the U.S.S.R. mellowed. If the U.S.S.R. *is* liberalizing, the West ought to indicate how far liberalization has to progress before the U.S.S.R. will be considered "mellow," and under what conditions and in what institutional forms the Cold War and the arms race might be replaced. The West, under these conditions, ought to present a much more elaborate, concrete, and comprehensive picture of the kind of world it is seeking than it has provided so far. (Some such indication is given in the U.S. proposal for complete and general disarmament; still this proposal deals largely with questions of verification and enforcement of disarmament and has little to say about the nature of the political community the United States is aiming for and the place it sees in this community for nonaligned, as well as "mellowed" Communist, societies.) A more specific image of the world of peaceful coexistence is particularly necessary since the measures sporadically suggested are likely to make more sense to Russians, neutrals, and allies if placed in such a context.

Those who view the changes in the Soviet Union as unstable and expect an attempt at neo-Stalinist reaction sooner or later, must ask themselves two quite different questions: Is duopoly the most effective way the West can use its limited influence on Soviet affairs to counter such a revision? And is duopoly still a supportable strategy if fifteen years of application have not seen either the disintegration of the U.S.S.R. or a genuine change of its regime? Is there no strategy better able to serve Western objectives and to help avert regressions in the Soviet Union?

EFFECT ON THE SOVIETS: FOREIGN AFFAIRS

In discussing the relationship of American foreign policy to domestic developments in the Soviet Union, we have progressed—as has duopoly—on the assumption of a close correspondence between Soviet domestic developments and Soviet foreign policy. There is, however, much room for doubt that such a direct relationship exists in any nation. Indeed, there are many instances of drastic changes in foreign policy that involved surprisingly little change in internal social or political structure. Britain's democratic procedures have changed little from the days when it was the mother country of an empire stretching from Canada to New Zealand, although it is now largely a nation like others, without an empire. And the degree to which they have changed cannot be accounted for by the loss of an empire. The structure of U.S. society hardly changed as its foreign policy shifted from isolationism before World War II to the postwar position of a global power with far-flung interests and commitments. Similarly, few internal changes occurred in either the U.S.S.R. or the United States as their relationship shifted from World War II alliance to Cold War hostility. On the other hand, drastic changes have occurred without bringing significant changes in foreign policy. For instance, the relations of Farouk's and Nasser's Egypts to Israel are quite similar, and the foreign policies of Czarist and Soviet Russia have much in common. Close ties between the structure of a society and its foreign policy cannot be assumed, and the effect of duopoly on Soviet foreign policy therefore needs to be examined independently of whatever effect it might have had on internal Soviet evolution.

Many experts rely heavily, in their studies of Soviet foreign policy, on analyses of speeches and publications by Soviet leaders. Since the positions expressed in these sources often lag behind changes in foreign policy and in quite a few cases are more bellicose than the policy they seek to justify, the nature of the Communist expansionist policy is misinterpreted again and again. For a long period, for instance, the United States considered an all-out Soviet attack, if not on America then in Europe, the most likely form of Soviet challenge. A study of *actual* Soviet behavior rather than of foreign-policy pronouncements suggests that the Soviets were and are expansionist, but that their willingness to risk war with the West was and is, the Stalin period included, quite limited and probably declining. While the Communist camp did, and in my judgment does, seek to extend its way of life and form of government to non-Communist peoples, it was and is willing to attempt this only at low risks, and—which is crucial—*the level of violence considered "low-risk" has continuously declined over the years.*

The Soviets put the protection of the achievements of their revolution at the top of the list of their foreign-policy objec-

tives. This can be interpreted cynically: the Russians can be
depicted as using the Communist parties in other countries
exclusively to forward their own national goals; or it can be
viewed neutrally, as the natural and common tendency of a
nation to put its national interest, especially its survival, first,
while it may still be genuinely committed to other values
such as world socialism; or it can be said that a Russian Communist is likely to feel that if the U.S.S.R., the "homeland
of socialism," is lost, the Communist movement itself will
be undermined. Whatever interpretation one accepts, the result remains the same: the U.S.S.R. has been extremely reluctant to endanger its survival in its expansionist efforts.

SHIFTS IN MEANS OF EXPANSION

What has changed over the past fifteen years is not so much
the Soviets' willingness to take risks as the level of risks involved in the use of various kinds of instruments of foreign
policy to advance political goals. There are four basic categories: (1) The actual use of *nuclear arms,* which has not
occurred. (The tendency of both sides to threaten the use of
nuclear arms has also declined over the years.) (2) *Armed
invasion,* including mass shipment of volunteers from one
country to participate in a civil war in another. (3) Reliance
on indigenous forces with some provisions from the Communist-bloc countries, referred to as *armed subversion.*
(4) The use of political, educational, and economic means,
referred to as *nonarmed capabilities.* These means of expansion differ in the visibility of their deployment and in
the number of casualties they are likely to cause in a given
situation. In general, the greater the visibility and the larger
the number of casualties, the more likely the aggressor is to
be identified and the conflict to escalate. *The central change
in Soviet conduct of foreign policy seems to be toward exclusion of armed invasion, less use of armed subversion, and
greater reliance on nonarmed capabilities.*

In the first postwar years, from 1945 to 1947, the Soviet Union was particularly anxious to establish friendly governments in neighbor states. It did not hesitate to use the Soviet Army, which had liberated these countries from Nazi occupation, to assist in the establishment of Communist or Communist-controlled governments in Hungary, Bulgaria, Poland, Rumania, and East Germany. On the eastern frontiers, the Soviets extended their control into Mongolia, Sinkiang, the Kurile Islands, and North Korea.

Although there were large and effectively organized Communist parties in Italy and France, attempting to take over these countries was considered too risky. The formation of NATO and the Berlin airlift seem to have indicated to Stalin that further westward penetration would involve more risk than he was willing to take, though some of his advisers probably favored more adventurous moves.[6] It should be emphasized that the cessation of armed expansion into Western Europe was not decided upon because the Russians were shown to be militarily inferior on the battle grounds, but because of the high risk involved in testing their strength. Few observers believe that the infant NATO of 1949, in its initial organizational stages, could have stopped an all-out attack by Soviet troops, or that West Berlin could have been defended militarily at that stage. Nor was it certain that the West would have used atomic weapons for its defense at this time. There was, however, the *possibility* that the United States would engage in a conventional or atomic war. Stalin preferred not to take the risks involved in exploring the extent of the U.S. commitment in Europe. Instead, the front of the Communist challenge was shifted to the Far East, where, Stalin felt, the West was less committed. But neither there nor in any other subsequent place were Russian troops en-

6 For an account of the evolution of the Soviet strategic outlook in this period see Marshall D. Shulman, *Stalin's Foreign Policy Reappraised* (Cambridge: Harvard University Press, 1963).

gaged in taking over a territory that was on the Western side
of the containment line. (On Cuba, see below.)

The 1950 invasion of South Korea by North Korean troops
was the last instance when Communist troops of a Russian-
controlled country engaged in an outright invasion. Moreover,
several Western observers have suggested that Stalin agreed
to the invasion only because he thought the West had written
South Korea off, or at least was not committed to its defense;
in other words, he thought the risk was low.[7] In any event,
no Russian ground troops were used and even later, when
U.S. troops (under the U.N. flag) were fighting on the side
of the South Koreans, the Russians did not become directly
engaged; the volunteers who fought on the side of the North
Koreans were Chinese. When the battle turned against the
Communists, Stalin preferred to forego efforts to help the invaders—direct Russian involvement *might* have escalated to
world war, a risk he was not ready to take.

Again and again the Communist camp let tempting opportunities pass by—in Iran in 1953, in Syria and Egypt in
1956, in Iraq in 1962—avoiding the risks involved in massive
military intervention from the outside. This self-limitation was
observed even when the other side did send troops. In 1963,
for instance, the United States was assisting the Diem government in South Vietnam with over fourteen thousand military
personnel and large quantities of supplies and weapons; no
Russian or Chinese troops came to the help of the indigenous Viet Cong, and only limited military supplies were sent
to them. The Viet Cong had to rely largely on their homemade weapons or those captured from the American-supplied
Diem troops, though North Vietnam provided training bases
and some supplies.

The policy of taking low risks and providing low visible aid,

[7] Vernon V. Aspaturian, "Soviet Foreign Policy," in Roy C. Macridis
(ed.), *Foreign Policy in World Politics* (Englewood Cliffs, N.J.: Prentice-
Hall, 1962), p. 146.

while the other side stands out as the one sending troops and massive shipments of arms, has some advantages, especially as far as public opinion is concerned, which may explain in part why the Communists prefer it. They also seem to be more successful at armed subversion than the democratic countries are in countering it (though the West has lately improved its capability to wage this kind of warfare). Whatever the motivation, after the Korean invasion the Communists refrained from using the more escalation-prone methods of expansion: outright invasions and massive shipments of volunteers and arms. Cuba seems, but in fact is not, an exception.

The Communist take-over of Cuba has become a highly charged subject, but the sad fact is the Communists gained control without firing a shot. They did not trust Castro during the period of his guerrilla activities, and only after he overthrew the Batista regime and established his control did they join forces with him; they took Cuba over gradually, without a coup, without an armed showdown. Russian troops were sent to Cuba after the 1961 attempt by CIA-guided Cuban exiles to overthrow Castro's government. The troops, like earlier shipments of conventional arms, were sent at the request of the established government of Cuba. Thus this positioning of troops cannot be considered an invasion force.

The Soviet shipment of missiles to Cuba has been given a large variety of interpretations, and is for many people a major point in the argument against the view advanced here that Soviet foreign policy follows a low-risk line. It might, however, be viewed rather as an exception, a concession to the military or to the "Chinese" faction in Russia. Another interpretation that makes sense in terms of the preceding analysis, is that Khrushchev thought little risk was involved. The United States has positioned missiles in countries closer to Russia than Cuba is to the American mainland. Note, too, that no actual violence was involved. Most important, when confronted with the American blockade and a near-ultimatum to remove the missiles or face the danger of war, Khrushchev preferred retreat to the risk of holding out.

According to a report by the Center for International Studies at the Massachusetts Institute of Technology, "The change in Soviet strategy began to take shape in the summer of 1951, and rapidly gathered momentum after Stalin's death in March, 1953. This strategy recognized that, whatever Communist gains from the Korean war may have been, the American and United Nations reaction to overt Communist aggression was, on the balance, exceedingly costly to the Soviets; and that there were greater possibilities for the extension of communism by political, psychological, and economic means."[8]

In the immediate postwar years the Soviets encouraged the use of violence by local Communist parties in their efforts to gain control of Asian governments. The Indonesian Communist Party was one of the first to rebel, in 1948, and one of the first to lay down its arms and turn to political activities along constitutional lines.[9] The Indian Communist Party engaged in limited guerrilla warfare under Ranadive. The Japanese Communist Party tried its hand at terrorism in 1950. In the Philippines, a Communist armed rebellion, led by Luis Taruc, subsided late in 1952. The party in Burma put down its arms at about the same time, and the one in Malaya followed suit soon after.

The transition from reliance on arms, rebellion, and direct action to participation in the politics of the countries took

[8] The Center for International Studies, Massachusetts Institute of Technology, "The Historical Background of United States Foreign Aid," in De-Vere E. Pentony (ed.), *United States Foreign Aid: Readings in the Problem Area of Wealth* (San Francisco: Chandler, 1960), p. 19.

[9] See Bernard S. Morris, "Recent Shifts in Communist Strategy: India and South-East Asia," in John H. Kautsky (ed.), *Political Change in Underdeveloped Countries* (New York: Wiley, 1962), p. 297.

place neither overnight, nor simultaneously, but in all these nations the new line was advanced by 1952 and fully endorsed by 1956 as "the peaceful road to socialism," to be traveled together with, rather than over the bodies of, the "bourgeois-national" governments. Progress was now to be attained by cooperation with non-Communist parties and social groups rather than exclusively with workers and peasants. To win the cooperation of these parties and groups, the use of terror and armed rebellion was sharply downgraded, and, in most countries, ruled out as an instrument of political action. When necessary, as it was in India and Japan, Moscow intervened with the local Communist parties, to support the factions that favored the new line and to overcome the "left deviationists" that held to the old and violent one.[10] The same trend was manifested recently in Cuba, where Moscow was reported in 1963 to have exerted pressure on Castro not to train other Latin Americans in armed subversion (though nonviolent maneuvers have not been discouraged). "Peaceful coexistence requires not abdication of the war of ideas," Khrushchev emphasized. As one Western authority put it, "It has been the Soviet belief in recent years that the 'liberation' [of the less developed countries] can best be achieved by supporting—politically and economically—independence movements."[11]

According to figures supplied by the Bureau of Intelligence and Research of the U. S. Department of State, there was practically no Soviet foreign aid prior to 1954. Only $13 million was spent by the Russians in grants or credits in 1955.

[10] In February 1948 Stalin was so concerned about American power and Soviet vulnerability that he reproached the Yugoslavs about the Greek civil war: "What do you think, that . . . the United States, the most powerful state in the world—will permit you to break their line of communication in the Mediterranean Sea! Nonsense. And we have no navy. The uprising in Greece must be stopped, and as quickly as possible." Shulman, op. cit., p. 285, n. 16, citing Milovan Djilas.

[11] H. J. P. Arnold, Aid for Developing Countries (Chester Springs, Pa.: Dufo Editions, 1962), p. 94.

The amount jumped to $365 million in 1956, and increased to
$403 million in 1959, where it leveled off. It was about the
same in 1963. In the same period the ratio of Soviet military
aid declined proportionately. In 1955, close to 75 per cent of
the total aid given by the Soviet bloc was military; in 1957,
less than half; in 1960, less than a quarter ($58 million out
of $236 million).[12] At the same time, the Soviet bloc in-
creased its technical assistance to underdeveloped countries.
In 1958 it sent about 4500 technicians; in 1960 the number
had grown to 7900 in twenty-three underdeveloped countries,
of whom 6510 were nonmilitary specialists. By 1962 the number had further increased to 8400. According to reliable Western sources, these technicians generally refrained from subversion, concentrating instead on their proper functions.[13]

The Soviet bloc has also greatly increased its trade with
underdeveloped countries, as the following figures, which
compare the amount of trade in the years 1954 and 1958,
show:

	1954	1958
Soviet Union	$215 million	$676 million
Communist China	$216 million	$409 million
European Communist nations	$438 million	$1036 million

The trade of the Communist bloc as a whole with underdeveloped countries increased from 1954 to 1958 by more
than 143 per cent. By 1962 Soviet trade alone totaled $1200
million with the less developed areas.

Part of this trade is strictly economic; the Soviets, for instance, mass-produce machine tools, which allows them to

[12] By early 1960 Communist-bloc countries had extended $3800 million
in credits and grants to less developed areas; of this total, $800 million was
for military assistance—the other $3000 million was for economic purposes.
[13] Arnold, *op. cit.*, p. 114.

sell machines of adequate quality to underdeveloped countries
at a fraction of the price these machines cost in the West.[14]
Part of the trade is highly political: for instance, when U.S.
relations with Cuba deteriorated in 1960, imports of Cuban
sugar were restricted; shortly thereafter the U.S.S.R. agreed
to buy most of the sugar the United States had refused. Western observers tend to emphasize the political use the Russians make of their trade (though the Cuban example shows
that the West also uses this technique).[15] In any case,
whether it is "economic" or "political," as far as the
changing means of Soviet foreign policy are concerned, increased reliance on trade, coupled with the reduction of the
use of arms, is surely welcome, and in tune with the general
pattern toward less reliance on means of violence to keep the
risk of war low.

In addition to increases in trade and in economic and technical assistance, the Communist bloc has greatly increased its
propaganda activities in recent years. In the field of radio
broadcasting, Communist-bloc international transmissions increased from about 609 hours per week in 1948 to 1675 in
1954; by the end of 1962 total weekly broadcasts had reached
3846 hours. Transmissions are sent in all the major languages of the world and in such less-known tongues as
Pushtu in the Middle East and Hausa in Africa; Communist
radio stations even broadcast in Esperanto. The Russians
have also stepped up the sending of films and exhibits to
other countries, exchanges of cultural delegations, and the
publication of foreign-language newspapers, booklets, and
pamphlets.

[14] Seymour Melman, *The Peace Race* (New York: Ballantine Books,
1961), p. 4.
[15] Willard L. Thorp, "American Policy and the Soviet Economic Offensive," in Philip E. Mosely (ed.), *The Soviet Union 1922–1962: A Foreign
Affairs Reader* (New York: Praeger, 1963), p. 326.

PARALLEL SHIFTS IN IDEOLOGY

Along with these changes in Communist conduct have gone ideological revisions reflecting the transition in emphasis from violent to nonviolent means of expansion. In the late 1940s war was considered not only inevitable but quite imminent; by the early 1950s Stalin admitted that war, while inevitable, was no longer an immediate danger; and in the mid-1950s came the pronouncement by the Soviet leadership that war between the Socialist and Capitalist camps was not inevitable at all. Along with this important doctrinal change, it was declared that Western "encirclement" of the Soviet Union was terminated and that henceforth the Communist camp was considered permanently secure, surrounded by friendly states in Europe and Asia. Support for "wars of national liberation" remains a keynote of Communist policy. But while it might be said that violence as a means of foreign policy has not been given up, it is not considered, either ideologically or practically, a necessary element of that support. As the Communists see it, they sent no arms to Cuba until its government requested them; and they sent no arms to Laos and South Vietnam until the Americans did.[16]

The central change that has occurred is not in Soviet society or in its expansionist goals, although these have changed, *but in what is considered a high and a low risk.* Acts such as outright invasion and armed subversion, which in the first postwar years could have been carried out with some degree of impunity (and thus were low risks) would now almost surely trigger a war and hence are considered high risks. War at any level is deemed more hazardous than before because of the danger of escalation, whereas the use of nonarmed capabilities is favored as the least volatile means of expansion. An

[16] See Dan Kurzman, *Subversion of the Innocents* (New York: Random House, 1963), p. 501. See also C. L. Sulzberger, in *New York Times*, April 24, 1963.

all-out strike, which might be considered if other expansionist means are frustrated, seems illogical under the balance-of-
terror (or deterrence) system. Hence, in my judgment, the
Soviets are pressed by the combination of containment and
deterrence to limit their expansionist efforts largely to nonarmed capabilities, though other means are not categorically
excluded.

TOWARD AN OUTLET SYSTEM

Containment and deterrence are often proclaimed successful because the Soviet Union has effected little expansion
over the last ten years and the decade was unshattered by
nuclear war. *But this is to confuse tactical goals with strategic
ones,* or to claim *post hoc*—in the face of strategic failure—
that the tactical success was all the West was aspiring to in
the first place. A central purpose of duopoly was to counter
Soviet expansion in order to bring to an end the Soviet expansionist drive and allow for genuine peaceful coexistence.
As the balance of terror has been added to the stalemate,
viewing duopoly as a permanent, rather than a transitional,
policy has become dangerous in itself.

Duopoly implicitly offers a deal to the Russians: if they
will accept the division of the world into an East and a West,
and refrain from interfering in the affairs of third countries in
any way, genuine peaceful coexistence can be worked out. In
1963 J. W. Fulbright, chairman of the Senate Committee on
Foreign Relations, put it in a way Kennan might well have
used in 1947: that ". . . it is not communism which is at
issue between the Soviet Union and the West but Communist
imperialism and that, insofar as it renounces expansionist and
subversive ambitions, the Soviet Union can enjoy a safe and
honorable national life without threat or danger from the
West."[17] This offer requires acceptance of the *status quo* by

[17] Clayton Lectures, given at Tufts University, April 29, 1963.

a dynamic global power, and expects that the Communists will refrain from responding to the call of anticolonial and revolutionary forces in the three underdeveloped continents; that is, stop supporting "wars of national liberation," *even with nonviolent means*. It might be asked if it is realistic to expect such a change in Soviet aspirations, and if, in fact, such change is necessary to Western goals. Would not providing legitimate outlets for Soviet ambitions and dynamism, to rechannel rather than to try to suppress them, be more responsive to the needs of the global social revolution, less apt to lead to nuclear war, and just as or more satisfactory to the West?

It has been argued that the whole purpose of containment is to buy time and that to attempt anything more specific is naïve. But as more and more time is bought, the price of waiting goes up. While the Anglo-Saxon countries of the West may be content to "muddle through" and deal with particular situations as they come along, the underdeveloped nations of Asia, Africa, and Latin America are neither so confident nor so patient as the West; they look for rapid and positive development and anxiously seek a blueprint to relate their aspirations of today to the world of tomorrow. More specific Western images of the future are called for, both to indicate acceptable outlets for Communist ambitions and to offer the new world a more effective alternative to the Marxist-Leninist approach than one that merely muddles through, avoiding the worst rather than actively pursuing the better.

What kind of international system might provide a fairly safe outlet for the Communist drive? The automobile market seems to supply an analogue, for illustrative purposes. Imagine two super-firms competing over the car market; one firm seeks to capture a larger and larger share of the market; the other firm follows a defensive policy, trying to hold on to its share. The competition is waged, let us assume, through changes in quality and in price; that is, the expanding company attempts to cut into the market of the other by offering automobiles of higher quality for lower prices. The defensive firm counters by matching the offers of the expanding firm. Each company has long since given up any realistic hope of pushing the other to bankruptcy and capturing the whole market for itself, though some of the executives—at least when they talk to the press—still ritualistically repeat such a hope. Both companies realize that price wars are ruinous for both sides, and that the buyers do not particularly benefit from them, since, once they are over, the companies tend to make up for their losses by producing cars that are more expensive and poorer in quality, and raising the prices of parts needed for repairs. Quality contests, in which each firm tries to excel over the other, are also expensive; but they are much more self-limiting and much less likely to win for the companies. The buyers' gains from such competitions are real ones; improved cars tend to stay improved even after a particular round of the intercompany strife is over.

For this reason it is more "rational" to limit interfirm competitions to quality contests, as indeed has been done for many years. But that is not the way all executives see it. The expansionist firm, set on gaining a larger share of the market, might any day turn to a price war if it finds it is making no progress in the quality contests; the defensive firm feels that its policy of attempting to make the other firm accept only a certain share of the market requires it not to allow even a small fraction of the market to shift. The defensive firm, it is hard to deny, might have to initiate a price war to retain its share of the market. Each firm realizes that by resorting to a price war it may undermine its own economic viability, but each hopes against reason that the price war will be limited and that it will be able to use it to show its determined commitment to whatever policy it favors, whether expansion or duopoly.[18] Theoretically there are several ways out of this potentially ruinous situation; in practice the range seems much more limited.

The solution advocated by the defensive firm is to formalize and legalize the existing allocation of the market; each firm will hold on to its part, and thus *both* price and quality wars will be stopped once and for all. The expansionist firm finds it difficult to accept this solution; it feels that some buyers, given a free choice, would prefer its product. Whether its ambitions are justified or its feelings valid does not matter; in either event it refuses to accept the duopolistic settlement, and the danger of a price war hangs in the air.

The frustration of the situation—either firm might suddenly find that a price war has begun—has led executives on both sides to consider an all-out price war to attempt to drive the other firm to bankruptcy; but this, the cooler heads on both sides point out, requires taking rather forbidding risks, actually endangering the very survival of both firms. Economics is not enough of a science and the information about the resources of the other firm is not adequate to provide any assurance about the outcome of such a showdown. In short, while this alternative is constantly considered, it has been avoided so far because it is believed too dangerous.

Still another approach, favored by a few, is to form a monopoly by merging the two super-firms. But practically everybody realizes that the two firms could never agree who the president of the merged corporation should be, what kind of cars it should produce, how to share the profits, etc. This solution is not dangerous, but seems unfeasible.

The favored solution builds on an extension of existing relations between the two firms. It seeks an agreement between them to avoid price wars, and the formation of a limited machinery that might prevent such wars, while allowing—within very broad limits—free competition over quality. Un-

---

[18] It should be made clear that I am not implying a moral symmetry between the two firms.

like the duopolistic approach, this one does not rule out competition or even some shifting by customers (obviously, the defensive firm would not agree to it unless it expected to be able to keep the bulk of its market by matching quality improvements of the other firm). Unlike all-out, cutthroat competition, it sets some limits on the competition, in the form of rules within which it is to be waged. *It should be emphasized that this competition under rules is not far removed from the existing relationship between the firms,* which in effect have limited themselves to quality contests and avoidance of price wars, but have formed no *explicit* agreement to so limit the competition, and provided no *assurances* that the implicit rules will be observed.

What does such a shift entail? (1) The participants have to change their view of each other from that of enemies locked in an unlimited conflict to one of rivals in a competition to be continued under rules. (2) Rules have to be formulated. (3) Machinery needs to be set up to effectively enforce whatever rules are agreed upon.

Economic history provides instances in which competition became so stabilized, for instance in the automotive and steel industries. It is my central thesis that the relationship of the United States and the U.S.S.R. is changing in such a way that they are gradually coming to fulfill the prerequisites of competition under rules, and that several limited steps have already been taken to shift away from cutthroat competition. The continuation and completion of the shift is by no means inevitable; it is both feasible and advisable. Each of the following chapters is devoted to the examination of one of the necessary elements of competition under rules on the international level. It will become clear that each prerequisite is already partially fulfilled; each needs to be further extended; and, most important, each is likely to gain the necessary support and be effectively implemented only as the emergent whole of the new international pattern is more widely recognized.

Chapter II

THE FUTURE OF BLOCS: CHINA AND FRANCE

The most important political factor making duopolistic strategy obsolescent and forcing revisions of both American and Soviet foreign policy is the decline of bipolarity. Yesterday it was the East versus the West; today, each camp recognizes divisions in the other and attempts to exploit them, while trying to cure the rifts in its own camp. Soon, the significant political forces undermining the cohesion of the blocs will be widely recognized and accepted; then the door will be open to a broad range of new possibilities. This will be the most important turning point since the postwar shift of the U.S.S.R. from a "strange ally" to the prime antagonist.

Yesterday, the West felt challenged by the specter of one united international Communist movement, directed from the Kremlin, and the Soviets suspended, after years of futile attempts, any serious hope of driving a wedge between the Western allies. Today, the bloc concepts of East and West still dominate the vocabulary of statesmen and many political maneuvers, but their relevance to international reality is steadily declining.

THE EAST: A MONOLITH TURNED POLYCENTRIC

Not so many years ago, any suggestion in the West of a significant Sino-Soviet dispute was met with disbelief or ridicule. The authors of a study published in 1957 for the distinguished Council on Foreign Relations under the title *Moscow-Peking Axis*, anticipated a durable union. Those who saw a rift developing were considered wishful thinkers, ill-informed, or the victims of Communist manipulation. "Even now surprisingly few politicians and political commentators in the West seem to have grasped the range and bitterness of the quarrel or to have understood its climacteric importance,"[1] despite the fact that in recent years there has been practically no international Communist gathering without some show of conflict between Moscow and Peking.

One of the early signs of a Sino-Soviet conflict came in 1959, when Khrushchev visited the United States. China, it became known later, objected to this trip, and chose the occasion for a violent press attack on the United States and Khrushchev's host, President Eisenhower. In the first half of 1960 the mutual criticisms were still indirect and opaque; China attacked Khrushchev's policy by criticizing Yugoslavia, and Khrushchev replied by commenting critically on Albania. The conflict broke into the open, as far as the Communist world was concerned, with bitter Soviet tirades against "left deviationism" in China, and vicious rejoinders from Mao against "modern revisionism" in Moscow. As early as 1956 the Soviets reduced their foreign-aid program to China; it has been estimated that no more than half the industrialization projects undertaken under the auspices of Sino-Soviet agreements have been completed. In 1957 and again in 1960 Russia reduced the flow of industrial supplies to China; and in 1960 most of the ten thousand Soviet technicians sent there were reported to have left. Russian credit extended to China to finance her imports was cut almost in half.

By the end of 1961 and especially in 1962, the conflict became evident to the outside world, with China and Russia competing for control of Communist parties in non-Communist countries, organizing pro-Soviet and pro-Chinese factions, trying to line up delegates to support their respective lines at

[1] Edward Crankshaw, in the *New York Times*, May 26, 1963.

congresses of the Communist parties, and circulating vast
quantities of literature accusing each other of numerous mis-
takes and offenses with a venom usually reserved for capitalists, imperialists, and their "social-democrat lackies." The Chinese delegation in Bern, Switzerland, serves as the Chinese
center for distribution of literature among the Communist
parties in Western Europe. When a passenger, flying from
Moscow to Peking, shifts to the Chinese airline at Irkutsk,
Siberia, he is given a choice of pamphlets, in half a dozen
languages, strongly denouncing the policies of Khrushchev.
Chinese travelers were accused by Russia of throwing them
out of the windows of the Moscow-Peking express.

The U.S.S.R. never met all the Chinese requests in foreign
aid, trade, or nuclear weapons. Among the specific Chinese
grievances were the high charges imposed for Soviet military
supplies provided during the Korean War (which the Chinese
said contrasted unfavorably with charges for supplies given
by the United States to the U.S.S.R. under the Lend-Lease
policy during World War II); Soviet efforts to control Chinese corporations through "joint" enterprises (which were
abolished); refusal to provide nuclear weapons and know-how;
plotting to seize part of Sinkiang; and Russia's refusal to help
China substantially following bad harvests that culminated in
a food crisis in 1961. Russia also refused to back Peking's ambition to "liberate" Taiwan by use of force.

Under Chinese advice and encouragement, in May 1961,
the Albanians forced the Russians to evacuate their submarine
base at Valona, depriving the Soviets of this Mediterranean
outlet. Several Russian consulates in China were closed.
China publicly denounced Russia's behavior in Cuba in 1962
as both too adventurous (in putting missiles there) and
"capitulationist" (in taking them out, under pressure). China
did not seek approval from the Russians for its attacks on India's border regions in the same period. The Russians, in turn,
provided India with arms during the course of the hostilities.

While Khrushchev promised Kennedy to support a neutral Laos and a cease-fire in the area, during their meeting in Geneva in 1961, China is believed to have given the Laotian pro-Communist forces weapons and training facilities and to have supported the resumption of fighting in Laos in mid-1963, against Russia's wishes.

To be sure, conciliatory moves have been attempted. All parties, including the Chinese, signed a joint statement after the 1960 Congress of Communist Parties to paper over the conflict. The statement expressed primarily the Soviet views on the disputed points, but made a few concessions to the Chinese. For example, the possibility of achieving power by a "peaceful transition" without civil war (the Soviet view) is emphasized, but it is also pointed out that the possibility of a nonpeaceful transition must be kept in mind (the Chinese position).[2] Earlier conciliatory moves included Russia's relinquishment of its control of railroads in Manchuria and the return to China of Port Arthur; the liquidation of Soviet shares in Chinese corporations; Khrushchev's visit to Peking at the head of a high-level Soviet delegation; and a good-will tour of Russia by Liu Shao-chi. In February 1961, upon the arrival of the Russian editor of *Kommunist* in China, Radio Peking still played the Soviet cantata, "Forever we are together."[3] More recently, in July 1963, Soviet and Chinese delegations, headed respectively by party Presidium member Mikhail A. Suslov and Deputy Premier Teng Hsiao-ping, held a series of "unity" talks in Moscow which, it appeared, came to naught.

Temporary pauses in the intramural conflicts among the Communists are by no means inconceivable, especially following the retirement or death of Khrushchev or Mao. The advent of a neo-Stalinist successor in the U.S.S.R. might help

[2] G. F. Hudson, Richard Lowenthal, and Roderick MacFarquhar, *The Sino-Soviet Dispute* (New York: Praeger, 1961), pp. 174 ff.

[3] *Ibid.*, p. 37.

to bridge the rift; or an agreement might be reached to grant
China a partial veto power on Soviet-led foreign policy of the
bloc; or the U.S.S.R. might agree to consult with China before any major act. Depending upon such factors as the nature
of the leadership in the two capitals, the trends of world affairs as they seem to reflect the efficacy of either the Soviet
or the Chinese approach, and the degree to which Peking feels
itself dependent on the military and economic support of
Moscow, the dispute might in the short run present a series
of ups and downs, with periods of cooperation followed by
renewed conflict. But in the long run, a complete healing of
the rift is most unlikely.

The roots of the conflict run far and deep. China, like
Yugoslavia and unlike most other Communist states, was won
over to Communism largely by indigenous forces and without the help of the Soviet Army. Russia was never anxious
to see a major power on its thinly populated eastern borders.
Stalin advised Mao in 1945 that the time was not ripe for a
revolution, and gave him little assistance. The Soviet Union
maintained correct relations with the Nationalist government
of Chiang Kai-shek almost until the time that Mao's forces
established control of the mainland. This Russian approach
not only left a residue of bitter memories in China; it
rendered the Chinese Communist Party independent of control by the Soviet party, and China free of the Soviet Army,
the two agencies through which Moscow exercises most of its
control over Communist countries.

Ideological disputes of the kind that has developed between Russia and China are rarely if ever completely recon-
ciled. Essentially they are formulated in terms of heresy and
orthodoxy: China is accusing Russia of compromising the
basic tenets of Marxism-Leninism, in espousing ideas of
peaceful coexistence with capitalism (China is opposed to the
Geneva disarmament negotiations in general and to the test-
ban treaty in particular, as well as to settlement of the

Berlin issue); of supporting "national-bourgeois" governments to the detriment of local Communist parties, for instance in Egypt and Iraq (where Communists were jailed while Russia was providing military and economic aid to the government); and of undue fear of nuclear war. Mao does not favor courting a nuclear war, but he is less fearful that it might occur and favors taking more risks. Khrushchev did not fail to note that the Chinese favor the *Soviets* taking more risks; they have been rather cautious in selecting targets for themselves. If they are so courageous about Cuba, Khrushchev asked, why did they not take Hong Kong, next door? Yes, Khrushchev admitted, the West might be a paper tiger, but, he said sharply, it has nuclear teeth.

While the Chinese accuse the Soviets of "betraying" and "abandoning" the proletarian revolutionary movement, the Russians regard the Chinese as dangerous "adventurers" and "dogmatists" who fail to realize the changed world situation and are incapable of appreciating "creative Marxism-Leninism." An added irritation is the Chinese view of Russia as a "have" nation which is losing its revolutionary momentum and growing soft; the Chinese point out that, instead of directing its "surplus" resources to the help of less developed countries, Russia is raising its own standard of living.

Such conflicts between true believers and the establishment sometimes lead to a revival of orthodoxy in the establishment; sometimes they are prolonged until the younger true believers also mellow. The initial Soviet reaction to Tito's "heresy" was equally violent, but within a few years the U.S.S.R. adapted its views by declaring that there may be various roads to socialism, and the relations between the Russians and the Yugoslavs have gradually improved. The policy favored by China might come under the same heading as still another "path" to socialism. But, while both sides may grow accustomed to the rift, and even find some way to make a virtue out of conflict, this will by no means restore unity in the Communist camp. Official permission to deviate from the established line is a sign of weakness, not strength. Yugoslavia has not returned to the Kremlin fold; and China—potentially much more powerful, with greater world ambitions, more overpopulated and less developed—is far less likely to become even as partially mollified as Yugoslavia. Lastly, the differences between the U.S.S.R. and Communist China concern foreign policy; the right to act independently in this sphere is more difficult to extend than is leeway in domestic affairs or even in intrabloc matters, since it endangers the status of the U.S.S.R. as a global power.

The intensity of the struggle lies in part not in China's quest for an independent course for itself, but in the contest for leadership of the international Communist movement. Both sides recognize the desirability of having one leader for the movement, but who will it be? China is less apt to toe the line again now that its economic and military power is growing and its prestige in the underdeveloped countries has been augmented, while it is quite unlikely that Russia will come to toe a Chinese line. Other forms of accommodation have and will be suggested, from "veto power" for China to "unanimity through consultation," but none of them will re-establish the united Communist bloc the West knew up to the late fifties, and the new arrangements themselves, if found, are likely to be temporary, unstable, and productive of new conflicts.

An irrevocable rupture is surely more likely than a complete reconciliation, but it may not follow. China has ideological, military, and economic ties to Russia that are difficult, though not impossible, to sever. The Soviet Union and Eastern Europe are by far China's largest foreign suppliers, with more than 80 per cent of all Chinese imports coming from this area. The share of capital goods in the total import, vital to China's industrialization, is still exceptionally high; it amounts to more than 95 per cent of the imports from the U.S.S.R. While the Sino-Soviet trade turnover declined from its record in 1959, when it came to more than $2 billion, it still amounted to $680 million in 1962, and China's trade with Soviet-led countries amounted to nearly 50 per cent of its total trade.[4] China has also found in the Soviet Union a vast market for its exports. Thus both countries have economic reasons for not pushing the rift to the point of complete rupture. Ideological ties, too, are far from negligible. Both are Communist countries; their interpretation of Marxism-Leninism differs and is a source and a vehicle of much conflict, but it also binds; the two will remain ideologically closer to each other than to any third major power.

As far as China is concerned, the most important tie is probably the 1950 Soviet-Chinese defense treaty. As long as China is not a nuclear power, that is, not capable of extensive production of nuclear weapons and means of delivery, it lives under Russia's nuclear umbrella, as Western Europe lives under America's. The Chinese, with their ultra-paranoid view of the West, cannot fail to worry a great deal about what their fate would be if a limited conflict with the West, for example in Southeast Asia, escalated and Russia did not deter the West's use of nuclear arms. In discussing the Truman-MacArthur debate, Western sources usually give the danger of involving Russia in a world war as the major reason for Truman's objection to the bombing of China. The Chinese have surely heard this. The explosion of a nuclear device by China, expected in the near future, will have some psychological impact, especially in Southeast Asia, and might increase China's intransigence toward Russia. But although China could do some damage even without a sophisticated delivery system and could threaten its Asian neighbors with even one bomb, a firm Western commitment to retaliate in case of any such attack might well suffice to cancel much of this effect. Not before the seventies at the earliest will China have enough nu-

[4] *New York Times*, July 15 and July 21, 1963. It was $1.23 billion out of $2.7 billion.

clear weapons and missiles to be an effective nuclear *power*. Until then, its basic dependence on Russia in security matters will be considerable. Mao's view of Soviet nuclear power, as reported by Edgar Snow, is that "Russia's nuclear arms provide the guarantee that the Americans would not resort to nuclear weapons in their counter-revolutionary responses to revolutionary situations."[5]

Russia has less reason to be satisfied with the "mutual" defense treaty. Chinese intransigence threatens to involve the Soviet Union in a world war it does not desire, without so much as previous consultation. Still, leaving China open to a Western offensive[6] would make Soviet defense guarantees seem unreliable to any present or future Communist country. As the leader of international Communism, Russia would find it extremely hard to lose the biggest Communist nation, with a population three times its own. And a final break with China would not eliminate but intensify the competition over the leadership of the Communist movement.

In short, the Sino-Soviet relationship in the next decade is likely to be much less intimate than it used to be, but it will not necessarily reach an irrevocable estrangement. The Communist bloc will become a loose camp, with two major centers of decision-making, two or more interpretations of Marxism-Leninism, and uncoordinated foreign policies. These policies will often clash, and, as Russia and China cross each other's lines, their movements will lack harmony as they sometimes support and frequently undermine each other's efforts and goals. This duocentric pattern of policy-making will, in turn, increase the opportunities for other members of the Communist camp to achieve some autonomy, a trend that will become more apparent the further the two Communist giants

[5] Edgar Snow, "The Chinese View," *The Listener*, May 21, 1963.

[6] Professor Zbigniew Brzezinski, for instance, suggested that the West extend its "counter insurgency" into North Vietnam, which is under China's wings. *Foreign Affairs*, April 1963.

move in different directions. Outer Mongolia, North Vietnam, and Rumania are each reported to have already gained various concessions, and even triggered a competition between Russia and China in providing aid. It is not inconceivable, now that the monolith has been broken, that third, fourth, and nth centers of independent Communist policy-making will emerge. Yugoslavia seems to have some such international ambitions, recently rewarded by support for its line from Guinea. Nor will Cuba, if it remains a Communist state, necessarily continue to follow the Russian or Chinese line. Even Albania, until now China's only European supporter, has manifested some willingness to move away by seeking economic aid in Italy, West Germany, and the Netherlands.

The actual degree of cooperation versus conflict that will exist depends not only on relations between China and Russia, but on the reaction of the West and the policy it chooses to follow. As far as the Communist camp is concerned, I expect the differences of interest and policy within it to be extensive enough for the Russians to be willing to make various arrangements with the West—similar to the 1963 agreement on partial cessation of nuclear testing—even if China continues to object. At the same time it might be futile to work toward an irrevocable rupture of the Communist bloc, or to expect Russia to agree to all or any interbloc measures that would require or lead to such a break.

THE WEST: HOW PERMANENT ITS DISARRAY?

THE NEW CRISIS

If in the past the West failed to see the growing split in the Communist camp, it has been equally reluctant to face up to the rifts in its own. The American public in particular tends to view the current disarray as largely the result of the personal whims and ambitions of one person, Charles de Gaulle, and is waiting, somewhat impatiently, for the gen-

eral's departure. His successor, it is widely hoped, will allow
the Western house to be put in order. To weigh the future
prospects of Western unity realistically, we must appraise the
historical forces that are working for and against the Atlantic
alliance.

The mold of the Western alliance was cast in the first years
of its existence. In the late forties Germany and Italy were
defeated countries, and most of the Western European nations were economically and militarily weak, dependent on the
United States for their defense, reconstruction, and balance
of payments. The United States provided most of the forces
and finances of NATO, reconstruction funds through the
Marshall Plan, and the dollars Europe's trade needed. No
wonder that, under these circumstances, there was little difference between the foreign policy of Washington and that
of Europe, especially as far as the U.S.S.R. was concerned.
Most Americans were not surprised by such harmony; they
had long believed that what was best for the United States
was best for the West, an attitude referred to by a Western
writer as "benevolent paternalism."[7] Up to the mid-fifties,
Europeans, whatever they believed, had little choice but to
follow the leader. The commander of the NATO forces was
always American; Norway and Denmark did not form a
Nordic defense union with Sweden in part because the United
States objected; Western Germany was rearmed and accepted
as a member of NATO in 1955 under considerable American
pressure; economic cooperation among Europeans themselves
was required by the United States as a prerequisite for receiving Marshall Plan funds; and the United States "encouraged"
Britain's withdrawal from Palestine, France's from Indochina, the Netherlands' from Indonesia, and Belgium's from
the Congo. Though most Americans never realized it, in the
process the United States became quite unpopular in Western

[7] Joseph Kraft, *The Grand Design* (New York: Harper, 1962), p. 60.

Europe. A French senator, expressing a widely held opinion, said in 1958: "At bottom the conflict is that America and France have neither the same world interests nor policy goals. America looks after her own self-interest, which is entirely different from ours." A former Italian Foreign Office official said: "The Americans have understood nothing of Italian and European affairs—and have learned nothing." While the German Christian Democrats were more charitable, a Social Democrat expressed the feelings of many of his party members about U.S.-German relations as follows: "We believe that Russia will make no concessions as long as it is convinced that West Germany is an American fief."[8] Many Europeans came to view America as "a youthful, rather simple-minded, unsophisticated, clumsy giant who unwittingly but persistently offended their sensitivities."[9]

The Western alliance was always an uneasy one. Italian voters reacted strongly when an American ambassador attempted to tell them what party to vote for; Britain resented U.S. pressures to make it apply for membership in the Common Market; France was displeased by American sympathies for the Algerian F.L.N. (Front de la Liberation Nationale); Portugal was offended when the United States disapproved of its colonial policy in Angola. Many European allies failed to meet fully their NATO obligations, either financially or in terms of the number of units assigned to the multinational command. Even when the economic situation improved markedly, no European nation matched the United States' contributions to Europe's defense. Dulles' "massive-retaliation" strategy did not enjoy Europe's approval, but the Europeans had to share its risks. Many Europeans objected to the U.S. decision not to recognize Communist China and its refusal to seat the mainland Chinese in the United Nations.

[8] Lloyd A. Free, *Six Allies and a Neutral* (Glencoe, Ill.: The Free Press, 1959). Citations, pp. 100, 117, 148, respectively.
[9] *Ibid.*, p. 117.

They considered the list of "strategic" materials unnecessarily long, and geared, in part, to American business interests. Thus while the United States had for a while the power to make its policy stick, it hardly won the Europeans' affection. Even in earlier periods they were not quite quiescent partners.

The history of NATO—the core of the Western alliance —is one of continual crises. The more outstanding political and military disputes occurred during the Korean hostilities, when most of America's allies were strongly opposed to MacArthur's intention to bomb Chinese bases in Manchuria; during the early fifties, when tension was generated between the United States and France over French opposition to German rearmament at a time when the United States had decided to rearm Germany anyway; during the Suez crisis in 1956, when the United States voted against Britain and France in the United Nations; during the late fifties, when both Greece and Turkey wanted to control the island of Cyprus while Britain wanted to retain it as a military base, and the United States tried to work out compromises that pleased neither side.

But these events were only preliminaries to the crisis that began in 1958–59 and became acute in 1961–62. In 1958 de Gaulle returned to power, and France began to defy the United States. It decreased rather than increased its contribution to NATO, at first because of the Algerian war (which the United States, and especially Senator John F. Kennedy, did not approve). And when the war was terminated in 1962, France still refused to assign additional units to NATO. The French navy in the Mediterranean had been withdrawn from NATO in 1959, and American bombers and missiles, which were to have been equipped with nuclear warheads, were ordered out of France. In 1963 France announced its intention of withdrawing its ships from the NATO Atlantic fleet by the end of the year. France favored a different policy toward Russia, including a "tougher" no-negotiation line on

West Berlin. At the same time, France was the only NATO country to support the Polish position regarding the Oder-Neisse border line between East Germany and Poland. Later it became the only Western nation that refused to participate in the disarmament negotiations at Geneva, and to sign the treaty on partial cessation of nuclear tests.

France has led the European Economic Community toward a policy that would dissociate the Common Market from the United States in matters of investment and trade; it vetoed the membership of Britain in the Common Market, which the United States desired; and it initiated a national nuclear deterrent that the United States most adamantly opposed. De Gaulle openly hopes for a Europe, led by France, that will not be part of either the East or the West, but a third force, free to follow its own foreign policy and capable of opting out of the conflict between the U.S.S.R. and the United States. Walter Lippmann has written that de Gaulle's Europe is envisaged as a power "to be led by the Franco-Germans and not by the Anglo-Saxons. It is to make itself sufficiently powerful to come to terms with the Soviet Union and thus to have 'Europe' extend from the Atlantic to the Urals."[10]

As France found a new leader in de Gaulle and Western Europe a new leader in France, the power of Europe, and hence its potential ability to act on its own, grew. By 1961, with the economic reconstruction of Europe long completed and the need for dollars satisfied, the United States for the first time had to turn to Europe to ease its balance-of-payments difficulties. As the successful Common Market seemed to turn Europe into a major industrial and commercial power competing with American industry, Europe became less and less willing to follow a foreign policy largely formulated in Washington and based on little genuine consultation with

[10] *Western Unity and the Common Market* (Boston: Little, Brown, 1962), p. 21.

allies other than Britain. The United States did take into account other countries' needs and viewpoints, such as German feelings over West Berlin and its objections to the recognition of East Germany, but this did not mean that America's allies had an effective voice in the formulation of Western foreign policy or that the U.S. conception of their feelings and interests was accurate. They were "looked after" rather than given a say.

In 1962 the United States undertook a major drive to preserve Western unity, to adjust the alliance to the growing power of Europe and the increasing desire of Europeans to have a greater voice in the shaping of Western policy, by attempting to form an Atlantic partnership. The idea was not new—such a partnership had been proposed in one form or another ever since World War II—but for the first time the idea gained momentum in Washington. The efforts to heal the Western rift have so far passed through two rounds, the first calling for a broad partnership with a united Europe, the second, for forming a multinational nuclear deterrent under NATO and freeing trade. A somewhat closer look at the outcome of these attempts tells much about the prospects for Western unity.

A PARTNERSHIP WITH A UNITED EUROPE

In several speeches in 1962, notably one on Independence Day, President Kennedy called for the establishment of an Atlantic partnership between a united Europe and the United States, in which the United States, he said, would deal with Europe on an equal basis. The junior partner's progress had been recognized, and he was offered the status of a full partner. This projected relationship was expected to solve several problems.

First, it was supposed to reduce the dollar crisis at a time when the United States was losing gold continuously as a result of the American foreign-aid program and U.S. military commitments around the world, both undertakings that are intended to benefit the entire West. The United States still contributed almost twice as much in these areas as did Germany or France and considerably more than the United Kingdom, not to mention other allies. Having Europe as a full partner in these commitments was expected simultaneously to increase the sum of funds available and to ease the burden of the American contribution.

Second, an Atlantic partnership was expected to better trading terms with Europe. Since President Kennedy's notable legislative victory in 1962 securing passage of the Trade Expansion Act, American representatives have been negotiating an exchange of tariff reductions with the Common Market to increase U.S.-European trade; their purpose is to ease the U.S. balance-of-payments problems and to bind the free nations more closely together.

Finally, Washington was seriously troubled by France's decision to build its own nuclear deterrent. In addition to its concern about the dangers involved in the spread of nuclear weapons to additional countries, the United States would like to retain the stature that accrues to the only Western country that possesses a full-fledged nuclear force. It was further feared that only an ally contemplating a foreign policy quite different from Washington's would go to the expense of building an independent nuclear deterrent. Even Britain, which is regarded as having "special ties" with the United States, did not escape the American pressure to maintain nuclear duopoly in the world, and U.S. monopoly in the West.[11]

Hence the United States proposed to share with United Europe its nuclear shield and sword. It had already increased its consultations with its European allies in the NATO Council and revealed for the first time to the Europeans its Russian targeting. Washington now considered a joint NATO

[11] On the way this pressure was exerted, see p. 45.

intelligence agency; more joint planning in the deployment
of Western military units, particularly nuclear forces; and an
Atlantic Assembly of Parliamentarians with advisory, but no
legislative, functions.

In short, a United Europe was invited to be America's partner. It was expected to be a political unit whose population,
economic capacities, and military power would approach
America's. Evolving from the Common Market, it was to
include—Washington expected—not only France, Germany,
Italy, and the Benelux countries, but also the United Kingdom and most of the other European NATO members, especially Denmark and Norway. Greece is already an associate
member of the EEC, and Turkey was expected to acquire a
similar status. But as these proposals were made, the United
States faced two serious difficulties: no United Europe evolved
to be partner with, and America had some second thoughts
about the whole business.

Europe did not appear to covet American political or economic company with quite the warmth Washington initially
expected. One European attitude was like that of the junior
member of a firm who for many years has been slighted
(through statements such as "governments in France are unstable," "Germany cannot be trusted," etc.), and who has
finally opened a shop on his own and is doing very well. When
suddenly the old man suggests a merger and offers to make
him a full partner, the former junior member, enjoying his
newly found power and status, is hesitant about dealing with
the old line or the old shop.

More specifically, the partnership suffered a major setback
when it became evident, by the end of 1962, that a United
Europe was still many years away. Washington had assumed
that Britain would be admitted to the Common Market, but
France was not willing to share its leadership of Europe with
Britain. There were many factors at work, one being bitter
memories in France of Britain's condescending treatment of

de Gaulle during World War II. Churchill once told de Gaulle: "Here is something you ought to know: whenever we have to choose between Europe and the open sea, we shall always choose the open sea." Britain, which was invited to participate in several European organizations after World War II, refused to participate in two (the European Defense Community and the European Coal and Steel Community), contributed to the ineffectiveness of those it did participate in (e.g., the Council of Europe), and quit negotiations over membership in the Common Market, when it was originally formed, to generate a competitive grouping of countries known as the Outer Seven.

De Gaulle also vetoed Britain's membership because the United States was so anxious for Britain to enter. The United States was afraid that France would guide Europe in a direction undesirable for the West and independent of the United States. Britain, as America's most trusted ally, was to be the guardian of the U.S. viewpoint in the United Europe. This was exactly what de Gaulle wanted to prevent. He had his own ideas on what was best for the West and for France, toward which he, not Britain, was to lead Europe. He saw Britain as a "Trojan horse."

The high point of this round of attempts to heal the Western rift came at the end of 1962. Without previous consultation the United States canceled the production of Skybolt, an air-to-ground missile that was to be supplied to Britain to carry its nuclear warheads from British bombers to enemy targets. Since Britain was counting on this missile as its main means of extending the life of its bomber squadrons (it terminated the production of its own missiles on the basis of the American commitment to provide Skybolts), the cancellation threatened to eliminate the British nuclear deterrent.[12] The United States had several good reasons for its decision:

[12] Later, Polaris-carrying submarines were offered to the British as a substitute, but even this offer had several hitches.

it found the Skybolt technically deficient and forbiddingly
expensive, and it did not favor its allies having their own
striking forces. After a brief protest Britain accepted this
unilateral American decision with a readiness that strongly
impressed de Gaulle, in the wrong way. He was now more
sure than ever that Britain-in-Europe would hew to the American line, thwarting his hopes for a more independent Europe.

As British membership in the Common Market was
blocked, the other predominantly Protestant, Anglo-Saxon,
Social Democratic countries—Norway and Denmark—decided
not to keep their applications for membership active, and
Britain renewed its efforts to strengthen the Outer Seven, the
competitive European trade group. By the beginning of 1963
Europe, far from being united, was divided into at least two
camps. Theoretically the United States could have formed a
three-pillar partnership, with a French-led Europe, a British-
led Nordic and Commonwealth group, and a North American pillar. But this would have entailed "abandoning" much
of Continental Europe to de Gaulle's dominance and reward-
ing his defiance. The United States still hopes to bring the
other five members of the Common Market, especially Germany, to seek reversal of the French decision to exclude Britain, to convince de Gaulle, or his successor, to give up the
French nuclear force, and to sponsor cooperation among all
the allies in one, united, American-led union.

At the same time, the United States has had some second
thoughts about the whole idea of nuclear partnership; the
Europeans increasingly expected to share the control of the
American nuclear force; but the more the United States
thought about it, the more it found such sharing not just un-
attractive, but clearly dangerous. Since this is the issue that
will make or break the effort to heal the rift in the West, it
deserves closer examination.

WHO WILL PULL THE TRIGGER?

The military alliance between one country that holds 98 per cent of the Western nuclear force and fourteen that hold little or none of it, was never an easy one. At first the Europeans feared that the United States would be trigger happy, then later they feared it would be trigger shy. They were never comfortable with an arrangement that required them in effect to delegate decisions over the life and death of their nations to a foreign government.

In the mid-fifties Europeans were worried by American declarations about "massive retaliation" that seemed to threaten to bring the world's roof down if one Russian soldier set one foot on the other side of the containment line. These fears were especially intense during the 1954 confrontation in Indochina, before it became clear that massive retaliation was not to be applied after all. A more recent case of European jitters over American action occurred during the 1962 Cuban crisis. Following the positioning of Soviet missiles in Cuba the United States decided to blockade the island to bring about the removal of these missiles. Although other NATO countries would probably have been bombed if the blockade had led to a war between the United States and the U.S.S.R., it was imposed without consultation with America's NATO allies. The United States acted as every other nation would probably have acted in a similar crisis: it moved unilaterally, in line with what it considered its vital national interests. The United States probably also assumed that there was a close correspondence between its interests and those of the West. But it would have acted the same even if this had not been the case.

The significance of the Cuban crisis in this context is illuminated by a fact rarely discussed in the American press: the Russians had, by 1962, a *comparatively* small number of long-range missiles and bombers capable of striking the

United States, but a large number of medium- and inter-mediate-range missiles and bombers able to lay waste Western Europe with little effort. The Institute of Strategic Studies in London reported late in 1962 that while the Soviets had only about 75 operational intercontinental ballistic missiles (as compared to perhaps 450 for the West), they had more than 700 medium- and intermediate-range missiles with ranges from seven hundred to two thousand miles (versus 250 for the Western allies). Similarly, the Soviet air force had relatively few long-range aircraft, but a large force of medium-range bombers suitable for use all over Europe. *Under these conditions Western Europe served as the major hostage of the Russians, with the Soviets capable of striking America's allies with much greater facility than could be directed against the United States itself.* If an American-Russian nuclear war erupted as a result of a confrontation in Cuba, Vietnam, Formosa, or elsewhere, Europe would in all likelihood be devastated. From this point of view unilateral American acts such as the Cuban blockade—even if Europeans see the particular act as fully justified—remind them that they stand to be exterminated without representation, to be destroyed because of a war in a far and foreign territory, over a matter they were not even previously consulted about.

Two recent developments have affected this situation. The Europeans have lost a good part of their concern about the quality of American foreign policy-making since the massive-retaliation approach was quietly dropped, and have acquired considerable respect for American strategic thinking. The Cuban blockade itself—once it was successfully terminated—was viewed by many Europeans as a masterpiece of restraint in the exercise of power. Increasingly, though, the opposite problem comes to haunt Europeans: the fear that the United States would be too slow to draw the nuclear gun when European vital interests were endangered. The fear has grown since the Russian space shots demonstrated their ability to deliver heavy payloads long distances—that is, to bomb the United States itself. And to make matters worse, leading American strategists publically raised the question of how many American casualties Europe is "worth."

A growing number of influential advisers to the President and the Defense Department have suggested that the United States explicitly renounce the first use of nuclear weapons and insist that its European allies build up their conventional forces, so that they would be able to defend themselves, with American help, but without involving the United States in a nuclear war for the defense of Europe. The Europeans, fearful of the cost of large conventional forces in both funds and manpower, and believing in the absolute deterring effect of nuclear weapons, have interpreted the emphasis on conventional forces as a weakening of the American commitment to defend Europe. There is a lingering fear that the United States will withdraw its bases and forces from Europe once the European conventional forces are built up. President Kennedy's statement, during his 1963 European trip, that "Your liberty is our liberty, and any attack on your soil is an attack upon our own," did not answer European questions as to the how, when, and what of such defense, and de Gaulle was quick to point out that such statements do not tie the hands of future American Presidents.

There can be no doubt that these European fears concern a fundamental issue: the conditions under which nations are obliged to commit suicide to defend the freedom of other nations and under which they give up, in effect if not in law, their sovereignty and allow the head of another state to preside over their fate in the nuclear age.

The United States has other nuclear worries of its own. The initial idea of bringing Europe into the planning of strategy and the direction of all strategic forces including the nuclear one was expected to have many salutary effects. The Europeans would realize how costly the American nuclear force is and hopefully would forego building their own and agree to share the costs of the joint Atlantic force; they would see that the United States deploys military forces and makes war plans in a way that indicates genuine concern for Europe's defense; they would realize the dangers involved in nuclear war as they became familiar with the details and thought through the various contingent plans; and they would thus become more willing to build up the conventional forces American strategists believe necessary. Finally, it was hoped that participating in the Atlantic force would give Europeans a sense of having a nuclear capability and so add yet another reason to discourage the building of national ones.

As the plan was initially unfolded, the Europeans, including the French, were quite interested. The influential Paris newspaper *Le Monde*, for instance, found the idea "exalting." But the Europeans seemed to have a peculiar conception of what partnership meant; they thought that under the Atlantic partnership they would share the control of the American nuclear force. But American law (the McMahon Act) forbids giving nuclear secrets and hence nuclear weapons to any other nation (with the partial exception of Britain). The Europeans wanted to know if the Administration was going to introduce legislation to change that law, because otherwise, they asked, how could The Trigger be shared? Then, as Walter Lippmann authoritatively reported, "After much debate and soul-searching, the Administration decided . . . that within the Western Alliance, the ultimate responsibility in nuclear affairs must be in one capital, not in two or three."[13] "Partnership," the State Department explained, meant exchange of information, mutual consultation, participation of Europeans in strategic planning; but control of The Trigger, that is, the decision to go or not to go to nuclear war, would have to remain American.

The onus for this decision is often put on the allies. How,

13 *Op. cit.*, p. 36.

it is asked, could the United States share its decisions with fourteen countries? There are only a few minutes, American sources point out, between the warning of a nuclear attack and the decision to retaliate. But these arguments are less than wholly convincing. First of all, even two governments (i.e., the United States and a United Europe) could not consult in the few minutes presumably available. Nor could the government of one country be "consulted." The strategic decisions would have to be made on a contingent basis, that is, various contingencies would have to be examined ahead of time and decisions made before the event on what action was to be taken under various possible conditions. The question was really whether the Europeans were to share in these all-important contingent decisions, or only to be informed, consulted, and the like.

This formulation of the problem brings up the crux of the matter. If the United States were to share these contingent decisions, it would be sharing the decision on the life and death of the American nation with other nationals; it would either have to face the possibility of going to war when the others felt it necessary and risking an almost certain devastation for a cause or battle it might not consider worthwhile, or it would have to refrain from going to nuclear war—let us say for the defense of Formosa—because the Europeans did not approve. In other words, if the decisions were really shared, either one vote would suffice under a given contingency, in which case the Europeans could engage the United States; or two votes would be necessary, in which case the United States decision could be vetoed.[14] Neither the Administration nor the Congress seems willing to surrender American sovereignty to an Atlantic partnership to such a degree. One day, if the Atlantic community grows and barriers

---

[14] This difference between sharing The Trigger on a basis of whether one green light suffices or two are needed is not noted in most discussions of the subject.

among its member nations are reduced, such a shift of
sovereignty might be possible; but surely such a day is not yet
in sight. Not only is there no United Europe to be a partner
with, but the United States is not at all ready to cast the
decisions governing its very existence into this or any other
partnership.

If such sharing The Trigger is out of the question, the Europeans could hardly be satisfied with sharing information, some
vague participation in planning, and largely perfunctory consultation. Thus one major source of the Western rift is that
the Europeans are losing confidence in the American commitment to undertake nuclear warfare for their sake; they suspect the United States is becoming more reluctant to use
nuclear weapons or threaten to use them than the Europeans
wish. (Technically, this issue came up in the discussions
about preparedness for a conventional war in Europe. European troops are prepared for a maximum of thirty-days
conventional war; the United States favored ninety days'
preparedness. In practice some of the Europeans would need
nuclear backing, in case of a major attack, after one to two
days, if not within hours). Nothing short of a grip on The
Trigger is likely to assure many Europeans in the long run.
Without it, they will continue to expect to be exposed to
nuclear bombardment if the United States should become
involved in a war with Russia, and not be sure they could
retaliate if they themselves become involved.

Widely expected developments in the technology of weapons are likely to increase further the Europeans' concern in
the near future. Over the next five years the Soviets are expected to increase their intercontinental missile force and to
reduce its vulnerability by putting their missiles on nuclear
submarines, moving platforms, and in concrete silos. The
more protected the Soviet force, and the greater the Soviet
ability to devastate the United States, the more reluctant any
American President would be to push the button.

SHARING A SMALL TRIGGER?

As it became evident, by the beginning of 1963, that the Atlantic Grand Design was a mountain that, after much labor, had not yet produced even a mouse of partnership, the United States made a new suggestion: if the Big Trigger could not be shared, what about sharing a Small Trigger? If sharing the control of the American striking force is impossible, what about providing the Europeans with one? This would be a force shared by several nations, and hence entitled the Multi-National Force (M.N.F.). The idea was in the air for quite a while, but only in 1963 as the grand design failed to take off was the M.N.F. officially unwrapped. The Europeans were offered participation, together with the Americans, in a new seaborne nuclear force, under NATO. There were many complex questions to be solved concerning the nature of the force—should it be of Polaris-carrying submarines or surface ships; who would pay for which parts; and what effects would staffing the ships with mixed crews have—but the basic political outline was simple. The M.N.F., it was admitted, would in itself have practically no military value since the United States already commands more than enough nuclear capability, but it was expected to have a psychological and political effect. The Europeans would man the ships, provide the command, and gain a "sense of participation." By these provisions many of the beneficial effects the partnership had been expected to bring would accrue. In particular, the M.N.F. was expected to prevent the proliferation of national nuclear forces, counter the French one, and prevent the Germans from asking for the right to build one or participate in a French-led force. The idea was referred to in Washington as one of "innoculation," giving America's allies a small "dose" of nuclear weapons to immunize them against the desire for bigger ones. Since Britain agreed to add its national force to the multinational one (subject to withdrawal in extreme national emergencies), France might be willing to do the same. At worst, if France chose not to participate in the M.N.F., that country would be isolated, left alone to maintain its own expensive force.

Such a plan looked feasible until its finer points were explored. First, there was again the question of the finger on The Trigger. Washington felt that the Europeans could man the ships, pay for them, provide port facilities and possibly even the commanding admiral. But control of the nuclear bombs turned out to be a different matter. Although the M.N.F. would be small by American or Russian standards, consisting of perhaps twenty-five surface ships armed with sixteen Polaris missiles each, it would be big enough to trigger a nuclear war with Russia if it were used; and since it would be a NATO force, such action would automatically involve the United States. "Behind this policy [not to share a trigger] is the obvious conclusion that if any European force starts a nuclear war, it is the United States that would have to finish it."[15] One foreign correspondent reported that an American presidential adviser was not speaking in jest when he said, "We hold these truths to be self-evident, that peace in the thermonuclear age can only be secured by American monopoly of thermonuclear weapons; and that although all nations are endowed with certain inalienable rights, these do not include the pursuit of thermonuclear happiness."[16] Thus, the United States came full circle; even the Small Trigger, it was felt, would have to be American.[17] The Europeans hardly found this satisfactory.[18]

De Gaulle's idea of Europe as a third force appeals to many Europeans, including those of the left, some liberals, and many anti-Americans.[19] Professor David Truman, a leading

[15] Editorial, New York Times, June 1, 1963.
[16] Peregrine Worsthorne, as cited in Current, February 1963, p. 27.
[17] Deputy Defense Secretary Roswell L. Gilpatric was reported by the press, on March 13, 1963, as stating that Americans will have sole custody of the nuclear warheads that will be placed aboard the multinational surface vessels.
[18] See Joseph C. Harsch, Christian Science Monitor, February 1, 1963.
[19] See also Altiero Spinelli, "Atlantic Pact or European Unity?" Foreign Affairs, July 1962, pp. 542–52.

American political scientist, returning from an extensive trip in Europe in 1963, put the matter succinctly when he stated: "In Europe, the Atlantic Partnership is an *American* idea." Fifty-six per cent of the French legislators favored increasing the French nuclear force in an opinion survey taken eight weeks before de Gaulle's access to power in 1958, and a majority of the legislators even at that time favored a France less tied to the West, with better relations with Russia, and standing on its own feet.[20]

The widest objections to any American proposal, however, have been raised against the Multi-National Force, presumably a U.S. concession to Europe's desires and needs. The French refer to it as the Multi-National *farce*. The Norwegians and the Danes have officially declared they will have no part of it. R.A.F. Marshal Sir John Slessor called it "monstrous military nonsense." The British Labor Party announced that if elected it would not agree to participate. The growing Italian left is against it. A meeting of NATO parliamentarians, as well as one of the Western European Union, passed resolutions in 1963 against the new force. The one nation that was interested from the outset, promising to provide about 70 per cent of the European part of the finance for the force and a large share of the manpower, and that sooner or later would request a major role in the command, was West Germany.[21] This was enough to give quite a few influential figures in Washington cold feet. The United States, however, continued to generate pressure in favor of the plan, and in October 1963 an agreement was signed between seven of the fifteen NATO countries to start preparations for the Multi-National Force.

[20] Free, *op. cit.*, p. 103.
[21] German Defense Minister Uhre von Hassel praised the decision to establish the allied nuclear force and stated that it would eventually give West Germany a voice in nuclear defense strategy; he listed among the goals of the Bonn government the importance of making such a nuclear force free of a U.S. veto and said that the force could never become "a genuine military instrument" until the veto was withdrawn. (The *New York Times*, May 28, 1963.)

AN ECONOMIC PARTNERSHIP?

The Atlantic partnership was intended to be more than a political and military alliance; it was to have economic foundations that were to be of importance for their own sakes and to strengthen other ties. When the Grand Design failed to materialize, economic cooperation was viewed as a minimum substitute and a possible basis for future cooperative efforts. But on this front, to put it briefly and hence without complete fairness, the West fared only slightly better than on the military-political front. The United States succeeded in getting its European allies to increase their financial contributions to NATO, but these still lagged behind the American contribution, even if the fact that the United States is larger and richer is taken into account.

Similarly, in 1962 the United States invested about 10 per cent of its gross national product in defense; Britain, about 7 per cent; France, 5.1 per cent (including expenses for its nuclear force); other West European countries even less.

The Europeans have somewhat increased their foreign aid but hardly have relieved U.S. commitments or channeled their efforts in the direction America would prefer. Most French and British aid goes to countries that have special ties to these ex-colonial powers, such as the members of their respective commonwealths. The use of this aid is not guided by any overall Western strategy; with the exception of India, the funds go largely to Africa, while the focus of the development race between the blocs is in South Asia and Latin America, and it is in these areas that the most of the U.S. commitment lies. (Foreign aid given by other European countries is comparatively negligible.)

The European central banks did come to the assistance of the United States during the 1960 dollar crisis, and some arrangements were made to ease the pressure on the dollar in future years. But the Europeans made it clear to the United

States that they expect it to put its house in order to prevent repeated American calls on their assistance. The United States has continued to lose gold and the danger to the dollar has not passed, nor do provisional arrangements made by the United States' NATO allies preclude future weakening of its position and status.

Growing apprehension, especially in France, but far from unknown in the other European countries, concerns American investments in Europe. Such investments increased 81 per cent in the first four years of the Common Market.[22] The total American investment in European countries, however, is small, even after its recent sharp rise; the percentage of American-controlled investment is 3.1 for Germany, 2.4 for Italy, and 1.4 for France. What made the American investment seem more threatening and visible than these figures would suggest is that it is highly concentrated in a few branches of the economy, and now often involves direct American control of European companies rather than the less antagonizing purchase of European stocks, which was common earlier. (In 1963 Chrysler's gaining control of the French firm Simca was much talked about). Also, American-owned companies are apt to violate established local practices. For instance, an American plant in France fired a number of workers without previously informing the authorities, as is the custom there to allow for the initiation of measures to counter local unemployment. As a consequence of all this, rather than moving toward a larger American-European capital market, the European Common Market is considering various steps to restrict and "regulate" American investment.

The greatest expectations the Atlantic economy aroused concerned the liberation of trade. The United States expected substantially to reduce, in part even to eliminate, tariffs on the

[22] This and other figures cited in the section on investment are drawn from Richard Grenier, "U. S. Investments in France," in the *Reporter*, June 6, 1963, and the *New York Times*, September 15, 1963.

exchange of American and West European goods, creating in effect one large free market that would include the six-country Common Market, the markets of the Outer Seven, and the gigantic U.S. market. Early in 1962, many American observers depicted in almost lyrical terms the scope and potency of such a tremendous free-trade area. As it turns out, a free market is gradually evolving (not without setbacks, strains, and many efforts), but it is only among the six European countries in the Common Market; other European countries are excluded, and their effort to forge a free-trade area of their own (the Outer Seven) has not been particularly successful.

By 1963 the United States was hard at work trying to reach some accommodation with the Common Market. As these lines are written, the negotiations are in progress; it looks as if nothing dramatic or far-reaching will be achieved. The Six, under French leadership, have realized that there is little they can gain from such an Atlantic market; they fear the competition of American industry, and they have their own farm surpluses. The United States has much more interest in lifting trade barriers, but because of its higher tariffs and various domestic considerations, it is in a weak position in these negotiations. When in May 1963 the U.S. special trade delegation to the Common Market proposed that the United States and Europe make large, across-the-board percentage cuts on many categories of goods, the Europeans refused. They pointed out that their tariffs are already generally lower than the American rates and that the U.S. tariffs cover far more goods (e.g., a fifth of all U.S. tariffs in 1963 were higher than 30 per cent, compared to a hundredth of Europe's). Whatever specific arrangements are finally worked out, the Atlantic partnership will hardly be saved by whatever degree of economic cooperation or trade liberalization is achieved. Here, even more than in matters of defense and foreign policy, Europe is succeeding on its own; it surely will maintain some ties with the United States, but the idea of significantly tightening them has little appeal in the New Europe.

THE FUTURE OF THE WESTERN CAMP

There are too many unknowns in the equation to allow hard and fast predictions about the prospects of Western unity. A whole generation of older leaders is stepping out of the limelight and a younger generation is taking over. The United States began the sixties with the election of a forty-two-year-old president to replace a seventy-year-old one and President Johnson was fifty-five when he took office; sixty-nine-year-old Macmillan retired in the fall of 1963; aging de Gaulle might be removed at any moment or retire when his term expires in 1965; eighty-seven-year-old Adenauer was succeeded by sixty-five-year-old Erhard. Under conditions most favorable to the present U.S. policy, Britain under a new Conservative government, France under pro-American leadership, and Germany under Erhard might for a while continue to follow a Western foreign policy largely as formulated in Washington. More likely, Britain, its economy weak and its island an easy target in a nuclear war, may strive toward a less committed position in the interbloc conflict. Its recognition of Communist China, increased trade with the U.S.S.R., and support of a "softer" line on Berlin, are all possible forerunners of such a trend. A Labor government would give it further momentum. It is not often recognized that the key point of contention, French development of an independent nuclear force, was begun before de Gaulle (in 1957 by Guy Mollet and Felix Gaillard) and is likely to be continued, in one way or another, by de Gaulle's successors.[23] The degree to which France will continue to lead Europe is another matter; it depends partially on the degree to which Germany asserts itself and on the amount of confusion that results from de Gaulle's departure. But what-

[23] The expense of the French nuclear force has been greatly overstated in the American press; a Gaullist deputy in the French Assembly, replying to criticism of the financial burden of the *force de frappe*, declared that it would cost no more than "half as much as the government spends on subsidies to agriculture." ("Letter from Paris," *The New Yorker*, June 29, 1963, p. 72.)

ever the degree, little and at best transitory support for a tight Atlantic alliance is likely to emerge.

While all eyes are on France, the big question mark of the future of the Western alliance actually rests with Germany. Germany—its economy strong, NATO more and more dependent on its funds and manpower, its international status almost fully restored—will surely seek a greater voice in Western foreign policy. The direction Germany will take is far from clear; it might seek to lead Europe with, or in place of, France. It might develop a more assertive mood, reflecting presently latent nationalist and irredentist aspirations. Unlike most observers, who play down the significance of the German commitment to reunification, I see it as a potentially major force. Public-opinion polls conducted in 1963 show that 59 per cent of the West Germans consider the country's division "an unbearable situation"; 40 per cent consider reunification the nation's most urgent business, and only 17 per cent see the preservation of peace as taking priority over reunification. This is not a sentiment politicians are likely to ignore in the long run. It has also been suggested that by no means the least improbable direction German policy might take would be to go along with Germany's former ambassador to Moscow, Dr. Hans Kroll, toward a Russo-German *rapprochement*.[24] As one analyst noted, for Germany "the temptation to treat independently with Russia, to repeat the 1922 deal of Rapallo and the 1939 Nazi-Soviet Pact, is not some vicious concoction of the Free Democrats, the Ruhr industrialists and a peculiar ambassador in Moscow. It is an enduring possibility written on the map of Europe."[25] Which ever of these directions it follows, I expect West Germany to cause considerably more trouble to the Western alliance and its U.S. leadership in the next ten years than it did in the last; in the near future it might well replace France as the black sheep of the alliance.

[24] Lippmann, *op. cit.*, p. 25.
[25] Kraft, *op. cit.*, p. 64.

The trouble Germany gave the United States over the signing of a partial ban on nuclear testing is a preliminary illustration. Adenauer, while still Germany's Chancellor, denounced negotiations over the sale of American wheat to the Soviet Union. "Only the stupidest calves choose their own butcher," he stated in Bonn, on October 5, 1963. But at the same time West Germany increased its trade with the U.S.S.R. The U.S. policy of pampering the Germans to punish de Gaulle's France merely accelerates the coming of the day when German power and prestige will be too great for their present secondary, and comparatively subdued, position.

Beyond these short-run fluctuations lies a much more basic problem: *the issue of nationalism in the nuclear age*. On the one hand, security and prosperity require action in unison on a multinational scale. In itself, the desirability of interstate cooperation better to serve the states' respective interests is hardly new; the ancient Greek city-states formed military alliances and cooperated in economic matters. But never was the need so great as it is now. In my judgment, however, the attempts to meet this need are failing because *the loyalties of the citizens have not extended to match the scope of the new multinational organizations, which hence are not granted the necessary social-political support of the citizens' communities*.

This becomes evident when the central question over which the Atlantic alliance is splitting is examined: that of control of The Trigger. Theoretically NATO requires that its members be willing to put their very existence on the line to assure one another's survival and freedom. The logic of such cooperation seems unassailable; one for all and all for one. But the question remains, who is to decide *under what circumstances* to raise the stakes? All fifteen nations might agree that West Berlin ought to be defended; but who will decide how? With conventional arms only? With tactical nuclear weapons? Or by an ultimatum—to withdraw or an all-out strike will follow? Facing such questions, each nation, conscious of its distinct identity, realizes that it has distinct interests: the next-to-the-Russians Germans, the comparatively unthreatened French, the sitting-duck British, and the most-likely-to-be-devastated (in a nuclear, but not in a conventional war) Americans.

Since the member governments and their people do not see themselves as citizens of one Atlantic community but of fifteen nations, the basic foundation for solving such a problem is lacking. There is no commitment to one center of decision-making that is accepted by the whole community, no one symbol to which they all respond. Hence the Europeans are uneasy under an American-controlled deterrent, and the Americans feel they cannot allow the Europeans the capacity to involve the United States in a nuclear war, either by giving them a small trigger or a finger on the big one, or by allowing them to build their own.[26]

It is extremely difficult to launch a community of fifteen nations, the needs of the nuclear age notwithstanding. Even efforts to form one political community of six nations in Europe, nations much more similar and geographically closer to each other than the fifteen, are far from sure to succeed. The Atlantic rift can be mended, if my analysis is valid, only if a community of the fifteen nations is formed to support joint institutions, unified decision-making, and one nuclear force. This is not likely to happen in the foreseeable future.

There will probably not, however, be a complete rupture in the Western camp. Even if the NATO treaty is not renewed in 1969, when it comes up for review, or if NATO is dissolved, the basic affinity between the two important centers of Western civilization will remain. At least for the next few years Europe will depend for its major deterrent on the United States, and the United States is unlikely to pull its forces out of Europe. In the longer run all Europe may become as

---

[26] If they do, I expect the United States to find ways and means to disassociate itself from allies moving on their own. This is one function the "hot line" between Washington and Moscow is designed to serve.

nonaligned as Sweden is now, that is, technically neutral and not a member of NATO, and well-armed with defensive weapons (potentially even nuclear ones) yet committed to Western ideals and institutions. Or, NATO may be formally maintained, but substantively weakened, with forces withdrawn from it and deployed outside of it. Whatever degree of cohesion persists, our analysis suggests that bloc ties will decrease, not increase as many in Washington hope and, which is worse, still expect.

PLURALISM AND WESTERN STRATEGY

Although the East and West blocs were always very different in their degree of integration—the East being much more monolithic and Soviet-dominated than the West was American-dominated—both are today breaking up, albeit in different ways and for different reasons. I expect that the next five to eight years will demonstrate conclusively that a complete recovery of the former state of unity is impossible in both camps, although there will probably not be an irrevocable rupture in either. And once both camps accept their inability to close the rifts with their allies, they will be more ready to deal with each other.

This evolution outdates the duopolistic strategy. Duopoly assumes solidarity on the side of the containing power and an inability to pry away major "chunks" of the expanding power; it neither provides guidelines for the dangers or consequences of a rift in the containing power, nor suggests ways to exploit rifts in the expansionist camp. The whole conception of maintaining a global *status quo* breaks down once the expanding power can make major gains or even envisage a chance for such gains by exploiting a split in the West. Thus the United States might be holding the line in West Berlin, expecting to show the U.S.S.R. that its so-called "salami" tactics will not pay off, while the U.S.S.R. might be preparing to negotiate with France or West Germany or both over "neutralization" of all of central Europe. As acute an observer as Walter Lippmann no longer considers such a development inconceivable; he points out that a *rapprochement* between a French-and-German-led Europe and the U.S.S.R. could lead to a deal involving the reunification of Germany, the disbanding of NATO and the Warsaw Treaty Organization, and the formation of a nonaligned Central Europe.[27] Duopoly orients U.S. policy to counter the loss of a "slice," but a whole "chunk" might be lost without even a trade-off.

Duopoly also gives up the hope of making a major inroad into the other camp, not by military rollback, but by winning over a major member following an internal rift. It has seemed to be this strategic outlook, drawing heavily on a belief in the monolithic nature of international Communism, that for years prevented the West from giving credence to reports about an evolving Sino-Soviet rift; from correctly assessing its depth; and, to this day, from adequately responding to it. Similarly, the Russians gave up, at least until recently, any serious hope of successfully dealing with the Western powers separately.

Each super-power would, of course, like to increase the rifts in the other's camp without allowing those in its own to grow. The United States would like the U.S.S.R. vigorously to encourage China to adhere to a treaty banning nuclear tests without itself having to apply similar pressure on France; Russia would like to benefit from the strains produced as the United States tries to prevent France from testing nuclear arms, without its having to face up to this question in its relations with China. (In propaganda terms, the United States emphasizes that France is an independent country, and that the United States cannot be held accountable for French testing; the

[27] The prospects of such a German move are discussed in a brilliant article by Hans J. Morgenthau in the *New York Times Magazine*, September 8, 1963.

U.S.S.R., on the other hand, has pointed out that China has never tested a bomb, while France has.)

An effective give-and-take between the United States and the U.S.S.R. requires both to be less sensitive to their respective allies and more ready to make interbloc arrangements, be it arms control or a settlement of such political issues as the status of Berlin. Yet so far both have largely avoided such arrangements. This avoidance seems to stem from, among other reasons, the desire of each not to undermine further the solidarity of its camp. While the world powers structure moves closer to a pluralistic state—a movement which we have seen is likely to continue in the next decade—basic Western and Soviet strategic thinking seems to be fixed to the bipolar state of the early fifties. The more the two major powers accept the possibility of a give-and-take relationship, the further we would move toward a pluralistic world. This implies not the severance of all political ties or ideological affinities, but a readjustment of attitudes to accommodate and utilize the declines in bloc solidarity that are already occurring and cannot be prevented.

Some limited accommodation has already taken place. Examining it, one might extrapolate the directions American (and Soviet) foreign policy may take if this mutual accommodation is extended. Both super-powers, I expect, will eventually draw on the psychological impact of the rifts, to form various interbloc arrangements now prevented by, among other things, the objections of their allies.

THE PSYCHOLOGICAL IMPACT

The psychological effects of the Cold War have often been emphasized. Over the years, it is said, both sides have built up a wall of hate, suspicion, and fear that makes them unable to see each other as they really are. The average Russian is taught to view the United States as a country of warmongers, capitalist exploiters, and imperialists. The average American

sees the West as representing the forces of light against those
of darkness, of freedom against slavery, of democracy against
totalitarianism. An illustration of the effect of these charges
is provided by the psychologist Urie Bronfenbrenner, who
showed photographs he had taken in the Soviet Union to
some American fifth- and sixth-grade school children. Asked
why the Russians planted trees along the road, a little boy said,
"So that people won't be able to see what's going on beyond
the road," and a little girl volunteered, "It's to make work
for the prisoners." Bronfenbrenner then asked why *our* roads
have trees beside them. Answers: "For shade"; "To keep the
dust down."[28]

This Cold War mentality hampers even the most limited
and innocuous interbloc arrangements. Thus, for instance,
when the United States and the U.S.S.R. were negotiating
the creation of a direct teleprinter line between the Kremlin
and the White House, aimed at easing communication between the sides, many American popular newspapers objected.
The New York *Daily News*, for example, editorialized that it
distrusted the "hot-line" arrangement as a gimmick that
offered Khrushchev "a golden chance to keep the White
House bemused and befuddled" because the Soviets could
send a long message at the same time they launched a surprise
attack.[29]

Although neither the popular press nor public opinion
directly determines American foreign policy, most politicians
find it difficult to resist them continually and on a wide front.
Russian foreign policy is much less influenced by public
opinion, but even in the Soviet Union it cannot be completely disregarded. Not that the leadership of either country
is exempt from the influence of these psychological processes. This means that any wider interbloc agreement will

[28] *The Saturday Review*, January 5, 1963, p. 96.
[29] June 21, 1963.

require some modification of the Cold War atmosphere, some psychological disarmament.[30]

Various means have been suggested to reduce interbloc hate and fear and thus the public suspicion of proposed interbloc arrangements. These include increased visits of Russians to the United States and of Americans to Russia; more cultural exchanges; and more joint American-Russian projects, following the pattern of the International Geophysical Year.[31] Several such steps have been taken in recent years; there has been, for instance, a considerable increase in interbloc tourism. But so far the effect on the Cold War atmosphere seems to have been limited. The surprise appearance of Russian missiles in Cuba did more to intensify the Cold War mentality then all these steps did to reduce it. A major breakthrough in Cold War psychology seems to be forthcoming, however, but from a quite different quarter and without anyone having planned it. It is an unexpected dividend of the rifts in the two blocs.[32]

The psychological equivalent of bipolarity is a world split into two parts, the free and the slave. This simple dichotomy fits well into the mass psychology that sharply divides the good guys from the bad guys and needs a villain (on whom all sins can be projected) and a hero (on whom all virtues can be bestowed). Rarely was this popular tendency to polarize more fully apparent than in pitting the free world against international Communism. There was no dirty trick in the book the Communists were not believed capable of; and whatever the West did was viewed as justifiable. (One of my students concluded that if in the disarmament negotia-

[30] President Kennedy, in his "Strategy for Peace" speech at American University, June 10, 1963, called for such a change of atmosphere.

[31] On these measures and their rationale, see Charles E. Osgood, *An Alternative to War or Surrender* (Urbana, Ill.: University of Illinois Press, 1962), and my *The Hard Way to Peace: A New Strategy* (New York: Collier, 1962), Ch. 4.

[32] The following discussion focuses on American public opinion, since information on the Russian side is not available.

tions the Russians agreed to an inspection scheme, this in itself would be sufficient proof that they had found a way to
circumvent it!) If the majority of the American people feel
this way, it is very easy for their elected representatives to
support increased arms production, to favor sending troops to
third countries, and to be "tough" in general, but very difficult
to support arms reductions, interbloc agreements, or disengagement. *Fortunately, the same processes that reduce the
blocs' solidarity also disarm them psychologically by weakening Cold War stereotypes.* Such "disarmament" is far from
complete or even widely shared, but it appears to be extensive
enough to provide a foundation on which our political leaders
could build the needed public support for interbloc arrangements.

This reduction in the Cold War atmosphere is not occurring
because the American people are suddenly deciding that Communists can be "trusted" or that "the differences between
the sides are not worth fighting for," or because tourism and
cultural exchanges are breaking either side's stereotypes of
the other. *It is occurring because of a split in the two
images of the East and the West.* China has become, more
and more, the focus of hate, viewed as a barbarian horde, a
"yellow menace," about to descend upon the world. At the
same time, some of the loaded slogans by which Russia was
characterized are receding in the popular vocabulary. For the
first time the general public seems to feel that perhaps the
Russians (note, not "the Communists") are not such bad
guys after all, and the idea is suggested—at least jokingly and
tentatively—that the United States might even have to fight
again with Russia, this time against China.

The New York *Herald Tribune* put it cautiously: "The
threat to the free world from Moscow may become smaller,
but the threat from Peking to both the free world and the
Soviet world could become greater. And it is not altogether
beyond the realm of possibility that those who oppose

thermonuclear war, Communists, non-Communists, and anti-Communists, may have to join forces some day to contain those who favor it."[33] More explicitly, Karl Deutsch, Yale professor of political science, suggested that the nuclear powers (i.e., the United States and the U.S.S.R.) agree to threaten with bombardment any sites where above-ground nuclear tests of any power are readied.[34] Various sources are beginning to emphasize the fact that Russia, like America, is now a "have" country and as such has an interest in a secure, orderly world in which the "have-not" countries, including China, will have to refrain from violence. Even the fact that Russia, like the United States, is predominantly white and China is not, is mentioned. The sum total of these changes in sentiments is not to increase global understanding or eliminate international suspicions, but to shift their focus from Russia to China and break up the sense of a totalistic confrontation, a dichotomy of "we" against "they." There are, increasingly, no more simply good and bad guys, but also gray ones, whom we may not like but whom we might have to tolerate or even cooperate with, and with whom we share disapproval of the "bad guys."

This reorientation is reinforced by a split in the image of the West into "we" and France (or "we" and the Common Market). A few years ago France was still, as far as the wider American public was concerned, a cherished ally; de Gaulle was a favorite friend and a hero of World War II who was seeking to stabilize the economy and government of France, to terminate the Algerian War, and to lead a European Common Market that was to be a major power on our side in the struggle against Communism. In 1963 France was considered a precarious ally, ungrateful, capable of secret dealings with the Russians, and de Gaulle was characterized as an egomaniac, concerned with false glory, arbitrary and ambitious.

[33] Editorial, November 25, 1962.
[34] The *New York Times*, June 14, 1963.

On the eve of de Gaulle's return to power in 1958 he was
". . . a profoundly sophisticated man with a far-ranging mind,
a shrewd insight into people and an ironic sense of humor."
In the United States and Britain it was felt that de Gaulle
". . . might contribute more to the defenses of the West
than all the lip service paid to 'Western unity' by all the
weak premiers of France in the past decade."[35] In 1963 the
general was referred to as "an uncomfortable, stubborn, self-
centered man, sometimes incredibly wrong."[36] Thus the West,
too, is split into good guys and not-so-good guys. Cartoonists
compared President Kennedy's troubles with de Gaulle to
those of Khrushchev with Mao, portraying the American and
Russian "masters" as having similar difficulties keeping their
unruly French and Chinese "pets" on the leash.

POST-RIFT STRATEGIES

The decline of bloc solidarity has opened both the public
mind and the international political arena to a new range of
maneuvering and flexibility. The first reaction on both sides
has been to try to heal their own rifts while increasing their
opponent's. Gradually, though, the possibility of and interest
in implementing interbloc arrangements is growing.

There is still discussion in the West about how to exacerbate
and exploit the rift in the East. There are those who favor a
"soft" line toward Russia and a "tough" line toward China,
on the grounds that the West should show the Communists
that it will support steps in the direction of genuine peaceful
coexistence and react harshly to expansionist efforts. On the
other hand, it has been argued that seeking accommodations
with Khrushchev will only weaken his position in the Communist camp, as a collaborator with capitalists, and will
force him to follow a "harder" line. A third position is that
whatever the West does will have little effect since the

[35] *Time*, May 26, 1958, p. 29.
[36] *The Reporter*, January 31, 1963, p. 23.

Russians will interpret it as indicating that their approach is superior, while the Chinese will claim it shows that their approach is needed.

Moscow has not yet revealed its strategy toward the Western rift; it is possible that the U.S.S.R. decided to refrain from any major drive to make the Western rift to grow, sensing that renewed pressure on its side might bring the Western allies back together. It is significant that ever since the rift between France and the United States came into the open Russia has dropped its insistence on an early settlement of the West Berlin question. It is logical, however, to expect renewed Russian efforts to deal separately with the Western allies at a later day.

FROM RIFTS TO RULES

The nature and the success of the rift-building efforts of both sides will depend largely on their aims. So far these have been governed mainly by the basic political instinct that it is better to have the opposing camp split than unified, but by little, if any, more specific strategy. If both camps are in the long run likely to continue to split whatever the other side does, little can be achieved by such subtle maneuvers as being "warmer" to the Russians and "cooler" to the Chinese, or by the Russians sending different diplomatic notes to the various Western powers. The response to the decline of bloc solidarity must be fit into an over-all strategy that relates efforts in these matters to those in other areas. Instead of simply building up rifts for rifts' sake, we might use them to gain the kind of interbloc arrangements the United States desires, the U.S.S.R. might be ready for, and the world needs. To return for a moment to our automobile-company analogue: suppose that both firms—the expansionist and the defensive—are faced with new, small but vigorous firms that not only cut into their respective shares of the market, but violate every rule accepted in the trade. After some efforts to absorb the newcomers (by offering partnerships) have failed, the two super-firms would be working in their own interests, and in the interest of all buyers, if they were to formulate some rules within which the competition between all could continue, and devise some machinery to enforce these rules. The time when the two super-firms are still dominant in the market is the best time to set up such rules and make explicit arrangements for their enforcement. Earlier, there was little motivation to do so, and later, it will be more difficult, because the full consent and cooperation of four or more firms will be required.

To put it differently, the two super-powers used to regulate international affairs by ruling their blocs, which focused tensions and disorder solely on the interbloc front. The rise of pluralism, the decline in both super-powers' ability to regulate their blocs, makes universal rules jointly formed and enforced by the two the major feasible mode of regulation available. The ban on nuclear tests is a fine illustration of such a rule that Russia and America seek to impose on all other nations, to avoid nuclear anarchy and preserve their status as superpowers.

Many specific plans have been forwarded for other interbloc arrangements. On the political front, several plans for a settlement of the Berlin question have been offered. In April 1962 Secretary of State Dean Rusk initiated proposals that included a plan for an international authority, controlling access to the city, based upon an international guarantee of unimpeded access.[37] This plan was widely reported as acceptable to the Russians, but was withdrawn by the United States when West Germany resisted it and France supported Germany's demand for a "harder" line. Seen as an isolated measure, in a world where the Western alliance is otherwise compatible, the introduction of such an agreement over Ger-

[37] *New Republic*, April 30, 1962, pp. 3–5.

man protest might well seem unwise, an attempt to please the other side rather than one's allies. But when the same measure constitutes part of a more general effort to bring the interbloc conflict under control, the fact must be faced that allies' disagreements are likely in any case. Some additional disagreement to attain a major accommodation is inevitable but not disastrous, and it becomes much more politically worthwhile.

The American-Russian treaty on partial cessation of nuclear tests is another case in point. The value of the treaty lies in part in the ban itself—stopping the increase of radioactive fallout and curbing the further development of nuclear weapons. But its main value lies in its potential as a step toward more important interbloc measures of arms control. Assume that such an agreement would be followed by the formation of denuclearized zones in the Far East, the Middle East, Africa, and Latin America.[38] A non-nuclear club would be established to which more and more countries would subscribe, committing themselves not to produce and not to possess nuclear weapons and not to allow other countries to station them on their territory. In this way nuclear anarchy might be prevented.

This raises a more general question. If the super-powers are willing to face disagreements with their allies and to assume the risk of some increase in the rifts in their respective camps, can the agreements they make be enforced on their reluctant allies? Does not the decline in bloc integration by the same token spell a decline in the ability of the super-powers to speak for their camps and to implement interbloc agreements?

The answer lies largely in the nature and scope of the agreements made. Paradoxically, I submit that the more important and broad in scope an agreement is, the easier it would be

[38] On this proposal, see below, p. 99–100.

to enforce. The super-powers can no longer command the almost automatic compliance of their allies. They even find it difficult to achieve agreement on matters close to their own national interests, such as the U.S. quest for certain tariff concessions from the Common Market. How can the United States sanction France if the French impose higher tariffs on U.S. agricultural imports? The United States might impose higher tariffs on French exports to the United States. But this would result in additional French tariffs on American products, and the United States would be the loser because it exports more to France than France does to it.[39] What can Russia do if China invokes its displeasure? It could and did cut its economic aid; but once this has been done, little leverage is left. Yet, as so often happens in power relations in the nuclear age, there is a considerable difference between minor and major issues.

It is the super-powers that hold the nuclear umbrellas over their allies, deterring a nuclear attack on them by the other side. More technically, they hold the strategic deterrent forces. One day China and France may each have its own deterrent; but for at least the next five years this will not amount to even a half-effective minimum deterrent force. If these countries should act unilaterally, or refuse to cooperate on major issues, the super-powers' warning that the umbrella might be removed is likely to suffice—for a few years at least—to bring them into line. China would not attack Formosa without Russian consent, and France had to retreat in Egypt in 1956 because the United States let it be known that it would not come to the defense if the Soviets carried out their threats to rain missiles on France. By their nature, the umbrellas the super-powers hold over their allies cannot be credibly folded

[39] In 1962 U.S. exports to France amounted to $575,014,800; French exports to the United States totaled $424,277,574. (Source: French Commercial Information Service, New York.) Also, American tariffs were higher to begin with, hence the marginal effect of their increase is lower.

to gain minor concessions, but can be used to generate support for major ones, such as *significant* interbloc arrangements. Hence, it is most difficult to enforce limited interbloc arrangements on reluctant allies, such as cessation of testing on France and China or solution of the Berlin dilemma on the Germanies. Only if such steps are accompanied or at least followed by other, more inclusive steps, which are part of a new over-all strategy, can the heavy levers be brought to bear.

Once again the effectiveness of a particular measure cannot be judged unless placed in a general context. Many solutions to specific problems that seemed quite unacceptable in the bipolar, Cold War context of yesterday might seem much more acceptable in tomorrow's emerging pluralistic context. It will no longer be two camps facing each other in an uneasy balance, but two super-powers that recognize that they have some common interests and responsibilities, above and beyond their commitments to their respective allies. These common interests and responsibilities might well find their expression, at least initially, in setting some limits or rules under which the intercamp conflict could continue with less danger. The factors other than the decline in bipolarity that determine whether such a strategy of competition under rules will indeed provide the framework for American (and Russian) foreign policy in the years to come, and what specific developments they might bring about is the subject of the following chapters.

Chapter III

THE CONTEST OVER THE THIRD WORLD

The decline of bipolarity has been manifested in two ways: in the weakening of ties among the members of the two super-blocs, and in the rise of nonaligned nations and third blocs.[1] While the full consequences of the waning of bloc solidarity are only gradually becoming understood, the limitations the duopolistic strategy sets on an effective American policy toward third-force countries have been recognized for some time. It is in this area that the most progress has been made toward a new approach. An examination of the changes in attitudes toward nonalignment is therefore of interest both for its own sake and as an example of the possibilities and risks involved in the competition strategy. It will be seen that some of the dangers that have arisen have been created by the incompleteness of the shift, the "mix" of old and new perspectives.

THE DECLINE OF DUOPOLY

During the fifties John Foster Dulles maintained that a country uncommitted to the West was necessarily opposed to it. Neutrality, he added, "except under very exceptional circumstances, . . . [is] an immoral and obsolete conception."

[1] *Nonaligned* countries are those that do not have permanent ties with either of the super-blocs. Alignment refers primarily to military and political ties. Nonalignment does not imply neutrality in the East-West contest; countries may acquire various shades of neutrality, or be pro-West or pro-East. As long as their sympathies, expressed in their favorable orientation toward one bloc as against the other, are not transformed into permanent ties, they remain nonaligned.

Stalin, too, consistently attacked the position of nonalignment, and during the period of his rule the Soviets viewed the world as split into "two major camps; the imperialist and antidemocratic camp, on the one hand, and the anti-imperialist and democratic camp, on the other."[2]

The strategy of containment assumes such a world, and third, or uncommitted, parties, which, by refusing to choose sides, rendered the drawing of a clear line impossible, were a constant harassment. How were such countries to be restrained from submitting to expansionist overtures and pressures? Between 1948 and 1956 the United States exerted considerable diplomatic and economic pressure to establish a grid of alliances with third countries, while the fall of Czechoslovakia, the Berlin blockade, and the invasion of South Korea accelerated the Western formation of military alliances geared to counter Communist expansion. At the same time, the Communist bloc employed a combination of occupation troops, propaganda (from the outside), and Communist organizations (from the inside) in an attempt to extend its influence in countries on the containment line (e.g., Iran, Indochina) and behind it (e.g., Indonesia). If the world did not fit their respective outlooks, both sides seemed to agree, the world must be tailored to fit the strategic cloth.

The U.S.S.R. was quick to recognize the limitations of the bipolar concept and to adjust its policy accordingly. In 1953, although they still hoped that the less developed continents would find their way into the Communist camp, the Russians began to foster nonalignment rather than alliance among third countries under the banner of a "vast zone of peace." In supporting non-Communist governments and independence movements, the U.S.S.R. sometimes neglected the Communists in these nations; it even backed govern-

[2] Party ideologue Andrei Zhdanov, cited by Vernon V. Aspaturian, "Soviet Foreign Policy," in Roy C. Macridis (ed.), *Foreign Policy in World Politics* (Englewood Cliffs, N.J.: Prentice-Hall, 1962), p. 146.

ments, like those of Nasser and Nehru, that jailed Communists and suppressed Communist parties. Soviet technical and economic aid to these countries rapidly increased, but no effort was made to send large military missions or "volunteers." With the single exception of Cuba, the twenty-odd underdeveloped countries that have received Soviet aid since its initiation in 1954 have continued to maintain their independence and their status of nonalignment.

The West, somewhat slower to respond to emerging multipolarity, continued throughout most of the 1950s to try to fit a changing world to its static duopolistic concept. Three American allies, Korea, Formosa, and Vietnam, received approximately half of all the aid handed out by the United States from 1948 to 1960, with members of the Western ranks such as Turkey enjoying as much as four times the amount of aid granted to nonaligned states such as Egypt.

As nationalism swept the less developed continents, it gradually became apparent that the nations that detached themselves from the West, or refused to become aligned with it in the first place, were not, contrary to expectations, joining the Communist camp. Apparently, in a contest for men's minds, as long as occupation by Communist troops—as threatened in Korea—is prevented, "military alliances are likely to be at best of minor importance, and at worst a political handicap."[3]

Western concern over nonalignment as a road to Communism was substantially reduced under the impact of what might be called the "Egyptian lesson." Measures against Communist organizations in Egypt were intensive during the years when the country was receiving a preponderance of its military and economic aid from the Soviet bloc. And the introduction of Nasser's brand of socialism was not followed by alignment with the Communist bloc.

[3] Hans J. Morgenthau, "The American Tradition in Foreign Policy," in Macridis, *op. cit.*, p. 214.

In 1955 Nasser undertook several steps that incurred American annoyance. Egyptian recognition of Communist China and purchase of Soviet arms was followed by the Aswan Dam transaction. Although it is difficult to establish with certainty the sequence of events surrounding the question of financing the Aswan Dam, Nasser's success in conveying the impression that the Soviets had offered to finance the entire project dealt the final blow to Western consideration of underwriting it. In February 1956 the State Department and the British Foreign Office announced their decision to withhold aid. Shortly thereafter an Egyptian request for American wheat and flour was turned down and $55 million in food to be donated by CARE was "buried in red tape."[4] Nasser's nationalization of the Suez Canal appeared to be the culmination of Egyptian estrangement from the West. In 1956, when the Western leaders blocked Egyptian government funds and cut aid to Egypt, the Soviets proved only too willing to step into the gap with increased military, economic, and technical assistance, and they offered to buy Egypt's chief export commodity, cotton, when the Western market became sated.

The ensuing military action against Egypt by France, Britain, and Israel, aimed at unseating Nasser, was stopped only by the objections of both super-powers. Russia threatened to rain missiles on the "imperialist" invaders; and the United States, anxious to touch up its image among the new nations and offended by the precipitate action of its allies who had failed to consult Washington, expressed strong reservations over the invaders' move. Because of its ties with NATO partners France and England, however, the United States was forced to mince words, while Khrushchev vigorously denounced the "imperialist violation of peace." Thus Russia reaped what appeared to be a significant propaganda gain; it

4 Keith Wheelock, *Nasser's New Egypt* (New York: Praeger, 1960), p. 249.

had provided assistance without strings to fill the gap left by Western withdrawal and called a halt, many Egyptians believed, to a Western invasion.

If Egypt had proceeded according to Western fears in 1956, Nasser would have crossed the bloc line at this time. Instead, he continued on the path of nonalignment. Anxious to receive all the aid he could from whatever source, he was at the same time concerned about being "taken over" in the process. He adamantly restricted the number of Soviet military missions and technicians and vociferously denounced local Communists, breaking their organizations and jailing their leaders.

By 1958 Western policy vis-à-vis nonaligned countries had begun to shift. A *rapprochement*, temporarily eclipsed by the Iraqi coup and the Lebanon crisis, was effected, and Egypt now received substantial economic aid and technical assistance from both blocs. But just as he did not allow Soviet aid to affect Egyptian domestic policy, Nasser has not allowed renewed Western support to set Egypt's course. In 1961–62, as relations with the West continued to improve, he nationalized large numbers of foreign and Egyptian banks, along with insurance companies, export-import houses, and other businesses, and formally introduced Arab socialism in Egypt.

In sum, Nasser, in accordance with the practice widely followed by nonaligned nations, has sought aid and trade from both sides, on the best possible terms, with as few strings attached as possible. Always careful to preserve Egyptian independence, he has over the years succeeded in eroding the power positions of both the local Communists and the pro-Western business groups. In the United Nations, Egypt has voted about as often with the United States as with the U.S.S.R. and frequently with the nonaligned Afro-Asian camp. Nasser clearly views membership in either the Communist or Western bloc as a kiss of death to his regional, national, and personal ambitions.

Another example of a third country determined to remain nonaligned is Guinea, which is run by a Marxian socialist elite and, for several years, was nearly written off Western books as a potential Communist satellite, the first in Africa. In 1956 de Gaulle, in a typical duopolistic move, offered thirteen French African colonies a choice between continued dependence or independence within the French Community, and striking out on their own. A welcome response of twelve *"oui's"* for independence along with Community membership was marked by one dissenting vote, the blatant *"non"* of Guinea. Guinea's defiant preference for "poverty in freedom" over "prosperity in servitude" incurred severe retaliatory measures from the angered de Gaulle, who immediately cut aid to France's former showcase and ordered the recall of French administrators and military units. As trade plummeted (80 per cent of Guinea's exports had been sent to France prior to 1958) and the United States hedged, Guinea turned to the East. The Sino-Soviet bloc's quick recognition of the new state (the United States was the fifty-first nation to recognize Guinea) and its offer of aid, technical assistance, and trade agreements were eagerly accepted by Premier Sekou Touré, who had been caught off balance by de Gaulle's vehement reaction. Many Westerners were quick to label Touré a Communist puppet.

But the West was forced to re-examine its position when, late in 1961, the Guinean leader denounced Ambassador Daniel Sold, a ranking Soviet expert on African affairs, for meddling in Guinean politics, giving the Russian diplomat forty-eight hours to leave the country. Subsequently, Touré jailed local Communist leaders, restricted Soviet and Chinese propaganda, and during the Cuban crisis of 1962 refused the use of Guinea's airstrip to Soviet planes, despite the fact that the Soviets had built it. The Soviet bloc continues to supply a substantial amount of aid and technical assistance to

Guinea, but it now faces French and American competition. Increasingly, the West regards Touré as he regards himself— "first an African and second a Marxist."

The story of many other countries in the less developed continents is similar to that of Egypt and Guinea. For some time, every coup in Iraq was expected to signal a Communist take-over, but it never materialized; in 1963 the Communists were ruthlessly purged, and Iraq continues to maintain its independence and its policy of nonalignment. Syria, widely expected to fall under Communist control in 1958, is still nonaligned. Indonesia was written off Western books half a dozen times, yet it still manages to balance between East and West. More recently, Algeria has been a source of much concern, as have British Guiana and Burma. The fact remains that over all these years the Communist bloc gained one country, Cuba (probably only a temporary gain), and lost one, Yugoslavia (perhaps a temporary loss), while seventy-odd underdeveloped countries successfully maintained their independence. Many of these countries have pursued policies of nonalignment under leftist governments, such as Burma and Ceylon in Asia, Mexico and Bolivia in Latin America, and Ghana and Senegal in Africa, to mention a few. But although these countries could not be tied to the West, they did not trade their nonalignment for more assistance from the East. An approach other than one based on duopoly was obviously called for.

The change, initiated near the end of Eisenhower's second term and carried considerably further under the Kennedy Administration, was reflected in several ways. Slowly, nonalignment became a position the West found tolerable and legitimate, although not desirable. "It would be an erring logic," stated McGeorge Bundy, Johnson's special assistant for national security affairs, "which would set our unaligned friends always behind our allies. We have chosen neutrality for enough of our history to recognize and respect the similar choice of others."[5]

The amount of economic aid given to nonallied countries in comparison to allies had grown considerably, with India taking the first position among aid-receiving countries as of 1960. And support for non-Communist governments, whatever their domestic and foreign policy, is increasingly regarded as wise policy.

The change in the Western approach to nonalignment is by no means complete, for although the Kennedy Administration appeared to favor the new policy, Congress, several government agencies, and large segments of the public continued to cling to the old approach. When India's border zones were attacked by Communist China in 1962 and the country turned to America for military aid, several congressmen favored leaving it to its fate to "show" all countries what happens to those who prefer nonalignment.[6]

There is still a feeling that allies are more "safely" anti-Communist than nonallied nations, and there is much less than full recognition of the broader strategic significance for East-West relations of approaching third countries with a pluralistic rather than a duopolistic concept.

LIMITED SHIFTING AND THE COMPETITION

THE CONTEST'S PRIZES

The United States and the U.S.S.R. are competing for the minds of the people of the three underdeveloped continents. They are motivated in part by humanist considerations (being "have" countries in a world of "have nots"), in part by a search for trade advantages or protection of investment, and in part by considerations of prestige, power, and security.

[5] McGeorge Bundy, "Friends and Allies," *Foreign Affairs*, October 1962, p. 17.
[6] *New York Times*, July 6, 1963.

Both sides and many onlookers have come to measure the relative global standing of the two blocs in terms of their successes and failures in the underdeveloped world. As far as foreign policy is concerned, the major prizes are shifts in bloc sympathies of the third countries, reflected in votes in the United Nations, public pronouncements, foci of trade, and the like. Since neither bloc any longer realistically expects to increase its membership significantly, the prizes do not include alignment but more limited shifts within the non-alignment context, such as from a pro-Eastern to a somewhat less pro-Eastern position (Indonesia in 1963), or from a quite pro-Western to a somewhat more neutral position (Brazil and Cambodia in 1962).

A typical American news item reads: "The Chinese Communist invasion of India affected Afghanistan profoundly. India moved closer to the Western powers in a defensive alignment. Pakistan, in consequence, moved closer to Communist China and away from the West. Then the Afghan government changed. . . . Under Dr. Yousuf [the new Premier], the Afghan pendulum is swinging back toward the West."[7]

Each year both sides can report some losses and some gains, but the stock does not become depleted for two important reasons: even the countries most sympathetic to one bloc, with one exception, Cuba, have stayed nonaligned, and neither side has been amassing the sympathies of all or most of the countries. Like the "floating vote" in national politics that both sides keep trying for, the nonaligned camp has not run out of prizes for the bloc contestants, nor does it seem likely to in the near future.

The patterns of voting in the United Nations illustrate this point. Studying eighty of the most important roll-call votes in the Fifteenth and Sixteenth General Assemblies (1960–62), Francis Wilcox found that in those instances in which the

[7] *New York Times*, June 20, 1963.

United States and the U.S.S.R. voted differently, 26.1 per cent of the votes cast by fifty nonaligned states (who constitute the decisive weight in the Assembly) coincided with the United States and 29.1 per cent with the U.S.S.R.[8] In about one third of the votes (31.3 per cent) these countries' votes differed from both the United States and the U.S.S.R.

To be sure, the voting statistics of the United Nations do not accurately reflect the realities of international power politics since each country, regardless of its power, has one vote, and the freedom to shift from voting with one bloc to voting with another is large. But they do serve to illustrate, in exaggerated fashion, the general nature of the emerging pattern of global politics, one in which nations that are not members of either of the two blocs constitute the majority and, anxious to maintain their independence, "move" back and forth between the sides, shifting their sympathies from one to the other, or withholding them from both.

MODERATION IS PRIZED

The "floating vote" of third countries is affected by foreign aid, ideology, personalities, geopolitical factors, and many other considerations. But it also responds to the international conduct of the two super-powers. With some exceptions, the voices of most nonaligned countries in international forums, from the United Nations in New York to the disarmament negotiations in the Palais des Nations in Geneva, have been raised in support of moderation in the interbloc conflict. They have tended to be on the side of measures restricting the conflict to nonarmed competition, have favored arms-control and arms-reduction proposals, and have urged that the peace-maintaining capacities of the United Nations be strengthened. The nonaligned have often taken these positions in self-in-

[8] Francis O. Wilcox, "The Nonaligned States and the U.N.," in Lawrence W. Martin (ed.), *Neutralism and Nonalignment* (New York: Praeger, 1962), pp. 127–30.

terest (e.g., fear of devastation such as Korea and Vietnam have known); in other instances, their support of moderation has been a result of their being at least temporarily under the influence of one bloc or another (e.g., India and five other nonaligned countries sponsored a proposal for a moratorium on nuclear tests in 1961 after the Russians had finished their round but before the Americans had completed theirs). But these nations have eloquently raised the tired voice of a mankind that seeks escape from war, relief from hunger, and freedom from oppression; refusing to place all the blame for the arms race and Cold War on any one side, they have been anxious for interbloc accommodation even if the last ounce of justice is not exacted.

More specifically, when East-West confrontations have occurred or appeared imminent, many nonaligned countries have pressed for moderation on the part of both blocs, although they have tended to be less critical of the East than of the West. One reason massive retaliation was jettisoned was the loud protest its announcement provoked in nonaligned countries. Later, in 1961, one of the reasons the United States did not come more openly to the aid of the Bay of Pigs invaders was that the nonaligned countries were expected to see such assistance as a revival of "gunboat diplomacy," a label the United States is trying to shed. Similarly, in condemning British, French, and Israeli action in the 1956 Sinai campaign, both the United States and the U.S.S.R. addressed themselves largely to the public opinion of the nonaligned countries. And although the nonaligned were more circumspect in their criticism than the Western allies when the U.S.S.R. suppressed the Hungarian uprising in 1956, and when it abruptly resumed nuclear testing in 1961, the U.S.S.R. did not escape expressions of their disapproval.

Among the nonaligned countries' numerous proposals for strengthening the United Nations' peace-maintaining powers and for reducing arms have been suggestions for denuclearized zones in Latin America and Africa; the establishment of a U.N. agency to study disarmament methods and instruments; and the creation of a special U.N. peace fund which would allow citizens of all nations to contribute directly to U.N. peace forces (proposed by Ghana in 1963 when lack of funds threatened to undercut the peace-keeping operations). Several nonaligned countries provided military units to restore peace and order in the Congo.

To put it more technically, the stabilizing role of the third states in a "loose bipolar system" has come to the fore in interbloc competition for their support, constraining the blocs "to phrase their demands upon each other in ways more consonant with universalistic standards than if the blocs were in an unmediated face-to-face relationship. In addition, the existence of such uncommitted nations permits the blocs to accede to the conciliatory efforts of the uncommitted states —a procedure that is more politically acceptable than accession to the demands of the opposing bloc."[9]

In general, nonaligned countries, even when acting in unison, are a weak, if growing, element on the global scales. Much of their influence on the super-powers stems from the fact that direct confrontations have become too dangerous. The blocs have shifted their attention to sparring in the underdeveloped continents, measuring their success in terms of their achievements in courting these militarily and economically marginal, but psychologically and politically significant, nations. These countries are more effective in preventing negative acts and moderating aggression than in promoting positive changes, such as improving the U.N. peace-maintaining activities, but by and large their influence supports the incipient movement away from the concept of duopoly. Providing an outlet for both sides' ambitions through nonarmed

[9] Morton A. Kaplan, "Bipolarity in a Revolutionary Age," in Morton A. Kaplan (ed.), *The Revolution in World Politics* (New York: Wiley, 1962), p. 252.

competition for the support of the nonaligned does not magically remove the danger of an interbloc showdown, but it reduces its likelihood and supports other factors working toward an international situation of peaceful competition under rules.

THE MIX

At first glance, it would seem that the United States and the U.S.S.R. have already initiated a process of competition, admittedly a limited one, in which they tolerate each other's "presence" and compete with nonviolent means, thus providing—in line with the requirements for more constructive interbloc relations specified above—an outlet for expanionist ambitions coupled with respect for the independence and nonalignment of third countries. A second look reveals that the nonarmed quality of this competition is not effectively safeguarded, and that while present interbloc relations are far less volatile than those of the duopolistic days, they are still potentially too explosive for safety in the nuclear age. The transition from duopoly to competition stopped halfway, leaving an unholy mix of armed confrontations amid the unarmed contest.

The two sides, it must be noted, never agreed to compete peacefully or set up the necessary machinery to contain the competition within its peaceful boundaries. They are increasingly competing by nonarmed means, but the limits of this contest are neither agreed upon nor enforced. There is no agreement not to interfere by the use of arms, and no consensus on what constitutes interference (except as each side so labels the efforts of the other).

The Communist bloc is quite aware, though the West is less so, that unless the Red Army is positioned in a nonaligned country, that country cannot be converted to the Communist bloc even if, as happened in Egypt and Guinea, there is a potentially promising radical revolution there. Native "counterrevolutionary" forces and "deviationists" have time and again stood in the way. On the other hand, Castro's Cuba, as long as the Soviet Army can be used to guard against "counterrevolutionaries," is safely within the bloc, and so are Hungary, Poland, and East Germany.[10] Therefore, as long as armed intervention is not ruled out, the Communist camp can, when expedient, convert sympathizers into full-fledged bloc members. And, although its motives are different, the West, too, arms governments and groups within the nonaligned areas.

The West, of course, claims that it would not do so if it were not for the Communist challenge; but as the Communists see it, no Soviet troops were sent to Cuba until Cuban exiles, financed, armed, trained, and guided by the United States, invaded the island at the Bay of Pigs in 1961, and Communist arms were not shipped into Laos and South Vietnam until after the West had shipped its arms into these areas.[11] As the West sees it, it tried to help the Cubans liberate their country from a Communist government, and to help the legal government of South Vietnam retain its power in the face of insurrection. One can hardly expect the sides to see these matters in the same light; the main point is that armed intervention in the nonaligned areas, though largely curtailed, has not been outlawed; there is neither an agreement nor machinery to enforce an embargo on arms. The main limitations are expediency and power considerations. The blocs fear that being too deeply involved in a local war, as in South Vietnam, may drag them into larger and larger conventional and potentially nuclear wars. The danger

[10] Communist countries that "rebelled" against Moscow are those in which Communism was introduced by indigenous forces without the help of the Red Army, namely, Yugoslavia, China, and Albania.

[11] C. L. Sulzberger in the New York Times, April 24, 1963. See also Dan Kurzman, The Subversion of the Innocents (New York: Random House, 1963), pp. 489 ff.

of continued armed sparring in the underdeveloped countries, it must be emphasized, is the very real one of escalation.

The West, increasingly concerned with leapfrogging over and breaking through the containment line, is building up counterinsurrectionist units ("Special Forces") and antisubversion networks to combat Communist thrusts. Armed competition is at least potentially present in every underdeveloped country: tomorrow Algeria, Indonesia, India, or Venezuela might become another Korea or South Vietnam. Although no large-scale interbloc military confrontation has occurred since the early fifties, it has been avoided rather than eliminated. Under the present system the danger is ever present. Until now the super-powers have managed to keep from being so ensnared in local conflicts that they could not extricate themselves. The Russians and Chinese did not match the more than fourteen thousand American troops sent to South Vietnam, nor did the Americans match the seventeen thousand Russian troops sent to Cuba, although both sides were under pressure to do so. After each close call that ends without a major blow-up, brinkmanship appears less dangerous; but this appearance is lulling and misleading. The fact that you were not killed driving at high speed on a slippery road is no assurance for the next ride.

REMOTE DETERRENCE: THE PRECEDENTS

It is both feasible and desirable to constrain armed intervention by either super-power in nonaligned countries. This can be done by what we will refer to as remote deterrence or holding from the outside. The essence of this approach is that both sides refrain from using arms in the third area as long as the other side holds back and that forces ready to counter violations are posted *outside* the third area. Past developments already point in this direction; the reliance upon armed expansion has declined steadily over the past fifteen years, although, with the exception of the Berlin crises, practically all interbloc confrontations in the fifties and sixties have occurred in third areas.

The present mixture of armed and nonarmed competition is unstable; we have to progress in order not to regress. As long as the use of force is not effectively ruled out, the result of any significant change in circumstances—if, say, one side decides that its nonarmed capacities are declining or that its armed position has markedly improved—might bring regression to armed competition. Actually some such signs were on the horizon in 1962–63 as both sides reversed to a limited degree earlier trends toward nonarmed competition by decreasing their foreign aid and increasing their defense budgets and, in particular, by augmenting forces for use in third countries.

THE PRECEDENT OF AUSTRIA

The containment line, it is widely believed, is maintained by troops of one kind or another. There are American troops directly facing Communist troops in Germany, Vietnam, and Korea. In countries such as Pakistan and Iran, where there are no American troops, arms are supplied by the United States, and local troops and countersubversion units are trained by American military missions. Any proposal for withdrawal of American troops and arms from these areas would seem, correctly in my judgment, as opening them to potential Communist control. Remote deterrence is an alternative method for holding the line, not by positioning troops on it, but by protecting it from the outside. Though it is rarely discussed, this is neither a new nor an untried idea; Austria provides a major precedent.

Austria separates NATO-member Italy from Warsaw Pact-members Hungary and Czechoslovakia. As long as its neutrality and integrity are not violated, it "protects" Italy from a Communist-bloc attack as if it were itself a NATO country.

How is Austrian nonalignment maintained, and how "safe" is it?

After World War II, Austria was a divided country with an Eastern, Russian-occupied zone and a Western zone governed by the United States and its allies. Vienna, like Berlin, was jointly administered. After years of negotiations, East and West agreed to withdraw their troops and refrain from interfering in Austrian internal affairs as long as Austria maintained strict nonalignment. Since the removal of troops in 1955, Austria has successfully done this. It has not been challenged by invasion or subversion, nor has it joined a bloc. It receives neither American nor Russian arms; and it spends little of its national income and only a small proportion of its budget on defense.[12] At the same time it benefits from trade with East and West and enjoys a large tourist business from both blocs.

What safeguards Austria's independence? Its people first of all; any power attempting to occupy Austria would have to impose its regime upon people who would prove extremely uncooperative. They would have to be watched constantly, and their level of production would fall as the costs of running the country increased. (East Germany is one such dubious blessing for the U.S.S.R.) Secondly, although the Communist Party has not been banned, it enjoys little support among this educated, affluent, democratically governed people. There is little room for Communist appeal and small chance of engineering an insurrection to which outsiders could rush support.

Thirdly, Austria, although unallied, is still militarily protected by the super-powers. If the Russians were to violate the treaty that established Austria's status, the West would feel free to move in to counter the Communist attack, as would

[12] Only 1.3 per cent of the gross national product, and 5 per cent of the budget, compared to 10 per cent and 50 per cent, respectively, for the United States. Figures for 1963 from the Austrian Trade Mission, New York.

Russia if the West were to move first. The fact that there is no explicit legal commitment to this effect is of little importance. Commitments to defend countries allied to the West are not particularly explicit either. Under the SEATO treaty, for example, parties are obligated in the event of aggression merely to consult with one another and to "act to meet the common danger" by unspecified means. Moreover, the West has provided military assistance to countries under attack that were not its allies. When India appealed for help late in 1962 after China attacked its northern borders, U.S. arms were rushed to the subcontinent and agreements for more arms and military advisers were concluded without delay.

Lastly, and least important, Austria's independence is protected by a treaty barring outside intervention. This in itself is a minor factor—treaties have been violated before. It should be pointed out, however, that in general, contrary to popular belief, the Soviet record of observing treaties is not much worse than that of most nations, including many Western ones.[13] This is *not* to suggest that one should rely on an international treaty to protect the integrity of a country. Austria's independence—and its place in the containment wall—is protected by the strength of its political and economic institutions and by *external* military support. Under *these* conditions the treaty helps to formalize an understanding, and, if violated, serves the nonaggressor in its appeal to public opinion.

Another characteristic of the "Austrian way" should be pointed out. As far as the U.S.S.R. is concerned, Austria is a neutral neighbor, not a member of a hostile military bloc; as the Russians see it, neighbors aligned to a hostile bloc amount to potential troop or missile bases for action against the Soviet Union (let us say in the event of another uprising in Hun-

[13] See A. Glenn Mower, Jr., "The International Morality of the Soviet Union," in DeVere E. Pentony (ed.), *Soviet Behavior in World Affairs* (San Francisco: Chandler, 1962), pp. 179–98.

gary). It prefers a nonaligned Austria, even though capital-
istic-democratic and flourishing, to an ally of the West. It
does not follow that therefore the "Austrian way" is undesirable for the West. The assumption that whatever benefits one
side necessarily is disadvantageous to the other has little basis
in reality. Austrian neutrality, which reduces the likelihood of
a clash between the nuclear giants, is beneficial to both
camps, to Austria, and to the rest of the world. But is Austria
a "way" or an exception?

ARE THERE OTHER "AUSTRIAS"?

The containment line, often depicted as a twenty-thousand-
mile-long barrier held by Western troops and allies, is actually
often "held" by a nonaligned country, backed up by outside
forces. North of Austria the containment line is held by
NATO-members West Germany and Denmark; farther
north, by nonaligned Finland. Americans occasionally refer
to Finland as a Soviet satellite, or a country living under the
Russian thumb. In reality Finland is largely a free country,
in a world where no small power is completely free. Since
it is nonallied and committed to remain so, it—like Austria
—is not free to join blocs and military alliances, but it does
participate in the Nordic Council. Because Russia is a major
customer, buying approximately 25 per cent of Finland's exports, and a big power whereas Finland is not, the Finns consider it unwise to offend the Russians unnecessarily; but by
and large they live their independent lives. Like Austria,
Finland's foundation of independence is its people.[14] Russia
learned from the bitter experience of 1939–40 that to try to
conquer the Finns can be a very costly endeavor. Being an
educated, rather affluent, people with effective, democratic

---

[14] Also like Austria, Finland spends comparatively little on defense.
From 1950 to 1960 it allocated 4.7 per cent of its budget to defense, and
1 per cent of its gross national product. Figures supplied by the Finnish
Mission to the United Nations.

institutions, Finland is unlikely to witness an internal insurrection initiated by its native Communist party; and the West would be likely to come to Finland's assistance in the event of a Soviet attack. In short, while there are important differences between Finland and Austria, Finland too constitutes a neutral zone between the armed camps.

South of Austria the containment line is held by Yugoslavia. Although internally communist, Yugoslavia broke away from the Soviet bloc in 1948. The West provides Yugoslavia with military aid, but Yugoslavia is hardly a member of the Western camp. In a sense it is an Austria in reverse; its internal institutions are strong but neither democratic nor capitalistic. In many ways, its people are sympathetic to the Communist bloc, just as Austrians are sympathetic to the West. Like the Austrians, however, the Yugoslavs are adamant in opposing the re-entry of Soviet troops, even if the Russians promise to withdraw later or propose merely to pass through. There is little doubt that the Yugoslavs would fight bitterly, with massive assistance from the West, in the event of a Soviet invasion. Thus, Yugoslavia is a communist, nonaligned country, which does not provide bases for American missiles or forces, but which stands in the way of Soviet military expansion. (It goes without saying that if the West ever invaded Yugoslavia it would be bitterly resisted, with strong Russian support of the Yugoslavs.)

In Asia, too, the containment line is held by Western allies bordered by nonaligned countries. Next to CENTO-members Turkey and Iran, equipped with American arms, military missions, and countersubversion commissions, we find Afghanistan (between Russia and Pakistan), nonaligned India, as well as Nepal, Sikkim, and Bhutan, and nonaligned Burma. Laos and Vietnam deserve special attention in this context. While the southern flank of Asia is generally nonaligned, the eastern one—the Philippines, Japan, and South Korea—is allied to the West; that is, while one flank is held by troops on the line, the other is largely held by remote deterrence, by forces that might be committed if these countries were challenged, but which are not positioned within their borders.

REMOTE DETERRENCE IN ASIA

Several observations about these Asian countries are pertinent. First of all, there have been no attempts at armed expansion in countries bordering the U.S.S.R. since Stalin's death; all such efforts, whether outright invasion or external assistance to insurrectionist forces, have occurred in countries bordering China. Russia is known to have denounced the Chinese action against India and to have provided India with arms and economic aid before, during, and after the clash. Russia, together with Britain, called for a cessation of hostilities in Laos, and there is no evidence or reason to believe that it would not have preferred a neutral, Austria-type Laos to one in China's sphere of influence. The pro-Communist forces in South Vietnam are helped by the North Vietnamese, who in turn are reported to be encouraged by China but discouraged from aggressive activities by Russia.[15] It helps no one to view all these aggressive acts as if they had been conducted under the control of one, united international Communist movement, directed from one central command in Moscow. The fact is that since 1953 there has been no instance where remote deterrence—when applied—did not contain the Russians.

In fairness it should be pointed out that some experts on Chinese affairs regard Chinese expansionist threats in a differ-

[15] Russia is also reported to have advised the FLN to negotiate with de Gaulle, while China preferred offering arms to the Algerian Communists; the Soviets encouraged the Iraqi Communists to cooperate with the Kassim government, while the Chinese favored an armed Communist underground; the same conflict of lines is now taking place in Indonesia, where the Soviets favor cooperation of the Communist Party with Sukarno's government, and the Chinese an armed underground. See G. F. Hudson, Richard Lowenthal, and Roderick MacFarquhar, *The Sino-Soviet Dispute* (New York: Praeger, 1961), p. 19.

ent light. I see China, unlike Russia, as an expansionist force, willing to take high risks. In my view, China does not yet understand the basic facts of nuclear life; it believes in absolute deterrence, i.e., as long as the Russians possess a nuclear force large enough to stalemate the Western one, the Chinese feel they can advance by means of conventional forces and armed subversion with impunity—or at least with "calculated" risks. Some Western experts, however, believe that China is merely attempting to make sure that its borders are rimmed by friendly, nonaligned, small-power nations, with whom it is willing to coexist peacefully. These analysts point out that during recent years the Chinese have signed and put into effect border-delimitation treaties with a large number of adjacent countries, after these countries agreed not to serve as bases for aggression against China (as Burma served when its territory was used by Nationalist Chinese troops). China has come to terms with nonaligned Burma, Nepal, and, more recently, Pakistan. Thus it has been suggested that "China's main motive may not be 'Trotskyist' at all but the much more 'Stalinist' aim of safeguarding her own territory by creating weak buffer zones along her borders."[16] Only India, it is pointed out, refused to negotiate over border differences, and it continued to hold territories widely regarded, even by the Nationalist Chinese, as belonging to mainland China. When numerous Chinese appeals over a decade had failed to bring India to the negotiating table, China dealt with the border question by force. Once they had achieved their limited objective, the Chinese halted their advance, despite the collapse of the Indian army, indicating to some observers that China had no expansionist intentions.

Regarding Laos and Vietnam, the same school points out that both the Viet Cong and the Pathet Lao are not Communist, but pro-Communist, groups; they are indigenous, not

[16] Editorial, *The Observer* (London), November 25, 1962.

invading, forces; and the Chinese neither supported nor armed them as long as the United States refrained from arming and supporting the other side in these countries. Even after massive American shipments of arms had been sent to government forces in South Vietnam, Chinese assistance to the Viet Cong was apparently rather limited. According to an article in *Airman*, a publication of the U. S. Air Force, in June 1963, the Viet Cong was still using homemade rifles, rusty nails in lieu of mines, and even crossbows.

It is further claimed that the CIA—not the Chinese or the Russians—first precipitated violation of Laotian neutrality, throwing its weight behind a right-wing militarist (General Phoumi Nosavan) in opposition to neutralist Souvanna Phouma. Not until 1961, months after Phoumi's 1960 coup, did China and the U.S.S.R. begin to ship arms and supplies into Laos.[17] The aggressive language of the Chinese has been interpreted as masking inaction rather than signaling China's actual intentions. "U.S. aides doubt Peking will start aggression" headlined a *New York Times* story on June 18, 1963, drawing on U. S. State Department sources.

It is impossible to enter here into all these questions, most of which depend to a large degree on facts unknown to the West rather than on judgment. Probably the next few years will shed more light on China's intentions. For our purposes no decision on what China's "real" motivations and plans are is necessary; whatever its intentions, its limited economic and military capabilities will prevent it from directly challenging the West, at least for the next decade. Although China may defy Russia on minor matters, it can neither act unilaterally in significant matters nor refuse to accept a major interbloc arrangement backed by the U.S.S.R. If Russia should threaten to fold its nuclear umbrella, China could not but feel exposed and at the mercy of the West. The U.S.S.R. cannot exercise

[17] See footnote 11, above.

this power over minor issues, but when it comes to important ones—such as vetoing a Chinese invasion of Formosa or introducing a major interbloc accommodation—it can.[18]

Russia's control of its giant ally is likely to dwindle in the next decade. If interbloc arrangements are postponed until China is a fully industrialized nuclear power, we will indeed be vitally concerned with its intentions. The question is, what can be done in the time that is left? Is "buying time," as favored by duopolists, an appropriate policy under the circumstances? Or is there a more effective approach?

REMOTE DETERRENCE EXTENDED

THE NEW SCOPE

Recent years have witnessed a decline in the duopolistic efforts of the West toward third countries and the rise of an implicit Russian-American understanding that it is "all right" for a country to be nonaligned, to receive economic aid and technical assistance from both blocs, to trade with both, and to shift its "sympathy" toward one side or another—as long as it does not leave the nonaligned camp to join one bloc (as Cuba did). Among the countries in which the competition approach is most firmly established are: Egypt, which by the end of 1963 had received $500 million worth of aid from the East and from the West; Indonesia, which received about $1 billion worth of aid from the East and $700 million worth from the West; India, which received more aid than any country from both sides; Brazil; Iraq; Guinea; Ghana; Tunisia; Algeria; and, among smaller countries, Burma, Cambodia, Ethiopia, Ceylon, Nepal, and quite a few others.

But the change of orientation is far from complete, and the limited tolerance of competition is not assured. Remote de-

[18] A similar conclusion was reached by Alice Langley Hsieh, in *Communist China's Strategy in the Nuclear Era* (Englewood Cliffs, N.J.: Prentice-Hall, 1962). See also A. Doak Barnett, "The Inclusion of Communist China in an Arms Control Program," *Daedatus*, Fall 1960, pp. 831–43.

terrence has evolved largely unwittingly. It is rarely recognized
as a policy; and the rules to be followed are neither explicit
nor based on an interbloc agreement as they were in Austria;
hence they might be challenged or violated unwittingly. Any
aggression or testing of the rules might lead to a war, as one
side tries to defend its interpretation of the implicit understanding, and the other refuses to be strait-jacketed by it. The
question then becomes: what can be done to form explicit
agreed-upon rules, to safeguard the nonarmed competition
from violation and regression?

We suggest that non-Communist Asia and Africa, and
probably Latin America too, might be explicitly treated as
Austria is as far as deterrence is concerned, and as Egypt,
India, and their likes as far as disarmed competition goes.
Their nonalignment could be formally recognized by both super-powers; they would be committed to maintain their unaf-
filiated status, and the United States and the U.S.S.R. would
declare an embargo on shipment of arms and troops to these
areas, agreeing to do all they could to see that their allies
complied with such an embargo, as well as preventing actual
shipment if attempted. (See pp. 112 below on the instruments
available for effectively implementing such a plan.) The
embargo would forbid shipping arms to indigenous insurrectionist and counterinsurrectionist forces—to rebels *and* to
governments—thus preventing the entanglement of the two
super-powers over internal conflicts, whether between two
tribes in the African bush, or between the central government
and provinces in a Latin American country.[19] Before we sug-

[19] The effect of such a policy on the stability of these governments is
discussed in the following chapter. It suffices to point out here that stability
is not always desirable; a period of chaos can be a fertile state for the
emergence of a more acceptable government; and the countries in which
both blocs have refrained from intervening have been, on the average, more,
not less, stable than those whose governments were supported by the West
or the East. Finally, it must be emphasized that what is advocated here is
not a unilateral termination of American commitments to third countries,
but, to the degree that these commitments are incompatible with such an
interbloc agreement, a renegotiation of them. Actually, few are incompatible.

gest under what conditions such an agreement might be made and how it might be enforced, its effects should be briefly indicated.

Remote deterrence would abolish the most important sources of possible escalation by preventing armed interbloc confrontations in third countries. Almost all interbloc conflicts since 1950 have taken place in one of the southern continents, which would be covered by the suggested system. Moreover, a country engulfed in a civil war would escape the extra destruction that takes place when the two blocs become involved and provide both sides with massive shipments of modern weapons, as first occurred in Spain in 1936–39.

Third countries would benefit substantially from such an arrangement. Once armed intervention is ruled out, they would need much smaller military establishments, and the resources and foreign aid now channeled to these could be diverted, at least in part, to development. The considerable number of administrative, technical, and other personnel tied up in military affairs could to a large extent be released for other purposes. And finally, with the reduction of armed forces, government use of them to impose its rule on the political opposition (often with the tacit agreement or support of the super-powers) would be curtailed. Then, when alienation from the government became sufficiently widespread, a popular revolution—which is often needed in these countries to redress basic grievances—would be easier to carry out.

The skeptical reader may well feel that it is impossible to keep major shipments of arms out of the nonaligned area; that for the West to maintain its forces anywhere other than *in* those countries would be ineffective; and that the Communists would never voluntarily withdraw their support from "wars of national liberation." It should be emphasized once more that remote deterrence is simply an extension of an existing system that already functions effectively. What is "possible" as against "impossible," our experience shows, is difficult to foretell. If, for instance, in 1957 the reader foresaw the Sino-Soviet split of 1961 or the deployment of Soviet missiles in Cuba of 1962 or the partial nuclear test-ban treaty of 1963, then he did considerably better than most of the experts, who failed to anticipate any of these events.[20]

What we are presenting here is acknowledgedly what might be called an "optimistic scenario"; that is, we are asking what arrangement could be made *if* the U.S.S.R. and the United States were both ready to shift to the less dangerous world of competition under rules. If either side favors a different strategy, neither remote deterrence nor many of the other measures suggested in this book are likely to be implemented. But assuming that both sides are genuinely interested in some settlement, what steps would they take? The West is committed to counter armed expansion; the East has ambitions it will not relinquish. Conditions must be found that satisfy both these requirements if an interbloc arrangement is to be reached. Fear of nuclear war is not enough.

THE COMPONENTS OF REMOTE DETERRENCE

Remote deterrence requires that both sides refrain from shipping arms and armed forces, overtly or covertly, into nonaligned areas; that they genuinely attempt to prevent their allies from sending such forces;[21] and that they agree that if one side intervenes with arms in the nonaligned area the interbloc agreement would automatically be nullified and the other side not only free but expected to counter such an attack. Such commitments have already been undertaken in defense of the containment line; why not in deference to non-

[20] See Hanson W. Baldwin, in the *New York Times*, June 16, 1963.

[21] This is not without precedent; Russians were overheard during the 1962 Cuban crisis ordering Cubans to hold their fire when American reconnaissance planes were flying over the island, and after the crisis the Soviets insisted that Castro not send armed agents to other Latin American countries. At the same time the United States curbed armed raids by Cuban exiles.

armed competition, which would still rest less on mutual trust than on mutual deterrence. The main difference between the old containment policy and remote deterrence would be that instead of already being in the third area, facing each other over the containment fence, the two blocs' forces would be separated from each other by a wide nonaligned area.

It is true that in the event of a violation there would be some delay between the attack by one side and the response by the other. An aggressor would probably have about twenty-four hours to advance, encountering only indigenous resistance, before the counterforces of the other bloc became engaged. But this is not much of an advantage; indeed, the time could be reduced if counterforces were held, in bloc countries, in a high degree of readiness and mobility (if necessary, even on ships cruising in the area during tense periods). Recent developments in the technology of weapons, military tactics, and organization, and increased mobility of troops and arms have made remote deterrence much more feasible than it was a few years ago, just as they have made U.S. bases near the Soviet border less important.[22] It is now possible to make entire divisions airborne so that they can readily be deployed anywhere. It took sixty-three hours to fly the U. S. 2nd Armored Division fifty-six hundred miles, from Texas to West Germany, in Operation Big Lift in November 1963. But the first units of the 15,278 soldiers hauled were ready for combat in Germany within hours of the beginning of the operation.

One disadvantage remote deterrence seems to have is that

[22] As the Russians have built up their capacity to destroy bases and the number of long-range missiles has increased, the military value of U.S. bases near the Soviet border has decreased correspondingly. For a while yet such bases will continue to provide dispersal of targets, making a well-coordinated surprise attack difficult. But with the deployment of Polaris-carrying submarines in the Atlantic and Pacific oceans as well as in the Mediterranean, they are rapidly becoming superfluous even for dispersal purposes, as indicated by the recent closing of U.S. missile bases in Turkey and Italy and their replacement by missile-carrying submarines.

it would eliminate "trip wires," a term used for small contingents of American troops placed next to the containment line, not to hold it but to demonstrate the United States' commitment to its defense. The assumption is that any attacker will realize that he will have to kill several hundred Americans before he can pass a particular border, which may well involve the full might of the United States. In other words, these troops serve as a wire to pull in the major force. Such wires are not compatible with remote deterrence, nor do they seem necessary. First, they have been used mainly in West Berlin and hardly at all in nonaligned areas. Second, the West already has demonstrated, in Korea in 1950, in Lebanon in 1958, and in India in 1962, that its help is available without such devices. An explicit commitment and the availability of highly mobile forces can effectively replace whatever trip wires there are in the southern continents. An explicit commitment to defend third countries is not to be taken lightly. A super-power that would allow third countries to be taken over despite such a commitment could expect to lose all the nonaligned support it had been enjoying, and thus the big contest, once and for all.

Remote deterrence is applicable to Asia, Africa, and Latin America, from countries as pro-Communist (within the context of nonalignment) as Afghanistan to those as pro-Western as Nicaragua. Many nations on these three continents are nonaligned both in legal terms, with no military or political alliance with either bloc, and in terms of their actual foreign and defense policies. But others, including Iran and Pakistan, as well as the Philippines, Thailand, South Korea, South Vietnam, Taiwan, and Japan, are, formally speaking, allies of the West. How are they to be treated?

It should be noted that these countries constitute a distinct minority in the underdeveloped camp; and many of the more important ones, such as most of the Latin American republics, Taiwan, the Philippines, and Japan, are separated by sea from the Communist countries, which makes holding from the outside, by the use of air patrols and ships, comparatively easy. The few allies that have a land border with Communist countries are, past experience shows, *already held mainly through remote deterrence*, notwithstanding their formal allied status. That is, since the Western forces in these countries are limited to military missions or small units, and their own forces are rather weak, in case of an attack large reinforcements would have to be rushed from the outside to their defense, as they were into South Korea and South Vietnam. Although it is believed that if the West sends military missions, instructors, and weapons into these countries before they are attacked, they will be able to make a large contribution to their own defense, the record clearly shows that there is only a small difference in ability and willingness between these underdeveloped allies and the nonaligned countries. Somehow, it seems, we tend to confuse SEATO or CENTO allies with NATO allies, disregarding the fact that the former are largely paper allies. If seriously challenged, their independence depends on Western forces almost as much as does that of nonallies.

In short, from a Western, holding-the-line viewpoint, there are only limited differences between underdeveloped allies and nonaligned countries. Both, if not attacked, serve to hold the line, and, if attacked, need outside help. The fall of a nonally to Communist occupation would undermine containment about as much as the surrender of an ally. The independence of India is as vital to the West as that of CENTO-member Pakistan, and that of Egypt as that of NATO-member Greece. This is not to suggest that no differences between allies and nonallies exist, but rather that differences are small when it comes to a question of defense against armed expansionism. In this respect they all may be treated together as one big third area to be covered by remote deterrence.

The legal status of the Latin American republics under the

Rio Treaty probably makes them semi-allies, less tied to the United States than countries with a collective defense organization, such as NATO, and more tied than nonaligned countries. In effect, many of these republics—especially the larger and more important ones—are increasingly nonaligned politically and at the same time as much in need of U.S. military protection if seriously challenged as are other underdeveloped countries. However, being closer to the United States and more remote from the major Communist land bloc, they can be even more readily defended from the outside.

Remote deterrence is in many ways similar to disengagement, which has often been rejected. It does not, however, have the disadvantages of earlier disengagement plans. The *grounds* on which disengagement is offered, as Professor Henry L. Roberts has pointed out, are basically "that the status quo with its unresolved tensions will be increasingly precarious as time passes. The proponents of disengagement also proceed from the premise that the Soviet regime, for the foreseeable future, will remain intact and largely invulnerable to external influences. From this it follows that any arrangement for altering the status quo must be through mutual agreement. . . ."[23] The neutralization, disarmament, and unification of both Germanies are given as a prime example. But, as Roberts correctly emphasizes, this and similar disengagement plans run into an impasse: "The Soviet leaders have given no sign that they are prepared to witness the de-Communization of an area that has once been Communized; on the contrary, they stated explicitly that this is not to be permitted. Against this impulse toward disengagement there is a contrary one toward greater engagement. This may take the form of 'exchanges'—cultural, academic, technical and economic."

[23] "Soviet-American Relations: Problems of Choice and Decision," in Alexander Dallin (ed.), *Soviet Conduct in World Affairs* (New York: Columbia University Press, 1960), p. 301.

It is my central contention that the particular mode of disengagement involved in competition under the rules of holding from the outside does not have the critical limitations of the various disengagement plans Roberts alludes to, and does have some of the advantages of engagement. It does not call for "de-Communization," because this would be, at least at the present stage, unrealistic; it calls instead for disengagement in the nonaligned area populated by nations that are not members of either bloc and hence need not be either de-Communized or de-Westernized. It calls for *military* disengagement, but intensive *nonarmed* engagement with all the means Roberts mentions—cultural, academic, technical, and economic. It calls for exclusion of military forces, not by the unstable balance of power, not according to "rules" laid down by one side, but in accord with rules to be formed through mutual agreement, verified through U.N. observer forces, supported by world public opinion, and backed up by the very armed forces that are now used to hold and to undermine the containment line. I do *not* suggest shifting from a system that relies on power to one that relies on morality, or from the force of armies to the force of public opinion; given the present state of international relations, such a shift could be extremely hazardous. I do suggest making explicit and effective the rules that have evolved implicitly and are today imperfectly enforced and sometimes crudely twisted when they do not suit their initiators. I do not suggest that power politics will be abolished and the two camps will become uninterested in the large, third area; this is impossible and probably undesirable. I would like both sides, all the sides, to be actively engaged in the nonaligned area, provided the engagement is effectively and mutually limited to nonarmed means.

The use of nonarmed means by either side to pressure countries into forming permanent military and political ties obviously undermines the competition. Each bloc might well

seek support from third countries on any specific issue in the
United Nations or in other international organizations, to
form transient coalitions, or to advance its economic, political, and cultural values, as long as the countries' freedom to
shift their support, coalition, or values, is maintained. Regression to a duopolistic stance ("if you take my aid you must reject his") would destroy the very basis of the competition;
but attempts to gain specific concessions or support in exchange for economic aid, trade concessions, etc., are not excluded. This difficult line between duopoly and competition
is regularly maintained in national politics and is an irreduci-
ble prerequisite of democratic competition. Each political
party seeks the support of all the voters, but at the same time
realizes that if the majority of voters were *permanently* tied
to it, the minority party would lose its commitment to this
form of political procedure and turn to means of violence to
upset it. Hence, each party, while seeking in each election to
gain as many votes as it can, is also concerned in seeing to
it that the voters remain free to choose again in the next
election, and that the other party's stake in the system of
competition under rules is sustained.

COMMUNIST VIEWS

Will the Russians ever agree to such a plan? Will the Chinese? Can the West hold its own in a nonarmed competition with the Communists? Can an embargo on shipment of
arms be effectively implemented, particularly on arms to subversive forces?

In general, questions concerning the willingness of the
other side to agree or disagree to a specific proposal should be
explored by asking it, since no losses are involved in asking.
To sit back and postulate that the other side will not accept a
proposal anyhow, therefore we should not offer it, gets us no-
where.

Remote deterrence is not a new idea but an extrapolation

from an existing system; if the Russians have agreed so far, why would they not agree to extend to other countries the system of Austria, Finland, Afghanistan, and India?[24]

The Russians too face the danger of escalation; they too know what their fate would be if the balance of terror were to become unbalanced. So it is reasonable to assume that the Russians, for their own sakes, would be quite interested in stabilizing the interbloc competition. To be sure, accepting an effectively enforced embargo on shipment of troops and arms to the third countries poses a difficult dilemma for the Soviets. They may confidently expect left-wing revolutions to continue to erupt in these areas, especially when Western military support to some of the more unpopular governments is removed. But little gain will accrue to the Soviet bloc from these revolutions unless they have troops there, as experiences in Yugoslavia, Albania, and China have shown. To rule out the sending of troops is to rule out the Soviet bloc's major means of consolidating its gains in the third area. The U.S.S.R. can be expected to accept such a major damper on its ambitions only as part of a more comprehensive interbloc settlement. If remote deterrence is offered as an isolated measure, it may indeed not seem acceptable to them. If, on the other hand, it is an integral part of providing the framework for genuine peaceful coexistence, they may accept it. Every sign indicates that the Russians understand as well as anyone that if no effective curbs can be constructed to contain the means of violence, sooner or later all advances in the third area will be Pyrrhic; the super-powers and their "conquests" will turn into the same radioactive dust. They may not par-

[24] Negotiations are not the only way an arrangement can be offered and agreed upon. Duopoly was never "offered" directly; but the West acted in a certain way, and the American President and Secretary of State expressed the West's expectations concerning the Russians and announced the guidelines it would follow in determining its responses to Soviet actions. The same method can be used to communicate suggestions regarding the stabilization of competition in the nonaligned area.

ticularly like competition under rules, but they may see that
neither they nor the West has much choice left.

China might react differently. But there would be no unilateral cancellation of the Western commitment to hold the
line against military expansionism, whether overt or covert.
On the contrary, the commitment to counter such aggression
should be more explicit. The more clearly this commitment
is made, the more clearly the Chinese will see the risks involved, and the more likely they will be to decide such risks
are too high, even for them. After all, such considerations
were one factor in discouraging them from invading Formosa,
despite much bellicose talk to the contrary; in preventing an
attack on Hong Kong; in stopping more massive help to the
Viet Cong; and in keeping them from Quemoy and Matsu,
only three miles from the mainland. Hence, even countries
on China's border may be protected from the outside without
becoming involved in their internal power struggles (with
shipments of arms, military missions, Special Forces, or
troops) *until* it has been established that China or another
aggressor had indeed attacked or is attempting to subvert them
by the use of arms. Local forces, of the left or the right,
should be allowed to test their strength and their appeal to
the population without Western, Soviet, or Chinese armed
intervention.

We must realize that the autocrats who rule several of these
countries have picked up the most unfortunate feature of
American Cold War politics—the practice of labeling "Communist" all opposition, whether left, liberal, or even right-
wing. This device was used by the Christians in Lebanon
in 1958 against the Moslems (and brought them to call on
the U. S. Marines for help); by Diem against the Buddhist
majority of his country (to bring American military transportation, arms, and finance for his police raids against these non-
Communist priests);[25] and by practically every Latin Ameri-

[25] *New York Times*, July 5, 1963, and September 9, 1963.

can dictator who wanted more American arms to squelch internal opposition.[26] In 1963 the Argentine military junta justified its jailing of more than fifty non-Communist Frondizi supporters by calling them "Marxist-Leninists"; Guatemala's anti-Communist civilian President Ydígoras was ousted by the military as a "Castro supporter"; and the army overthrew Ecuador's left-leaning but non-Communist President Arosemena, charging him one day with drunkenness, the next with Communist sympathies. In each case, American-trained personnel, using American weapons, participated. America has largely learned to overlook this shoddy trick in domestic politics; it cannot long be fooled by it in alien terrains. There is an urgent need for the United States to develop the instruments needed to determine whether an uprising is genuinely indigenous or whether outside interference has occurred. Remote deterrence forces are not to be committed before the need for them has been demonstrated.

It is important to realize that in the past, whenever significant violations of curbs on shipments or levels of conventional arms occurred, the fact soon became known, whether the matter involved violation of the Versailles Treaty, the Washington Naval Arms Limitations, or the Korean Armistice. The British in Palestine were unable to find many of the caches of hidden arms, but their estimates of the forces of the Jewish underground were quite accurate. Soviet shipments of arms to Egypt and to Cuba did not remain a secret for more than a few weeks. In short, it is not difficult to get adequate information on a significant violation of an embargo on arms. This is particularly true when the area to which the embargo applies is separated by sea from the source of supplies, as are most of the countries in the nonaligned area. A land border is much more difficult to guard than the sea

26 For various operative factors, see Manfred Halpern, *The Morality and Politics of Intervention* (New York: The Council on Religion and International Affairs, 1963), pp. 13 ff.

lanes, but even this, as the experiences at the Gaza Strip, on the border of Israel and Egypt (where a U.N. force has been stationed since 1956), shows, is far from impossible.

A FLASHLIGHT FORCE

This precedent points to an important factor that would greatly enhance effective implementation of an embargo on shipment of troops and arms. The problem is, at least initially, that each side will suspect the other of violating the arrangement, and every time a government is toppled in the third area—or withstands a challenge—one bloc will suspect that the other had a hand in it. Even if both sides genuinely desire an embargo, an instrument must be found to counter such suspicions by making it unlikely that a violator could operate unnoticed. A U.N. observation force, positioned at borders, ports, and airfields, would suffice. We cannot, in the near future, realistically expect to have an effective U.N. police force that could counter aggressions (for reasons discussed below). But an observation force, armed only with flashlights, infrared instruments, helicopters, and the like, to check the borders, actually already exists. It would, of course, have to be greatly enlarged and required to function against the two blocs and not only between third countries, as has been the case so far. The personnel could be provided by third countries, whose men would be more trusted by the blocs and more acceptable to the countries on whose borders it would be positioned. The force should be deployable, without any need for negotiation by the United Nations, at the request of either bloc, and either side's refusal to allow it to operate or gross interference with its work would be viewed as sufficient evidence that the embargo agreement had been violated. If a third country refused it entrance, the force could be deployed next to its borders, on the side of the neighboring country (which probably would be quite willing to see that no more arms were amassed next door), as well as in international air-

and waterways. This force would, in effect, take over some of the "trip-wire" functions; any aggressor would realize that he would have to overrun several hundred U.N. observers before he could invade a country.[27]

Many of the details of such a force have still to be carefully examined and might well be changed; the virtue of the plan as a whole should not be judged in terms of the acceptability of one or more of its items. One might well reject every one of the suggested details and nevertheless accept the idea of remote deterrence, suggesting different procedures for it.

Remote deterrence is clearly a "minimum-regret" strategy; if the other side does not accept it, nothing is lost. If it were first accepted and later violated, no major or even minor damage to the security of the Western heartland could result, since the major strategic deterrence forces would not be affected. As the challenged independence of a third country was protected or restored, no loss would be incurred. This is not to take lightly the fighting that would ensue, but as this risk is taken every day to maintain the stalemated, no-exit, duopolistic system, it seems worth taking for the defense of peaceful competition. Most important, I believe that remote deterrence is likely to work and embargoes are unlikely to be violated, because this would benefit both sides and the third countries—it draws jointly on noble motives such as the desire for peace and less noble considerations such as the fear of the "remote" forces both sides will continue to maintain. It is when morals and power combine, rather than contradict each other, that international relations are most effectively stabilized.

In discussions of this plan with State Department officials

[27] I am indebted to Professor Richard Falk of Princeton University for pointing out the importance of the "presence" of the United Nations under these circumstances. It is also discussed in his unpublished report for the U. S. Arms Control and Disarmament Agencies, entitled "Indirect Aggression and Disarmament."

in Washington, again and again the question was raised: Assuming that an embargo can be effectively imposed on both camps, can the West effectively compete in a nonarmed contest? In view of the great ignorance and misery in the underdeveloped continents and our spotted past, may we not lose even if the suggested machinery effectively limits the competition in the third world to nonarmed means? Austria, Finland, and Yugoslavia are developed; but could underdeveloped Burma or Iraq be "held"? The answer is far from simple. The circumstances upon which an effective Western nonarmed capacity depend are the subject of the following chapter.

Chapter IV

INTERVENTION FOR PROGRESS

Closely associated with the shift from duopoly to competition is a redistribution of resources and efforts among the instruments of foreign policy in both camps. It is the package, rather than the contents, that is significantly altered; some instruments are emphasized while others are largely downgraded. Often such modifications in emphasis rather than substance initially escape notice. Increasingly, however, the change becomes manifest. Both the U.S.S.R. and the United States have nearly shelved the use of nuclear weapons as active instruments of foreign policy as they have moved closer to a total stalemate on this level. And, as we have seen, the Communist camp, to the extent that it is Soviet directed, has reduced the use of armed subversion and placed more reliance on nonlethal low-risk means to advance its goals.

In recent years the West, too, has expanded and improved its nonarmed capabilities. The proportions of aid devoted to economic as opposed to military purposes have been greatly enlarged—whereas the ratio was about one to three in 1953, by 1963 it was approximately one to one; the Peace Corps was introduced; and more attention has been paid to the trade needs of the underdeveloped countries, as reflected, for instance, in American support of prices for coffee and other tropical agricultural products. These improvements in American nonarmed capabilities are usually viewed as increasing the U.S. ability to counter Communist efforts to exploit growing social tensions in the underdeveloped countries. Increased American contributions to the realization of basic human values, to the flight from hunger and the quest for education, are also highlighted. In the context of the present analysis, another feature of the new trend stands out: it serves the transition from duopoly to competition. The stronger the Western ability to counter by nonarmed means Communist challenges, which are now almost exclusively focused on underdeveloped countries, the less likely the West is to have to resort to arms, and the less volatile the interbloc contest. On the other hand, the less effective U.S. efforts are, the more successful Communist expansion becomes, and the more likely the occurrence of armed clashes and eruption of wars. Therefore, we are particularly interested here in the conditions that affect Western nonarmed capabilities and their effect on United States' new policy.

DUOPOLY AND SUPPORT OF THE STATUS QUO

After World War II the three underdeveloped continents faced the dizzying acceleration of two closely related revolutions. *Nationalism* swept colonialism aside as forces of *social change*, usually of a leftist nature, challenged *status quo* governments. With few exceptions the two movements merged; Nasser, Nehru, and Nkrumah are leaders of both.

The American position vis-à-vis the national and social revolutions was ambivalent at first. The United States found that its sympathy, traditionally on the side of independence movements, offended its major allies, Britain, France, Belgium, and the Netherlands—the imperial powers. Time and again the United States was constrained to tone down its rhetoric and support, lest it alienate its allies unduly. This predicament was spotlighted in 1957 by an exchange between Secretary of State Dulles and a congressional critic of Administration policy in Algeria. On July 2, Senator John F. Kennedy urged the Administration to switch sides in the Algerian struggle; American assistance to the French against the rebels, he argued, "has affected our standing in the eyes of the free world, and our leadership in the fight to keep that world free. . . ." "Mr. Kennedy," Secretary Dulles rebutted, "ought to concentrate on the Communist variety [of colonialism] rather than the French."[1]

Allied to French colonialists in Indochina and British colonialists in Iran, the United States appeared guilty of colonialism-by-association to many Africans and Asians, while in Latin America it was still regarded as a semicolonial power itself. The Latin Americans were slow to forget the days of gunboat diplomacy, of occupation by U. S. Marines, and of rule by the United Fruit Company. The tag "Yankee imperialism" was exploited but not invented by Communist propaganda. At the same time the Soviet Union presented itself as the champion of the anticolonial forces, supporting them with effusive sympathy and, increasingly, with funds. Having never experienced Soviet rule, the people of the three southern continents paid little attention to Western warnings of Communist "imperialism."

If U.S. anticolonialism was restrained, its support for forces of social change was almost absent. U.S. foreign policy in the years between 1947 and 1958 supported the forces of *status quo* in most of the underdeveloped countries. Actually, American foreign policy was governed by an implicit sociological theory that saw a very close connection between the internal regimes of these societies and their foreign policy; certain social groups—those that favored the social *status quo*—appeared to be "safe" supporters of a pro-Western foreign policy. Thus the United States actively supported Syngman Rhee in South Korea, Chiang Kai-shek in Formosa, and Nuri el Said in Iraq. Groups supporting social change, particularly revolutionary change, were not trusted, including such anti-Communist, democratic, and wholly Western parties as the Swe-

[1] *New York Times*, July 3, 1957.

dish Social Democrats and British Labor Party.[2] Global *status quo* was to rest upon domestic *status quo* in allied countries.

American support to *status quo* governments took several forms. First of all, there were shipments of arms, military missions, and military-technical assistance, most of which were never used against outside aggressors. Second, there was considerable aid to bolster these countries' economies, much of which found its way into large salaries for large armies and police forces: 70 per cent of U.S. foreign aid between 1947 and 1958 was military or supportive to the military, and about half of it served to buttress such outright *status quo* governments as those in Turkey, South Korea, and Formosa. Third, in instances where this outside assistance proved insufficient, the United States stepped in with armed forces. For instance, in 1958 U. S. Marines came to the aid of President Kamil Sham'un in Lebanon. Sham'un called for Marines to counter Communism, but actually used them to maintain his Christian-based government in power over a non-Communist, Moslem majority.[3] From Syngman Rhee in Korea to Odría in Peru, from Duvalier to Salazar, arms and armies supplied directly or indirectly by the West were used to oppress Communists, socialists, and liberals—i.e., any and all forces of social change. As revolutionary and reform movements of all stamps learned not to expect much help from the United States, especially as long as they were not ensconced in government, bids for Russian support increased, especially after the early fifties, when the Russians decided to support not just Communist but progressive forces in general.

This aspect of American dealing, or rather not dealing,

[2] Truman's coolness to Britain's Labor Cabinet is seen as having hampered the new government's attempts to adjust the country to the demands of peacetime in 1945. George Lichtheim, *The New Europe* (New York: Praeger, 1963), p. 14.

[3] Manfred Halpern, *The Morality and Politics of Intervention* (New York: The Council on Religion and International Affairs, 1963), pp. 11–14.

with progressive forces is well known; it needs to be briefly recounted, because the memory of this period and the widespread anti-Americanism it generated are still very much alive, reverberating in reactions to contemporary U.S. foreign policy and affecting the interbloc strife. While some of the *status quo* governments supported by the United States, such as those of Franco, Salazar, and Trujillo, remained in office for surprisingly long periods, many were swept aside by progressive leaders and forces. Many African, Asian, and Latin American countries are already under the control of progressive groups, and most countries still controlled by *status quo* forces, such as South Vietnam, Nicaragua, and Paraguay, are widely expected to follow suit. Many of the new leaders were at least initially anti-Western, though not Communist. They chose not to align their countries with either camp. Duopoly required a world of *status quo*, but such a world is not available.

SUPPORTING PROGRESS

THE NEW FRONTIER'S THEORY

Throughout John Foster Dulles' tenure, American liberals argued that the socio-political theory underlying American foreign policy was invalid. Equating revolutionary and reform groups with Communists was decried as intellectually false and politically stupid. The non-Communist advocates of social change, liberals argued, constituted the most effective pro-Western forces; by introducing long overdue social, economic, and political reforms to the less developed countries, they would take the wind out of Communist sails, while the *status quo* forces perpetuated the poverty, political oppression, and ignorance on which Communism thrives. Most of the moderate left groups, such as the APRA in Peru and the Congress Party in India, it was emphasized, were regarded by the Communists as their chief rivals. Finally, the assumption of a close relationship between domestic regimes and foreign policy came under question: Was there evidence that leftist governments would join the Communist bloc?

During his 1960 election campaign, Senator John F. Kennedy propounded this liberal theory. His 1961 speech initiating the Alliance for Progress suggested a major shift in American foreign policy toward active support of anticolonialism and forces of social change. An array of goals was set in the Punta del Este Charter to be fulfilled by the *Alianza*, including such reforms as "more equitable distribution of national income" and "comprehensive agrarian reform." Countries that neglected to hold regular elections were to be barred from participating in the new alliance.

The Communists claimed a natural alliance with all progressive forces. Under President Kennedy, the United States was to challenge this claim. Both sides were to be ranged against the local *status quo*, competing for the support of the rising forces.

The Communists were not particularly worried by this new American counteroffensive. Can a tiger live on a vegetarian diet, they asked. The United States was deemed incapable of competing seriously over the leadership of forces of social change and anticolonialism. How in fact did the New Frontier fare on this front?

THE RECORD: U.S. ANTICOLONIALISM

After assuming office President Kennedy set out to support more actively anticolonial, nationalist forces and to increase pressure on America's European allies to eliminate the remnants of the colonial period. Less than a month after he entered the White House, as the world closely watched his steps to ascertain his policy, a minor incident occurred that was to symbolize his approach—and the difficulties it was to face.

On January 24, 1961, Associated Press dispatches reported

that a Portuguese ship, the *Santa Maria*, had been seized on the high seas by a group of passengers. The next day it was learned that the mutineers, led by a Captain Galvao, were political rebels protesting against the colonial and authoritarian regime of Portugal, and it was rumored that they were heading for Angola. The United States found itself in a quandary. According to international law, such seizures are defined as piracy, and the United States was expected to direct its navy to capture the ship and help its return to Portugal. However, most of the underdeveloped world and liberal public opinion in Western countries sided with the rebels. Portugal's status as an American NATO ally complicated matters further. The State Department was clearly uneasy; headline reports in the following week reflected its predicament. January 25: The State Department announces that the Navy will seize and return the *Santa Maria* to Portugal in line with the piracy act. January 26: U.S. vessels will accompany but not board the rebel ship. January 27: The United States is reported to consider halting its search provided that passengers not involved in the uprising are put safely on shore. January 28: Lisbon rumored to condition renewal of Azores base leases to the United States on return of the ship. On February 3 the *Santa Maria* was captured and handed over to Portugal after the rebels were set free in Brazil. The United States somehow worked its way out of this embarrassment, but it was a far cry from the "tough" anticolonial line earlier speeches had seemed to indicate.

Shortly after the *Santa Maria* incident, news of the Angolan rebellion and vindictive Portuguese reprisals again spotlighted the liability of America's association with colonial Portugal. Horrified by missionaries' reports of mass shootings and concentration camps, American U.N. Ambassador Adlai Stevenson joined seventy-eight other U.N. members in a resolution urging Portugal to "take steps to guard the rights and freedoms" of Angolans, a vote warmly praised by third nations. In similar resolutions passed during 1962 the United States again voted to censure its NATO ally. Portugal, however, once more succeeded in using the American lease of its bases as a lever to prevent more active U.S. support for the rebels. The United States continued to supply Portugal with arms, including napalm bombs, which were reportedly used to quash the rebellion.[4] U.S. assistance to the hundred thousand Angolan refugees huddled in Congolese camps was minor, and in 1962 the government proceeded to authorize a $55 million Export-Import Bank loan to Portugal.

While the United States successfully overrode the clamoring of the smaller colonial NATO powers in some instances—as, for example, in its support of many of the Indonesian claims in New Guinea against the Netherlands—its anticolonial drive was persistently dodged by its more powerful allies. Reluctant to antagonize France, the United States followed a largely "hands-off" policy toward the Algerian rebellion; President Kennedy in 1961 was not bound by Senator Kennedy's indictment of this policy in 1957. With the outbreak of the Congo crisis in 1960, United States' backing of United Nations' efforts to restore peace and order was nearly hobbled by the resistance of NATO-allies Belgium, France, and Britain. The U.N. operation against Katanga was completed only after a change of government in Belgium brought support to American policy in favor of unification of the Congo. Since then United Nations' forces in the Congo have been curtailed (in part because of lack of funds, though the sum required is comparatively small), and Belgium and France have re-extended their influence in the area.

Another factor hampering American support of anticolonial movements, also illustrated by the *Santa Maria* incident, is that a violation of international law is often involved which incurs condemnation as interference in the internal affairs

[4] *New York Times*, July 29, 1963.

of states, such as Portugal and France. This consideration has come up again as African nations launch new efforts to undermine remaining "colonial" governments in Africa. The Africans feel that legalism is inadequate in face of the gross violations of human rights in Southern Rhodesia, Angola, and South Africa. They point out that Western powers have violated the convention against interference before, often for reasons much less worthy than restoring freedom to their African brethren. Moreover, they tend to view the white man in Africa as an intruder in the first place, hence as interfering, not interfered with. But the United States found resolutions to expel racist South Africa from the United Nations and impose sanctions on it "rash." Expelling countries would create a dangerous precedent. Nor did the United States support African efforts to restrain Britain from transferring control of its troops to the white settlers in Southern Rhodesia, where Africans constitute more than 90 per cent of the population but are subjected to autocratic white rule.

In general, the United States—despite its revolutionary birthmark—is committed to law and order and favors constitutional accommodations. It is interested in strengthening weak international law and organizations as a basis for a growing world community. And it is particularly concerned with establishing and strengthening taboos against intervention; Washington believes that the Communist camp would benefit most from an international climate in which intervention was condoned. Since the law often protects the *status quo*, the Kennedy Administration ran up against this problem nearly every time it considered supporting militant anticolonial forces.

Despite the handicaps and limitations, the United States' efforts to improve its standing among the new nations have paid off. A long succession of visits of Africans and Asians to the White House, American state visits to the new countries, and increased U.S. support of new nations' positions in the

United Nations have helped the United States shake some
of its colonial guilt-by-association. The crucial test of the
new approach to third countries, however, lies beyond the
problem of anticolonialism, an issue now on its way out;
most countries have already obtained their independence—
and most colonial powers have resigned themselves to the
loss of their empires. It is in the vigor of American support
to the forces of development and democratization in independent countries that the major test of the U.S. position
vis-à-vis the third world occurs and that the ability of the
West to hold its own in the unarmed competition will be
determined. What is the New Frontier's record here?

THE RECORD: DEMOCRATIZATION AND DEVELOPMENT?

The New Frontier was committed to intervene on the side
of economic and political progress in the underdeveloped
countries in general and in Latin America in particular. A
combination of moral pressure, economic assistance, trade,
and regional cooperation, was expected to bring modernization, eliminate the appeal of Communism, and keep the
nonaligned free until these goals were achieved. The Administration's intention was to intervene to foster economic progress, not exploitation; democracy, not tyranny; and to use
peaceful means, not force. Illustrative of this new spirit was
President Kennedy's welcome to the visiting head of a leftist
government that had curtailed the concessions of American
oil companies, imposed high taxes on business, and undertaken land reforms. The leader of the largest capitalist nation
greeted Rómulo Betancourt of Venezuela as follows: "Your
liberal leadership of your country, your persistent determination to make a better life for your people, your long fight for
democratic leadership not only in your country but in the
entire area of the Caribbean . . . all these have made you,
for us, a symbol of what we wish for our own country and
for our sister republics." These were strong and courageous

words. To what degree did the New Frontier carry out the convictions underlying them?

The Kennedy Administration early discovered that the task it had taken on was gigantic, the resources meager, congressional support limited, time running out, and conditions in eighty-odd underdeveloped nations complex, unpredictable, and uncontrollable. Actually, if these countries are divided into five groups, the Administration was able to forward its program in one group, and to make limited headway in another, while states in the remaining three categories resisted the program.

Intervention for progress was most successful in alliance with *reforming, democratic* governments; some concessions were gained from *enlightened right-wing* ones. The U. S. Administration did not succeed in squaring its policy with the *radical-left* countries; it was blocked by *right-wing tyrannies*; and it ran into major difficulties with *counterprogressive* forces.[5]

The Reforming Democracies

Countries with democratizing governments which supported development and firmly oppose Communism were the darlings of the New Frontier. These incubators of progress offered an opportunity to improve America's reputation in liberal Europe and in the predominantly left-leaning non-aligned world, and to counteract Communism.

The Dominican Republic, testing its newly acquired demo-

[5] The technically minded reader will note that this categorization was arrived at by ignoring the empty cells of a multidimensional space, including development, democratization, and effectiveness. The left *radical* regimes are low on democracy and, on the average, high on development; the *reforming democracies* are high on democratization, on the average, but low on development; the *tyrannical right* regimes neither develop nor democratize; the *"enlightened"* right-wing ones make some progress on both fronts. *Counter coup* refers to a situation rather than a mode of government; in it a tyrannical or "enlightened" right-wing government is restored. Other combinations are theoretically possible but not found often enough to justify a separate category.

cratic wings next to Castro's Cuba, was selected in 1961 to be the showcase of intervention for progress, a kind of Caribbean West Berlin. Earlier Administrations had tolerated and often cooperated with the Republic's dictator, one of the most tyrannical in Latin America, Raphael Trujillo. But when Trujillo was assassinated in 1961, all stops on intervention were pulled. To accelerate development the United States granted and loaned the small republic, with a population of about three million, $47 million dollars. It sent scores of experts to advise all major branches of the new government on everything from training the army to conducting agrarian reform. The Peace Corps drilled wells and organized 4-H clubs. To shield the infant democracy from unsympathetic forces of the radical left and the radical right, the Los Angeles police department provided riot-control chiefs and the CIA pitched in as well. U. S. Navy destroyers cruised close by in moments of crises in 1962 to leave no doubt on whose side the mighty neighbor stood. All means formerly employed to sustain rightist dictators were now set in motion to defend an inchoate democracy. But, it turned out, these were not sufficient. After eight months in office, Bosch was unseated in September 1963 and democracy was suspended.[6]

Another favorite of the New Frontier in the Western Hemisphere was Betancourt's Venezuela. Democratically elected, engaged in a serious development campaign that ranges from fairly extensive land reform to substantial housing projects, the Betancourt government gained the moral backing and economic support of the Kennedy Administration. Ninety per cent of Venezuela's export income, an annual sum of $2.5 billion, derives from the oil industry, much of which is bought by the oil-rich United States. In addition, the United States provided Betancourt with the usual package of development loans, grants, Peace Corps, and military-training missions.

[6] See below, pp. 132–36, on these "countercoups."

Bolivia is a third reforming democracy that received much U.S. aid and favor; actually it gained more assistance per capita than any Latin American country—$220 million for a country of three and a half million inhabitants. Close behind is Colombia, the semiofficial "showcase of the Alliance for Progress,"[7] to which the United States committed its own support at the rate of $100 million a year and recruited for it from other countries and the international agency an equivalent sum. On other continents, democratic, developing, pro-West Nigeria is an African favorite, while in Asia, India is a key recipient of American economic assistance and political support.

Although support for progress has been extensive in these reforming democracies, its success is far from assured. By late 1963, development programs had come to a halt in the Dominican Republic. Expectations of a coup that would similarly affect Venezuela were widespread. Bolivia was viewed with special interest since it had introduced ten years earlier (between 1952 and 1962) many of the measures the Alliance for Progress advocates, and since it received massive aid. The net effect of the aid, as one source put it, "has been chiefly to maintain the present government in power rather than to make enduring contributions toward the country's viability and growth."[8]

Those who had called Colombia a showcase were eating their words because, while some progress was made, the fiscal confusions, raging terrorism, and serious economic difficulties due largely to the decline of coffee prices in world markets, made it anything but. Actually it was rather hard to find a showcase for the Alliance for Progress. The Alliance defined 2.5 per cent per capita as the *minimum* annual rate of economic growth to be achieved, less than half the growth rate

[7] *New York Times*, October 3, 1963.
[8] James H. Street, "What Is Wrong with the 'Alianza,'" *The Reporter*, February 14, 1963, p. 28.

maintained in affluent Europe. The actual growth of the economies of South America in the first two years of the Alliance was about 4 per cent but after adjusting to account for population growth, only a subminimal increase of less than 1 per cent *per capita* is left. It was lower for the second year (1962) than the first one (1961). Most countries did not introduce significant agrarian reforms (some progress was made in three countries) and most kept reforms of taxes and formulation of master plans for development merely on the books. In general, agricultural production lagged behind the general slow growth, intensifying the uneven structure of many of the Latin American economies, and exports failed to grow, deepening their balance-of-payment problems. Few consolations could be derived from reforming democracies on other continents. Nigeria's development was far from safely launched. India's economy, after receiving aid amounting to $5 billion (over ten years), and still the number-one recipient of Western assistance, was scarcely keeping pace with its population. There was little hope that it could in the foreseeable future reach a "take-off" stage, where it could continue to develop without massive foreign aid.

The laying of solid democratic foundations might take even longer than development in many of these countries, and it was not clear whether democratization, one goal of intervention for progress, did not hamper the other, development. The more responsive a government is to its people, the more likely it is to devote scarce resources to satisfying their immediate demands, making fewer resources available for development. In addition, the means available to organize development—such as relocating citizens and redistributing land—are limited to those allowed under the democratic process. To intensify the problem, not much time appears to be left for experimentation. Impatience with the progress of democratic reform is bound to intensify in this era of rising expectations. Parents whose children are starving are hard put to it to wait; intellectuals reflecting over the plight of their nation provide a potential revolutionary, often Marxist, leadership. As a result, to the left of Bosch, Betancourt, Nehru, and other democratic moderate-left leaders, are vocal, radical groups convinced of the need for iron-fisted, totalitarian organization to achieve rapid development. Persuaded that in efforts to win the cooperation of the *status quo* groups, the moderates favor, are doomed to failure, they cry for the uprooting of entrenched groups, and for forceful redistribution of land, capital, and labor force.

It is much too early to predict whether or not these reform governments, even with American help, will be able to hold their own against the challenge of the radical left (and, we shall see, the extreme right) and maintain, if not the active support, at least the acquiescence of the *status quo* groups for their development efforts. The picture changes with every roll of the newspaper presses; as these lines are written, India's government is faring best in terms of popular support, although much of it is tied to Nehru's personality and Indian development is slow indeed; strikes are rocking Bolivia; terrorism is uncontrolled in Colombia; there is considerable political confusion in Nigeria; Betancourt is directly challenged; and Bosch has just been unseated. Watching these countries in the next few years will tell us much about the fate of U.S. alliances with moderate, reforming democracies.

There are already those who predict that if the West is really intent on beating the Communists on this front and answering the swelling needs of the less developed countries, it will have to support more radical, less democratic forces. The New Frontier not only did not support a radical movement, party, or leader in any contest between radicals and reformers (of which there are many in Latin America), it

showed considerable uneasiness about radicals in general, even
those in control of their respective countries.

Radical Nondemocratic Governments

A test for the Kennedy Administration's position on radical
progress cropped up in Algeria after the 1962 Evian peace
settlement. Premier Ahmed Ben Bella, an iron-fisted radical
seeking to develop his country in a hurry, launched his reform
program in the face of staggering economic dislocation and
impressive political opposition. The French colonials, before
most of them left Algeria, broke, burned, and demolished
all they could, reducing Algeria's gross national product from
$2 billion in 1960 to $1 billion in 1963. Unemployment
was widespread, and rivalry among leaders of the Algerian
liberation movement threatened the country with political
chaos. Ben Bella imposed a one-party system, exiled, arrested,
or sidetracked the opposition leaders, and so established some
stability in the country without imposing a police regime.

Indications of American sympathy and projections of generous assistance, expressed during Ben Bella's Washington
visit shortly after Algeria won independence, cooled rapidly
as the Algerian Premier stopped in Cuba on his way home
and praised the reforms of Castro's regime. A limited amount
of technical assistance and some food surpluses were given
to Algeria, but compared to the help extended to Bolivia or
Colombia, Algeria was clearly "out."[9] Though Ben Bella
banned the Communist Party and curbed its activities, he
put his country "on the road to socialism." He might, Washington felt, shift to the East, or be taken over from within,
as Cuba was.

While the Kennedy Administration was more generous toward some one-party, socialist governments, especially that of
Egypt, it was uncertain about Ceylon, which nationalized

[9] According to the *New York Times* of September 29, 1963, even food
shipments were "tapering off."

American oil refineries without due compensation and increased its trade with the U.S.S.R., did not trust left-leaning,
tightly ruled, though developing, Ghana, and had no sympathy for the military-socialist government of General Ne
Win in Burma.

A major determinant of the New Frontier's coolness toward the radical left was Congress. The Kennedy Administration might have continued to grant aid to Ceylon, which
was after all not very radical, but Congress enacted a law forbidding aid to countries that nationalized American property
without due compensation. The Administration might have
been more generous to Ghana, but Senator Dodd called
Nkrumah a "Communist" and—who knows?—by the next
elections . . . "did you expect Cuba to go Communist?" The
pressure of domestic politics reinforces the liberal preference
for democratic reformers which prevails in the State Department, and its "let's-not-get-too-involved-with-radicals" attitude. Some aid is extended to all comers, but the amount of
aid, degree of red tape, approval of loans and grants encountered all indicate the true likes and dislikes. Washington's uneasiness vis-à-vis the radical left is expressed not only
in the withholding or dabbling of aid to many of these countries, but in the matter of official visits. Heads of radically
led states have not been invited to address Congress the way
Pakistan's President Mohammed Ayub Khan was.

The progressive American policy is caught in a dilemma.
The democratic reformers, responsive to the consumer demands of the masses, partially blocked by *status quo* groups
that have not been uprooted, are slow to develop. Some radically governed countries develop more rapidly, but they tend
to violate the tenets of democracy the United States is out
to advance and do seem not "safe" from Communism to
boot. The reformers might open the door to Communism
by being unable to answer the basic needs of their people,
bringing scorn to both democracy and the United States, their

patron. Actively supporting radical governments requires at least tentative endorsement of one-party states and might indeed involve an Administration in supporting a Castro of tomorrow. Moreover, any consideration of a change in policy is complicated by the general paucity of instruments available for U.S. foreign-policy makers, which was brought into sharp relief by the countercoups.

Countercoups

China was won by the Communists, an authoritative study concluded, because of the imbalance between ambitious ends and inadequate means that marked American policy toward China in the 1940s.[10] Any progressive U.S. policy is hampered by the fact that even a country as affluent and mighty as the United States does not have the resources and instruments necessary to carry out the goals of intervention for progress. As far as development is concerned, most economists seem to have seriously underestimated its costs. Even when the United States grants a fairly small country hundreds of millions of dollars over the years—as it did in Bolivia, for instance—waste, corruption, ignorance, resistance, malplanning, and the like, still leave it basically underdeveloped. When it comes to political goals, such as strengthening the hand of constitutional, democratic governments and keeping the military oligarchies out, all the instruments Washington commands—short of sending the Marines—do not suffice, and sending the Marines would undermine the very purposes of the policy. This problem is best illustrated when a government favored by Washington, because of its reforming and democratic quality, is challenged by a military, right-wing countercoup. The events of July 1962 in Peru offer a prime example.

[10] Tang Tsou, *America's Failure in China, 1941–50* (Chicago: University of Chicago Press, 1963).

In the early 1940s a trend toward fair elections and progressive government became evident in Peru, which for a century had known practically uninterrupted dictatorship. Upstaged for eight years by Manuel Odría's military-supported, rightist dictatorship (1948–56), this trend asserted itself in 1956, with weak democratic governments making some progress.

In 1962 elections favored Haya de la Torre's moderate-left APRA, a party which, unlike its domestic rivals, had a record of commitment to a dynamic program of progress. As the only other serious contender demanding social change, the APRA was viciously attacked by the Communists. The 1962 election reached a temporary deadlock when De la Torre's APRA fell short of the required 33 per cent plurality. While the APRA and the Popular Democratic Party were bargaining for support in Congress, where the election question would be decided, the army seated its candidate, General Ricardo Perez Godoy, using American tanks and American-trained personnel. President Kennedy immediately severed diplomatic relations and cut off military assistance as well as nearly all economic aid. However, after thirty days, diplomatic relations were resumed and most aid programs restored, including $25.3 million for housing, roads, and rural settlements; $4.5 million in technical assistance; and $36.9 million in Import-Export Bank loans.

The Peru story, it might be claimed, had a happy ending, since in 1963 the army decided to retire behind the scenes. It allowed elections to take place (though it seemed clear that not all candidates could be seated), and Fernando Belaunde, the newly elected President, was widely expected to introduce reforms and uphold the civilian façade, at least for a while. After a year's pause the violated reforming democracy was restored. But, as the pause indicated, the United States was unable to protect the reforming government it favored nor did it seem to be in a position to do so in the future, if Belaunde faced a military challenge.

In Argentina the United States supported the government
of Arturo Frondizi, whose life—but not government—was
spared because of U.S. intervention.[11] Here the United
States did not even protest the military coup; and here
again, after a year, the army, growing tired of having itself
to run the civilian agencies, retreated behind the scenes and
allowed half-free elections to take place (though many
candidates were blacklisted, especially Peronists and some
radicals). Dr. Arturo Illia, a fairly progressive man, was
elected and seated. But not only is a new military coup likely,
especially if Illia veers too far in the progressive direction, but
he must constantly clear his policy with the military, and
there is little the United States can do about it.

United States lack of response to these coups had some
immediate consequences. In 1962 various military juntas
throughout Latin America were closely watching Peruvian
and Argentinian events for indications of the U.S. reaction
to these unconstitutional, counterprogressive coups. As it became clear that the United States was neither able nor anxious
to prevent them, in the following year several other military
groups unseated American-supported, varyingly progressive
governments.

In rapid succession military coups against U.S.-supported
governments took place in Guatemala (March 1963) and in
Ecuador (July 1963), adding to the earlier right-wing military
takeovers of General Cemal Gursel in Turkey and General
Chung Hee Park in South Korea, two countries in which U.S.
economic aid and military assistance, and hence presumably
influence, had been most massive.

Late in 1963 Washington's favorite reforming democracy,
Juan Bosch's government in the Dominican Republic, was unseated by a military junta in alliance with business groups
that felt threatened even by Bosch's moderate reforms. The

[11] John Donovan, *Red Machete* (Indianapolis: Bobbs-Merrill, 1962), p. 23.

military accused Bosch of being "soft" on Communists and it declared plans to turn the country "into a rightist state." While the United States did not publicly react to the coups in Guatemala and Ecuador, it cut off all aid programs to the Dominican Republic and severed diplomatic relations. Still "inspired" by the mild U.S. reaction to earlier coups, within a week of the coup in the Dominican Republic, a right-wing, military coalition unseated the democratic reforming government of Ramon Villeda Morales in Tegucicalpa, Honduras. Again the United States cut off aid and diplomatic relations. But a few days later, Washington had second thoughts and talked about the differences between "good" and "bad" military coups, the former presumably more responsive to popular demands than the latter, though the *New York Times* duly reported that the Latin Americans failed to see the difference.[12]

The problem these right-wing unconstitutional coups posed for the United States is manifest. The use of force to counter such coups would evoke a renewed outcry of Yankee imperialism and unite the nonaligned world against the United States. Withholding diplomatic recognition (for a longer period than is required to see who is really in control) is considered ineffective and is not favored by most State Department experts, since they view diplomatic relations not as a seal of moral or political approval but as an opportunity for U.S. outposts, often used to keep in touch with democratic undergrounds in these countries, and as a channel of communication to be kept open at all times. Cutting aid to such governments is regarded as both unjustified ("the people will suffer") and ineffective (a military junta is unlikely to give up its power because of such pressure). To save face, a promise to hold elections is usually squeezed out of the new military rulers. Yet even when this promise is kept, as it was in Argentina, the government that follows such a coup tends to be less demo-

[12] *New York Times,* October 5, 1963.

cratic than the one that preceded it, if only because of the expectation that it will be unseated again, and the effectiveness of American support for progress is weakened.

In part the problem is semantic rather than real. These countries are not democracies, even when the military is in the barracks and elections are held. As long as elections are manipulated, and significant segments of the population or candidates are barred; as long as civilian governments find it prudent constantly to check their moves with the military chiefs, the unseating of such governments removes only a thin veneer that barely covers their political (right-wing) and unconstitutional (military-dominated) reality. This makes the task of intervention for progress still more difficult; the United States is faced with not only counterreform coups but pseudo democracies, and thickening the veneer so that it could serve as a real protection to democracy is a difficult task indeed. And while counterreforms and pseudo democracies alike undermine the policy of intervention for progress, American support of progress is further hampered by the extreme right.

Right-Wing Tyrannies

Among the right-wing, often military, governments receiving American support are a few tyrannies about which Washington is extremely unhappy. These have rulers who violate every human right and remember economic development chiefly on the speaker's platform. Providing excellent ammunition for Communist propaganda guns, they are embarrassing company for a U. S. Administration seeking to strengthen the U.S. image as the leader of progressive forces on the three less developed continents.

Raphael Trujillo was such a tyrant, a most unpleasant legacy handed down to President Kennedy by the preceding Administration. Luckily for the new Administration, the perplexing question of how to deal with Trujillo was solved by the dictator's own people, who assassinated him with arms smuggled in, it is reported, by the CIA.[13] The New Frontier would have liked to be rid of other tyrants with no more effort.

Haiti was expected in May 1963 to trace a pattern similar to its island neighbor. It is ruled by François Duvalier, the object of a personality cult second to none in Latin America, who has maintained a terroristic regime with the aid of a group of hooded thugs (Ton-Ton-Macoute, or bogeymen) supported by 60 per cent of the country's budget. With one of the lowest incomes per capita in the area, Haiti enjoys not much more development than it does democracy.

During its first two years the Kennedy Administration limited itself to well-concealed displeasure with the horrors of the Haitian government; military and economic aid were continued at the rate of about $6 million a year, as were shipments of arms and training missions. It was not until May 15, 1963, when Duvalier illegally appointed himself to a new, six-year term, that the United States saw an opening for breaking the tyrant's hold. After cracking down on economic aid, curtailing diplomatic relations, and reducing Marine and Air Force missions, the United States kept its aircraft carrier *Boxer* poised just outside Haitian territorial waters with two thousand Marines waiting in vain for the anticipated internal uprising. The O.A.S. refused to sanction a proposed invasion by Dominican armed forces, and no effective Haitian exile group was available. The United States, left with a choice between landing the Marines to free Haiti, against which a storm of protest was gathering, and allowing Duvalier to remain in office, chose the latter course.

Another somewhat less extreme Latin American police state is Paraguay. Under General Alfredo Stroessner it is a country of secret police, tapped telephones, prisons crowded with political opponents, and an almost incredible one sixth

[13] Norman Gall, "How Trujillo Died," *New Republic*, April 13, 1963, p. 19.

of its population in exile. The illiteracy rate of 80 per cent is among the highest in Latin America. In poor economic and financial condition when President Kennedy entered the White House, Stroessner's regime spent one third of the New Frontier annual allowance—about $10 million in 1962—to maintain the police and army. The story of Nicaragua under the rule of the oligarchic Samoa family follows the same outline.

Long-supported dictators cannot be expected to topple on a pre-fixed date, and Washington does not like strained relations with the government in control of a country for long periods. Once the inability to topple-on-order was demonstrated in Haiti, the less scandalous tyrants could expect to hold on to their reins without a U.S.-sponsored challenge. Thus, despite the policy of intervention for progress, a fair number of tyrants continue to rule as U.S. allies and friends, and continue to oppress their people and block effective modernization, preserving the conditions under which Communism thrives, as the rule of Czar Nicholas II in Russia, Chiang Kai-shek on the Chinese mainland, and Batista in Cuba have so effectively demonstrated.

If the United States had trouble squaring its progressive stand with its tyrant allies safely in the Latin American rearland, its relations with despots on the containment line have proved even more embarrassing. Among the less troublesome, but potentially embarrassing, was the military junta of Turkey which overthrew the government of Premier Menderes in 1960. After eighteen months of outright military dictatorship, it withdrew behind a thin democratic façade. General Gursel, head of the military regime, was elected President, and a civilian, Ismet Inonu, the Premier. The latter did not enjoy majority support in parliament, but had the confidence of the military. The year 1963 was marked by rebellions, martial law in the main cities of Turkey, arrests of hundreds of officers and political leaders, and death sentences for leaders of the uprisings.

South Korea's military junta had a hard time erecting a civilian façade, and General Park kept delaying the election he had promised the Kennedy Administration, only after much pressure was exerted. After several purges, arrests, and exiles of opposition leaders, elections took place on October 15, 1963, but the major opponent, former Premier Song Yo Chan, was conveniently jailed. Park's supporters stuffed the ballot boxes, registered children as voters, and used the police to bring out reluctant supporters.

These two U.S. allies, which, together with South Vietnam, absorb a large part of U.S. military and economic assistance, must have been grateful all during 1962 and most of 1963 to Ngo Dinh Diem, then despot number one, for deflecting public opinion from their autocracies. Diem's tyranny cast long shadows on the policy of intervention for progress when this playboy puppet, supported by fourteen thousand American troops, Special Forces, and military advisers, supplied with heavy modern weapons and massive U.S. aid (amounting to, 1962–63, $1.5 million a day), not only proved unable to suppress pro-Communist forces, but turned American arms and American-trained and -financed forces against the non-Communist Buddhist majority of his country, to implement his religious persecution laws, to snatch bodies of priests who had burned themselves alive in protest against his rule, to arrest teen-age students, to impose one of the most corrupt tyrannies on earth. If all the efforts for progress are put on one scale and those on behalf of Diem's government on the other, Diem's liability probably outweighed the progressive assets, at least as far as the nonaligned world is concerned.

As in other rim countries, the United States found it difficult, for long months, to bring itself to cooperate with an opposition to unseat Diem. You cannot take risks, it was said; the Communists will benefit from chaos in a rim country, especially one engaged in a civil war. The New York *Herald Tribune* expressed its support for Diem under these circumstances, recalling Al Smith's quip: "You don't change barrels while going over Niagara Falls." But, it seems to me, if you take no risks and continue to ride in rotten barrels to support the Batistas and the Diems, you provide the Communists with perfect ammunition in the all-important contest over the minds of people in the three underdeveloped continents. Hundreds of speeches about the Alliance for Progress and a year's work of the U. S. Information Agency cannot erase the picture of priests burning in the streets of Saigon, protesting the persecution of a tyrant propped up by the United States.

The "no-alternatives-available" argument has little validity. It was said that after three decades of Trujillo's reign no democratic leadership could be found for the Dominican Republic, and hence his tyranny was supported year after year. But shortly after his downfall, a leader was found in Juan Bosch. The *New Republic* provided a long list of "alternatives" for Diem.[14]

It may be that occasionally the man to follow a Diem will be no better, and then what I like to call the "multi-toppling" approach will have to be adopted, i.e., continued opposition will have to be encouraged until a leader more responsive to the people is found. There is no evidence that such a transition period would be nearly as harmful to the Western position as the support of Diem and his like. And in any case the Kennedy Administration finally had to give way and support the removal of Diem, but only after much damage was done to its reputation throughout the free world.

This point deserves some emphasis. Immanuel Kant was once asked if a person who is completely drunk and has lost control over his actions is morally responsible for a crime he commits. Yes, he said, because you should never get that

14 April 20, 1963, p. 4.

drunk. The 1963 Diem did not fall out of the sky; he was hated by his people long before he crushed Buddhist demonstrations. The majority of his countrymen always saw him as a continuation of the much resented French colonial rule, which resorted to the same methods to suppress political opponents and recruit peasants for forced labor to build *"agrovilles."* Nor was he new to the business of crushing religious groups; in 1955 he had turned his forces loose against two sects, the Hao and the Hoa. In 1960 his palace was bombed by his own military.

The same holds for other tyrants allied to the West. They rest now out of the limelight, oppressing their people and using American funds, arms, and military training missions. Tomorrow a Vietnam-like war might erupt in any one of these countries. Then the United States will rush to save its ally, and sooner or later the same difficult situation that prevailed in South Vietnam in 1963 will be reproduced. The time for the United States to take stock and find out what support for progress means in South Korea, Taiwan, Turkey, and the like, is now.

"Enlightened" Right Wingers?

To exhaust the categories of countries the United States faces, the "enlightened" right wingers must be included. There is some disagreement as to which countries are to be included in this category, but the fact is that some progress has been attained under some right-wing governments.

Iran, after many years of stagnation, seemed to initiate both a development and a democratization drive in 1962–63. The Shah was reported to have granted title for two million acres of land to the peasants who occupied it; he formed a number of rural cooperatives to buy seed, fertilizer, and mechanical equipment and to grant long-term credits, all essential concomitants to turn land redistribution into successful agrarian reform. The army was reported to have been used to fight illiteracy; the industrial workers to have been promised a profit-sharing plan in which they would gain 20 per cent of the net earnings of each industry. It is hard to judge how far and how deep many of these reforms actually ran. For instance, massive use of the army to teach vocational skills is reported, but the number of instructors provided is forty-four. Some questions have been raised about the accuracy of the two-million-acres figure, and though the 1963 elections may have been the freest Iran ever had, the Shah put the opposition under house arrest, closed seventy-five Teheran dailies and weeklies, and gained a surprisingly high percentage of the vote (close to 90 per cent).

It is even more difficult to predict how far the Shah will go with his reforms. Already his white (from above) revolution has provoked the ire of the landlords, *muafs* (religious priests), and business groups. An attempt at armed revolt took place in 1963. The Shah may still be unseated or scared into slowing down, though he seems to be moving in a progressive direction.

General (now President) Ayub Khan, after seizing power in Pakistan in 1958, removed the shambles of parliamentary democracy as practiced by this Western ally. He established an out-and-out dictatorship, but soon began an experiment to restore democracy gradually from above. As a first measure he introduced, late in 1959, local elections in the villages and urban wards. In 1962 he went a step further and set up an electoral college, in which some eighty thousand men (in a country of eighty-five million) were given the right to elect the President and the central legislative assembly. He hopes slowly to enlarge the electorate in this system of "basic democracy." While progress has been far from sensational, it is an interesting experiment in gradual democratization.[15]

[15] For a discussion of the difficulties Ayub encountered in his program for democratizing Pakistan, see J. H. Huizinga, "The Disappointments of Ayub Khan," in *The Reporter*, June 6, 1963, pp. 30–31.

The limited progress made in these countries is of special interest because of the growing support in Washington for development-through-the-right or "white revolutions." Painfully aware of the small number of reforming democracies, and not trusting radical ones, there is growing interest in a "safe" right-wing regime that develops and democratizes. State Department officials and consultants are particularly optimistic about progressive military regimes. The military is believed to be increasingly conscious of the need to modernize and to provide responsive governments; it is also said to be the best organized element in these societies and the most familiar with modern technology.[16]

In my judgment this theory, which competes with the liberal theory of social change, is prescribed more by a desire to make virtue out of necessity than by a sociological insight into the dynamics of these countries, or evidence to back it up. Military governments have recently been established in scores of countries, from Burma to Peru, Ecuador to South Korea, but very few are leading their countries on the road to progress.[17] The military is well equipped and organized—to run military affairs (though in general even their fighting record is far from outstanding). When it comes to governing a civilian society, the average officer has a "trained incapacity"—he tries to run a society like an army. He lacks a sense of both economic utility and political responsiveness, being accustomed

[16] See Max F. Millikan and Donald L. M. Blackmer (eds.), *The Emerging Nations* (Boston: Little, Brown, 1961), pp. 112 ff.; and Robert J. Alexander, *Today's Latin America* (Garden City, N.Y.: Anchor Books, 1962), p. 181.

[17] There are several exceptions, but most of them, upon closer examination, turn out not to be exceptions at all. The famous Mexican Revolutionary Army was created outside the traditional structure and after it was toppled; it was not a revolution carried out by a military that existed before the revolution. In other cases, the young officers made a coalition with progressive civilian forces only to leave them in the lurch when they seemed to progress "too much," as was the case in Brazil. My views on this issue are elaborated in "Democracy's Future in Latin America," *The New Leader*, November 25, 1963, pp. 13–16.

to function in an environment in which efficiency is hard to measure and discipline can be forced. Sooner or later, most military governments lead to economic chaos and political upheaval.

Even more important, the military tends to draw its officers from groups that support the *status quo*, making it a poor instrument to bring about the far-reaching changes in the social structure that can open the road to modernization. It is true that some services, often the air force, are more popularly recruited than the others, and that the younger officers are more "progressive" than the senior ones, but with a few exceptions (mainly in the Middle East), the military as such has not provided a sound administration for progress.

In sum, the New Frontier's drive has not advanced very far. The reforming democracies, the showcases of intervention for progress, are threatened from the extreme right and the radical left, and the ability to combine steady development with a democratic regime is far from established. The radical governments pose major difficulties; since they are not democratic and their non-Communist posture is not assured, to support them is to take risks with Congress and the voters. Counterreform coups that put right-wing military men in the place of elected, at least mildly reforming, governments are embarrassing because the United States lacks the means needed to back up the governments it favors (or is committed not to use them). Even more out of character are the old right-wing tyrannies the Kennedy and Johnson Administrations inherited as allies. Being faced with so many "exceptions" to the progressive rule, there is an increasing temptation to view "enlightened" right-wing governments as progressive, but evidence that they lead to development and democratization is scarce, and supporting them does not endear the West to the overwhelmingly left-of-center nonaligned world.

THE FUTURE OF INTERVENTION FOR PROGRESS

THE LIMITS OF PROGRESS

Many of the factors that dim the record of intervention for progress are in the category of givens about which little can be done. If in answering anticolonial appeals offends our NATO allies, U.S. is constrained to proceed cautiously if it is not to lose strategic bases and defense partners. If Congress insists on tying aid to private enterprise in countries where the state has yet to provide necessary economic prerequisites (technically known as "infra-structure"), including such unprofitable items as roads, communications, and schools, there is little an Administration can do. If Congress enacts a law forbidding aid to countries that nationalized American property without "prompt, adequate, and effective" compensation, the President can try to repeal it or work around it, but progressive U.S. policy is still hampered by it.

The policy also faces significant obstacles in the underdeveloped countries themselves, some of them insurmountable. Developing a country requires a considerably greater investment of funds and effort than has often been estimated, and many more social and political changes than is usually believed. The funds required are enormous, not simply because of the dearth of capital in underdeveloped countries, but because only a fraction of the capital granted ever reaches its destination. Booming populations eat much of it up; the appetite of the existing population grows as it comes into increasing contact with the modern world, an inevitable concomitant of modernization; and corruption and inefficiency, however countered, continue to siphon off substantial amounts.

Under these circumstances it is hardly surprising if more aid is lost than is effectively invested, and the ratio can be improved only very slowly. Whole institutions have to be adjusted, and much of the social fabric rewoven—all of which requires a supportive political context. But the governments often lean on groups whose fortunes are, or seem to be, enmeshed with the existing social structure. These often include the old coalition of landlords, army officers, and the church, and the new industrial classes that have acquired deep-seated vested interests in the existing social structure. For example, the industrialists in Latin America are as little interested in the progressive income tax, a central feature of the Alliance for Progress, as are the landlords. And the urban labor unions are often rather indifferent to unionization of the countryside, which might lead to increase of food prices. In short, the prospect of providing the political context for speedy development without radical revolution is not bright.[18]

Under the best circumstances it will probably take decades before the development of most of the eighty-odd underdeveloped countries is firmly founded, and their democratic forms of government soundly based, whatever the United States does. But one of the major flaws of the intervention-for-progress policy—and one that can be corrected—is that it does not fully recognize the dimensions of the task and draw the appropriate conclusions. Armed with native American optimism and a surprising sense of omnipotence, prompted by the necessity of convincing Congress and the taxpayers to relinquish billions for foreign aid, and anxious to counter Communist claims of being the sole champions of progress, the supporters of intervention for progress have seriously overstated the potency of this policy. Often it has sounded as if, given the requested billions, it could deliver—in a few years—a developed Latin America, if not Africa and Asia, populated with democratic governments to boot. The Administration would fare better if it did not build up such high expectations among congressmen, American voters, and the

[18] The factors hindering development and their international impact are discussed at greater length in Part III of my *The Hard Way to Peace*.

citizens of underdeveloped countries. Juscelino Kubitschek, former Brazilian President, has observed that "it would have been better to have silence than to have spread seeds of hope that will never grow and bear fruit." Promising less and doing more might prove to be not merely a more virtuous, but a wiser, policy.

BUILDING REALISTIC HOPE

No one can provide the peoples of the underdeveloped continents with the affluence of Western Europe (not to mention America) in a lifetime. If the per capita income of India were tripled within the next generation—an incredible feat—it would still be ten times smaller than that of the United States. In 1961 the average per capita income of Latin America was $84; of Africa $100; of the Middle East $87—compared to $2790 in the United States.[19] A steady increase in national income of 5 per cent per year is unusual; if attained, it would still take these countries generations to reach the *present* level of the United States. Similarly, democracy does not take root overnight; even in the West, where conditions were particularly favorable, it evolved over centuries. The question is not one of delivering affluence and all the freedoms of democracy here and now, but of moving in the desired direction; hope so reinforced will have to carry the rest of the burden. Thus, whether the United States stands on the side of progress or of the *status quo* vis-à-vis the underdeveloped world, is critically important. The United States is not expected, unless it generates this expectation itself, single-handedly to usher in an economic, social, and political millennium. Instead, it is examined to see whether it will reach out for leadership for progress and how vigorously and consistently it will pursue it.

[19] Figures are in terms of "money" gross national product, and were calculated by Professor P. N. Rosenstein-Rodan of the Massachusetts Institute of Technology.

The United States should be the first to point out that it does not command the resources to fulfill most of the needs; it can and will help, but it cannot be expected to carry most of the load. Its entire national income would not suffice to accomplish this task.

The United States should also actively dispel the impression that simply providing capital makes the difference, a fallacy that implies that the aiding nation is to blame for tardy development because it did not grant "enough" capital aid. It should make clear how much progress depends on the developing countries themselves, which must change institutions and habits that cannot be changed for them. And it should provide some realistic backdrop against which to measure progress, which will inevitably be slow, piecemeal, and uneven.

In a recent visit to several developing countries, I asked American representatives why they shied away from this "realistic" line and constantly promised more and claimed more than the United States could ever hope to deliver. One of them said: "Isn't this the essence of propaganda?" The others suggested that such a shift of policy would drive scores of countries away from the United States. However, a similar shift in line has been carried out by one agency to good effect. The U. S. Information Agency used to adhere to a black-white approach that sought to belittle all Soviet achievement and publicize all Soviet faults, while whitewashing American shortcomings and loudly playing up U.S. virtues. Under the Kennedy Administration, as Edward Murrow took over the leadership of this agency, a more "objective" line was adopted which admits American shortcomings (for instance, in racial matters) while stressing progress, and makes claims that are easier to live up to, in a more subdued voice. It is difficult to document, but I believe, from traveling widely and talking freely to many people, that the new "realistic" line is much more effective.

Officials who accept the "realistic" line as far as propaganda goes, object to extending its application; conversation on the subject is usually sealed with the statement: "If we point out the limitations of our development and democratization policy, these countries will turn to the U.S.S.R." This is somehow viewed as an immediate disaster, tantamount to Communist occupation of these countries. But, in point of fact, the yields of the Soviet foreign-aid program are rather meager. The Russians granted Indonesia a billion dollars worth of economic and military aid, only to see it moving closer to the West in 1963. Afghanistan was a Soviet favorite, but after many years of extensive economic aid, trade, military assistance, and cultural programs, it, too, increased its ties to the West. The same, as we have seen, occurred in Egypt and Guinea. There have also been the all-too-familiar signs of lack of gratitude, and complaints about slowness of delivery, products and experts unadapted to the tropical climate and circumstance, etc. Morocco found, in what is by no means an exceptional case, that a sugar-beet factory built at Sidi Slim, by Poles, had to be redesigned by French experts, and that the only offer Communist China could make, was to trade tea for phosphates. According to *Pravda*, of 480 projects initiated since 1955, only 120 were completed by mid-1963.

The vision of scores of countries turning to the Soviet Union for aid is quite unrealistic; Russian resources are badly strained as it is, and it could hardly provide aid to most of them. If it did, these countries would quickly discover that the U.S.S.R. can no more assure development than the United States can, actually less. That it will not support the evolution of free elections, democratic parties, and the like goes without saying. The United States has little to fear from an open competition over quantities and qualities of foreign aid, and much could be gained from adjusting the claims and reducing expectations to what can really be delivered.

THE REQUIREMENTS OF CONSISTENCY

But a realistic line alone will not do. If the American bid for leadership of progressive forces is to be convincing, consistency is all-important. We are dealing here with psychology and politics, not just with economics. The United States seeks the leadership of progressive forces, but it is suspect—too often in the past it has wielded the instruments of intervention to protect American private or national interests rather than to promote a country's progress. Every American act, at least initially, will continue to be examined to see if it provides for exploitation or development, for subjugation or democratization. Even the quasi-intervention by the United States in Haitian affairs in 1963 was viewed as "just one more example of Yankee imperialism" rather than "sincere concern for the welfare of Haiti."[20] Surely most Americans saw U.S. pressure against Duvalier as a selfless act, aimed at advancing democracy. It is therefore of interest to see how the same move seemed from a nonaligned vantage point. Why, the Mexicans asked, the sudden concern? Hadn't the United States cooperated with this and similar tyrants for years? In the whole hemisphere only two countries—Panama and Nicaragua—were willing to approve U.S. intervention, under O.A.S. mandate.[21]

A very sympathetic observer might understand why the United States supported, in 1962, both Duvalier and Bosch, Samoa and Betancourt, Diem and Nehru, Salazar and Tito, but the average citizen or even leader of these countries can see little sense and no consistency in this policy. To him, it seems like confusion at best, cynical politics at worst. Hence, the urgent need for the United States to make its policy more explicit and consistent, to increase its appeal. This can be done, within the framework of existing means and resources.

The U.S. claim to leadership of progressive forces would be

[20] Ramon Eduardo Ruiz, letter to editor, *New York Times*, May 22, 1963.
[21] *The Reporter*, June 20, 1963, p. 24.

more effectively advanced if, in its dealings with each country, it were to take more into account the impact of this relationship on its relationships with other countries, and on its global image. The cost of even relatively minor support to a right-wing tyranny ($2.4 million to Haiti in 1963), the long delay in renouncing Diem, are high in terms of nonaligned public opinion. Aid to a military junta that has illegitimately deposed a constitutional, reform government might be small enough to do little to assure its future, and cutting this aid might not bring its downfall, but such action will significantly clarify the U.S. stand for the opposition in these countries and others. Support to "enlightened" right-wing governments can be justified, for the period that they actually stay enlightened. As long as the Shah Riza Pahlevi of Iran effectively introduces land reforms that lead to his country's development and democratization, more power to him. But if he turns to toying with development and playing at elections, he will merely fan revolutionary flames in Iran, and U.S. support of him will undermine its role as a progressive leader in Iran *and* elsewhere.

The United States should tie its aid more closely to progress —not because it can assure development or buy democracy by extending or withdrawing it, but because it needs to wield these instruments to make more visible its commitment on the side of progress. The difference between the governments the United States favors and those it does not, or favors less, must be made much clearer. Looking back at the five kinds of governments the United States faces in the third world, what would such a policy change entail? For the *reforming democracies*, such as Bolivia, it would mean continuation of an all-out effort to make a success of *their* effort, without unduly building up expectation of rapid development or democratization without a hitch.

Ties to *rear-land tyrannies* of the Haitian variety would be reduced to low-level diplomatic relations, foregoing all economic aid, eliminating technical assistance, withdrawing military missions, and cutting off supplies of arms. Even small amounts of aid—similar to those given to Duvalier until mid-1963—are interpreted as an endorsement, therefore cutting off rather than simply reducing is called for. The claim that these tyrants will turn Communist if the United States cuts its aid is ridiculous; none ever did. On the contrary, supporting Batista opened the door to a Communist take-over.

Rim-land tyrannies, like Park's South Korea and Diem's South Vietnam, would be subjected to much greater pressure to liberalize; and effective opposition whenever it is found would be supported, even if this required "multi-toppling" and some degree of chaos. Changes of government in these coup-experienced countries often produce much less demoralization than support of tyrants. "Preventive" action should be taken, wherever possible, long before the situation deteriorates, as it did in mid-1963 in South Vietnam, and before the country is engulfed in a civil war. There is little hope that the United States will be widely followed as a leader of progress so long as the amount of help it grants a Diem exceeds what it provides for all the progressive governments in South and Central America together.

Again, the United States should not expect from itself, or lead others to expect, that it will topple tyrants at will and replace them, on a prearranged schedule, with level-headed progressive leaders. It should make it clear that it will support indigenous opposition to any tyrant, and meanwhile disassociate itself from tyrants as much as possible. The degree to which this is possible depends in part on interbloc relations in general and on the introduction of a remote deterrence system in particular.

The *counterreform* military juntas would be given the reverse example of the one they got in Peru in July 1962. The United States must find ways to point up more explicitly the difference between the regimes it approves and those that retard democratization and development. Occasionally, this difference is blurred when the military unseats a duly elected government that is not particularly favorable to the United States. For instance, in 1962 the United States was unhappy over Frondizi's refusal to support its efforts to oust Castro's Cuba from the O.A.S. When the Argentinian generals unseated Frondizi, there was next to no American protest. While the United States can hardly be expected always to like the outcome of an election or the policy of a democratic government, it can by the same token not expect the Latin Americans to learn to accept the rules of the game of democratic political life unless it sets a more explicit example. Similarly, talking about the virtues of democracies and continuing to support military juntas that topple progressive governments does more damage to the spirit and purpose of the New Frontier policy than many Communist agitators could. It is hard to imagine that generals will return to the barracks, or stay there, just to avoid displeasing the United States. But as the pressures toward civilian governments in these countries mount, and the military considers relinquishing its control of the government machinery, U.S. pleasure and displeasure is *one* factor affecting its decision. The more clearly known it is what U.S. pleasure is, the more effective it will be. Again, in countries where the generals are not considering a retreat, the civilians who work toward their removal and for the restoration of progressive government should know more explicitly that the United States is on their side.

The treatment of the *radical* forces must be determined in part by their status. If they are competing with effective democratic reforming forces over the future rule of a country, the United States will surely support the force that is on the side of both development and democratization. If the radicals challenge an established reforming democracy from the left, adding to the troubles it faces from the right, as they do in Betancourt's Venezuela and did in Bosch's Dominican Republic, they should expect the same cold-shoulder treatment we advocate for anticonstitution juntas of the right. But what position is the United States to take toward those countries already under radical one-party rule, like Ben Bella's Algeria, Nkrumah's Ghana, and Touré's Guinea?

When these radical governments are in effect Communist ones that look toward joining the Communist bloc, as Jagan's British Guiana was widely believed to be in 1963, the United States cannot be expected to treat them differently than it treats any other member of the bloc. But when they are non-Communist—as the large majority of them are—they would receive U.S. support under two conditions: that they develop, and that they avoid tyrannical procedures. The importance of these countries lies in the fact that they are trying another approach toward progress, making accelerated development the first step and leaving democratization for later. While the West, as its support to the reforming democracies and several statements indicate,[22] prefers the simultaneous approach, there have not been enough countries successfully taking on democratic reform and development for the United States to cold shoulder those who try development first. As long as the radical governments of the Ghanas and Algerias are making progress in developing their countries, full assistance should be extended.

There is, however, one condition that radical governments should be expected to meet: they should forego terrorist practices. It is one thing not to hold elections, or to require workers to move from an overpopulated area to a developing one, or even to limit political agitation, and quite another to establish concentration camps and firing squads, and exercise police brutalities. There is a minimum democratization a country should have to fulfill before it is allotted Western help, both because terror is morally repulsive and supporting

[22] Millikan and Blackmer, *op. cit.*; Henry A. Kissinger, *The Necessity for Choice* (New York: Harper, 1961), Chapter VII.

it corrupts, and because no ally of governments based on hang-men and secret police, who cannot lead their own people, can lead the forces of tomorrow.

Again, it would be naïve to expect a Ghana or an Algeria to give up government instruments they consider essential, to abolish imprisonment without trial to qualify for technical as-sistance or the Peace Corps, and to close forced-labor camps to gain a grant, unless they are ready for such steps. It is realistic to expect that when such a country hovers on the border line between terrorist regimes and "tight" ones, the focused public opinion of the West, backed up by the instru-ments of intervention for progress, could make the difference. Most of these countries are too far from the parliamentary democracy the West would like to see for any pressure to bring them, at this stage, to conform to its rules and spirit. Fore-going terror, on the other hand, seems within reach. But if it were not, the West still could not afford association with a terrorist government of the left any more than it can cooper-ate with those on the right, and still be considered a leader of progress.

"Enlightened" right-wing regimes might well be judged by the same criteria. Terrorist regimes of the right, like those of the left, should not get any Western support; they vilify our cause and undermine the effectiveness of our policy beyond any strategic or economic value they might have by other considerations. "Tight" regimes, on the other hand, might win the West's cooperation as long as they indeed developed or democratized. An earlier discussion of the qualities of these regimes suggests that their progressive potential may have been exaggerated; but the same pragmatic rule suggested with regard to the radical-left governments applies here. If Pakistan is indeed democratizing, if the number of persons granted the right to vote is increased, if elections are held more frequently and freely, and if opposition is allowed, this is progress, and the fact that Pakistan is under conservative military rule

should not stop us from hailing it. But when the democratic reform is running out of steam, when the "basic democracies" are under the aegis of police and internal-revenue administrators, this, too, must be recognized.

Democratization and development are processes, not qualities that you have or do not. Countries move forward, stand still, or regress on each of these fronts. If the United States supports progress, expresses displeasure at stagnation, and actively counters regression, it will build up its capacity and renown as a global leader of progress. It will then be more ready to compete freely and fully with the Communist movement over the nonaligned floating vote.

INTERVENTION FOR PROGRESS AND INTERBLOC COMPETITION

The policy of intervention for progress is closely tied to current changes in the interbloc contest, and the tie runs both ways. More successful support for progress requires a fuller shift away from duopoly toward interbloc competition, but the interbloc contest will not be effectively limited to nonarmed means unless intervention for progress is more successful. The picture is blurred in the present transitional phase, but the trend is increasingly evident.

PROGRESS REQUIRES COMPETITION

Since the tendency is to explain strategic innovations to the American people in terms of the old framework, to make them more acceptable, intervention for progress was initially introduced as another way of containing Communism. The reign of non-Communist governments on and behind the containment line was to be assured not by promoting the *status quo* groups but by neutralizing the Communist appeal; by providing the people of these countries with the desired progress. If the West could help engineer agrarian reforms, industrialization, housing programs, and new schools, and at the same time increase the responsiveness of the governments to their people, the oppression and misery on which Communism thrives would be eliminated, and containment strengthened.

But supporting progress in the old, duopolistic context required the United States to walk a tightrope, trying on the one hand to strengthen the position of the progressive forces, and on the other to keep these countries from stepping up relations with the Soviet bloc. In part the United States wished to avoid competition—if Ceylon bought Soviet oil, it might not buy American and British oil; if Bosch were allowed to import Soviet books (printed in Spanish in Cuba), this would make the task of the United States Information Agency that much more difficult. In part the United States feared that peaceful Communist penetration into the third area would be followed by armed penetration, leading to either occupation or take-over from within. Thus, despite growing recognition of the fact that the nonaligned countries did preserve their independence, and that the Soviets increasingly restricted their expansionist efforts to peaceful means, *the United States still puts much pressure on the third countries not to trade, receive aid, or allow their leaders so much as to visit the Soviet Union.*

The reluctance to accept the consequences of the shift from duopoly to competition in this area is well illustrated in the following report by Max Frankel from Washington:

> Diplomats engaged for years in efforts to warn other nations of the perils of trading with Communists are asking what to say now that Washington itself is taking a new look at East-West commercial relations.
>
> Propagandists engaged for years in arguing that the Russians cannot be trusted to keep agreements are asking what line they should pursue now that Washington itself is thinking of a whole series of agreement.

Americans who have worked overtime in recent years to deny the Soviet Union air routes into Africa and Latin America are asking what they are supposed to do now that the United States itself is close to exchanging air service between Moscow and New York.[23]

The answer seems to us to be that as long as Washington sincerely seeks to shift toward a world in which peaceful competition is allowed, even encouraged, it should not attempt to lock Soviet trade, agreements, and airlines out of the new nations, as long as satisfactory provisions are made that these will not, cannot, be used for purposes of armed expansion.

But this is not just a matter of policy that can be decided in the State Department. It is rapidly becoming evident that the progressive governments, although vigilant against joining or being joined to the Communist camp, refused to cease building up their contacts with the Sino-Soviet camp. It was only the tyrannies and, to a lesser extent, the "enlightened" right-wing governments, that could be relied on to adhere to the tenets of the duopolistic posture. Reforming democracies could barely be held in line, and the radical governments flatly refused to accept the limitation. The countercoup groups, on the other hand, while embarrassing the American progressive stand, brought their countries back to the duopolistic fold. For example, progressive Frondizi refused to cut ties to Cuba, but the right-wing generals who removed him were only too happy to second the motion. While the new support for progress and the old duopolistic approach did not jostle each other all the time, it was clearly difficult to bring them into line. One required "taking risks," the other, "playing it safe"; one opened the door to interbloc contacts, the other sought to keep it closed. Gradually, and not for all countries at the same time, the broader strategic framework has changed, but the transition is still not complete.

[23] "Problems of the Thaw," *New York Times*, October 25, 1963.

Intervention for progress can be more fully implemented if the United States is willing to take greater risks in supporting progressive forces and abandons pressures on all countries, not to expand peaceful contacts with the other bloc. To make this more acceptable to the West other elements of the competition strategy, especially remote deterrence and its related international machinery, ought to be set up.

Assume for the moment that the many difficulties involved in introducing such a policy can be overcome, that an embargo on shipment of arms into the third world will be established, and that both sides refrain from supporting either rebels or the government, insurrection or counterinsurrection, by the use of arms, armed agents, or troops. What effects would this have on U.S. foreign policy? One result would be to rid the United States of its tyrannical allies, for without the domestic power they gain from funds and arms provided by America, they could not hold out for long against their discontented people. Unable to continue using the ruse of claiming to be under Communist attack (now to be systematically checked out by the U.N. observer force as well as partisan intelligence sources), they would lose their gambit for involving the United States in their internal struggles. One line that tied America to nonprogressive forces would be severed.

At the same time remote deterrence would reduce many of the risks now seen in an all-out support for progressive forces. The Kennedy Administration, partially influenced by pressure from Congress and the voters, saw reduction of aid to a military right-wing regime or, conversely, increase of assistance to a radical one, as increasing the chances of its turning to Communism. Actually, however, since nonaligned countries jealously guard their independence, beyond complete Western ostracism, only an armed force could push them to join the Communist camp. (As we have seen, over the last decade, only Cuba voluntarily joined the Communist bloc, and it probably would have returned to the nonaligned fold long ago, were it not for Soviet troops stationed there, and for American ostracism.) An effective embargo on the positioning of bloc forces in third countries would practically eliminate the risks involved in a much more determined but unarmed intervention for progress, one that more freely supports radical governments as long as they refrain from terrorism and actively develop, is less reluctant to withdraw support from right-wing ones that combine tyranny with no development, and is more ready to encourage indigenous opposition to tyrants.

One major misunderstanding should be avoided here, a confusion inherent in the term intervention. Many Latin Americans are quick to denounce Yankee intervention and, in the same breath, to blame the United States for not intervening more effectively in favor of progressive forces. Several U.S. writers have pointed this out as being highly hypocritical, suggesting we are "damned if we do and damned if we don't." This is not necessarily fair; many Latin Americans draw a line between armed and nonarmed intervention. Following and supporting the evolution of competition under rules, the United States would refrain from the use of force in support of progressive groups, but would use all other means available (granting of aid, assistance, trade, credits, Peace Corps, public statements, state visits, etc.) to assist the groups it favors and avoid association with those it does not. Unlike the use of force, these means cannot guarantee immediate delivery. Sending the Marines to Haiti in 1963 would have toppled Duvalier's regime; cutting him off from all aid has a slower effect as far as Haiti is concerned—though the gains for the American position, in terms of building up its reputation for forwarding progress, are immediate. The use of U.S. armed forces, even against a tyrant, would be denounced by most supporters of progress, and is contrary to the international system the United States seeks to promote and the basic values of the American people.

COMPETITION REQUIRES PROGRESS

Some years back, when the United States was still largely committed to holding up *status quo* governments and the Communist appeal to the oppressed people of the under-developed countries was believed irresistible, the notion gained currency that until these people gained a better standard of living, more responsive government, and education, the United States had no choice but to defend them from Communism by the use of arms. The Communists were, and often still are, expected to use peaceful means as a wedge to be followed with armed subversion or invasion. It was pointed out that the apparent Russian strategy followed for the past decade, of using peaceful tactics, was introduced under certain circumstances, and if those were to change, might well be abandoned. But today an order seems to be evolving in which reliance on peaceful means, initially introduced for reasons of expediency, can be stabilized. It is not a question of trusting the other side's word to stick to peaceful means only, but of introducing actual checks and safeguards. American confidence in the United States' ability to secure and advance its values without resort to arms will also play a large part in making the shift to peaceful competition complete and stable. The more effective its intervention for progress is, the better equipped and more ready the United States will be to enter a strictly disarmed contest. The change in interbloc relations and the shift from support of the *status quo* to support of progress reinforce each other.

INTERVENTION FOR PROGRESS AND THE COMMUNIST CAMP

Suppose the two sides in a period of equilibrium agree to enter competition under rules, and one soon finds itself far behind the other. Will the loser then not resort to arms, putting us back where we started?

Such a regression cannot be ruled out, but the likelihood of its happening is small—small enough surely to give this approach a try. After all, this is a "minimum-regret" strategy; the remote-deterrence provisions as well as the maintenance of strategic deterrence (see next chapter) assure that only minimal losses will be incurred if it fails. If it works out, all the promise of disengaged blocs and accelerated progress of the third world will be at hand.

The very assumption that rests behind the question is the mistaken zero-sum notion that often comes to haunt the strategist. Either East or West is likely to have the upper hand in the development race, it is said, and the loser will be under much pressure to broaden the means of conflict. Hence, it is concluded, any limitation of the conflict will be temporary. This view overlooks, first of all, the vagueness of the measuring rod in the development race. For the last fifteen years, each side has claimed to be doing better in developing countries in its sphere of influence; in Asia, for instance, China and India have been watched as test cases for the Communist and democratic ways of modernization for more than a decade, but no evidence of a "victory" is in sight. Which is doing better, India or China?

Second, the nonaligned countries tend more and more to receive aid from both sides, to trade with both sides, to invite each side's technical assistance, and to send leaders to visit Moscow and Washington, without joining either bloc; gains in the sympathies of these countries are transient; the total stock of floating vote, which both blocs court, is not depleted. Gradually the two blocs might realize that neither will be victorious in this race, but both will benefit as the "have-not" countries' standards of living and, even more, their hopes for a brighter tomorrow, rise, and their stakes in world order are enhanced. Peace, freedom, and social justice are the real winners, and third countries as well as bloc members benefit from their advance. Competition, as Americans have long known, often benefits all participants by increasing the sum total of values available rather than building up one at the expense of the other, and both at the risk of nuclear war.

Chapter V

TO ARMS CONTROL AND BEYOND

THE VISION OF ARMED DUOPOLY

Duopoly is both a political approach and a military strategy. It is supposed to provide security for the West and stability for the world by building a counterforce to checkmate whatever force the Communists may wield. Under duopoly aggressions are to be deterred by making military advances seem unprofitable. If deterrence does not work, they are to be repulsed. He who wishes peace, the Pentagon recites, prepares for war.

The military instruments of duopoly are many and complex, but there are two major components: those that seek to deter a nuclear attack on the heartlands of the West, and those aimed at holding the containment line. The larger nuclear weapons, strategic bombers, and long-range missiles serve mainly the first purpose; conventional troops and subconventional forces, the latter. The two components are closely related, however. Each side has to feel that it has adequately countered the nuclear threat to its own security as it seeks to expand or to counter expansion in a third country. Without feeling that their heartland is effectively protected, the Communist bloc could not attempt expansion with impunity; and without such a shield, the West could not effectively counter the challenge. Similarly, an ineffective conventional or subconventional capacity would either allow a violation of the containment line, as happened in Indochina in 1954, or to threaten a nuclear war to deter a local, limited challenge.

Although the Kennedy Administration took some steps to supersede military duopoly, its first years were spent trying to perfect it. Its main innovation was to strengthen and vary the West's non-nuclear capabilities so as to be better able to counter "low-level" Communist challenges without having to resort to nuclear threats or war. The active-duty strength of the army (by early 1963) had been increased from 860,000 to 960,000, and the number of combat-ready divisions from eleven to sixteen. The drive to convince the European allies of the need for larger conventional forces was renewed. Marine Corps strength was increased by fifteen thousand men. The Special Forces, the United States' primary counter-insurgency capability, were tripled during the first two years of the Administration.

As far as the major deterrent force went, the main objective was to evolve a better-protected nuclear retaliatory force. Reliance on strategic bombers was reduced, and reliance on "hardened" missiles, protected in deep cement silos (the Minuteman ICBM), and on nuclear submarines (carrying Polaris missiles) increased. The major result of this has been to strengthen the U.S. ability to strike back even after suffering attack. This second-strike capacity is expected to make an attack on the West seem senseless to a potential enemy. It also allows the United States to refrain from striking first when an attack appears imminent but not certain. Thus, in many ways, deterrence seems more "in" than ever.

The Kennedy Administration, however, viewed armed duopoly with increasing concern. President Kennedy, addressing the United Nations on January 25, 1961, said: "Every man, woman, and child lives under a nuclear sword of Damocles, hanging by the slenderest of threads, capable of being cut at any moment by accident, miscalculation or madness." Nevertheless, this sword—the policy that maintains peace on a balance of terror—has been subjected to less revision and less public criticism than any other aspect of duopoly. Most Americans still believe in the stability of the deterrence system. An often-repeated view is that "this system has kept us alive and free ever since the 1940s; why should it not continue to do so?" Only very slowly and gradually has the false logic behind this statement come to be recognized—more in the White House than on Capitol Hill, and more in Washington than in the country at large. No one would accept the advertising slogan of a fallout-shelter manufacturer which guaranteed a foolproof shelter, "If not satisfactory, double your money back"; yet most people accept a national-security system that has very much the same quality. Obviously, if we are still alive to say so, the major deterrent system has worked; but *one* blowup of this tenuous balance and the few who live to tell about it will find little value in their testimony.

The false confidence gained from riding to the brink of disaster without toppling over makes the next round more perilous. President Kennedy's masterful exercise of power during the 1962 blockade of Cuba exhilarated many Americans (that is, after the blockade was over and the results were in). Little recognition was given, especially outside Washington, to the fact that the results were attained by leaning far over the brink, a brink a hundred megatons deep; that special circumstances had favored the United States in this round, and that the next time might be the last.

The Administration is by no means indifferent to these dangers; the build-up of non-nuclear forces is itself in part an expression of growing concern. The use of conventional and subconventional forces to counter Communist expansion is surely less dangerous than the threat of nuclear bombardment or the use of tactical nuclear weapons, but this does not mean that such alternatives are safe enough. The use of conventional forces is very unpopular in both Europe and the United States, as was seen during the Korean War and again during the fighting in South Vietnam. And even limited engagements entail the danger of escalation.

INSTABILITIES IN THE NUCLEAR DETERRENCE SYSTEM

Many military strategists still hold to the notion that two piles of nuclear arms balance each other and make an attack by one side on the other suicidal. It therefore seems necessary to review briefly the ways in which this seemingly stable system might be unstabilized on extremely short notice.

WAR BY ACCIDENT

The United States has paid considerable attention to the danger of nuclear war touched off by accident, and a large variety of mechanical safety devices have been introduced to avoid the unintentional triggering of a nuclear device or accidental transmission of code communications that read Fire! A communication link has been established between the White House and the Kremlin to be used if an accident is imminent (to warn) or has occurred (presumably, to apologize). But despite all efforts, no responsible expert would claim that accidents are ruled out. Near-accidents and close shaves have been frequent enough.

According to a study of the accident problem made by an independent, non-military group, nuclear weapons have been involved in about a dozen major incidents or accidents, mostly plane crashes, both in the United States and overseas. In one of these incidents, a B-52 bomber had to jettison a 24 megaton bomb over North Carolina. The bomb fell in a field without exploding. The Defense Department had adopted complex devices and strict rules to prevent the accidental arming or firing of nuclear weapons. In this case the 24 megaton warhead was equipped with interlocking safety mechanisms, all of which had to be triggered in sequence to explode the bomb. When Air Force experts rushed to the North Carolina farm to examine the weapon after the accident they found that five of the six inter-locks had been set off by the fall! Only a single switch prevented the 24 megaton bomb from detonating and spreading fire and destruction over a wide area.[1]

In a public debate on this subject at Columbia University, Herman Kahn explained to me that even if there were an accident, it would not lead to a nuclear war. If New York, for instance, were suddenly wiped out, he said, the President would appoint an investigating committee that would probably conclude that no sane person would have designed such a one-bomb attack deliberately. I tend to concede that, in part because of the work of Kahn and his associates, a panic, hit-the-button response that would set off a "spasm war" might well be avoided, though the possibility cannot be ruled out. But, at best, several million lives would have been sacrificed, not to assure peace and freedom but because the military machinery made a mistake. Thus, such an accident would at best lay waste a city; at worst, trigger an all-out war.

UNAUTHORIZED ACTION

is another way a nuclear holocaust might begin at any moment. While there are now double locks on many American missiles (though not on the tactical nuclear weapons deployed in Germany) which prevent their being fired by any one person, any commander of a Polaris-carrying submarine can shell sixteen Russian cities if he violates regulations forbidding him to take such an initiative. As a sociologist who has examined the major instruments used for selecting personnel, I can state without qualification that there is no satisfactory way to select the personnel with access

[1] Ralph E. Lapp, *Kill and Overkill* (New York: Basic Books, 1962), p. 127.

to triggers, command, and communication posts. Former General Edwin Walker, who took a leading part in a riot against officials trying to maintain law and order during an attempt at desegregation of the University of Mississippi, is the same gentleman who, a short time earlier, commanded American forces in Germany—forces equipped with an abundance of nuclear weapons. When international tensions mount, as the SAC bomber crews and Polaris submarine captains are put under increasing strain, the chances increase that sooner or later one of them may act out the suspicions or fears he harbors. Occurring in an already strained situation, such as the Cuban blockade, a false move might bring down the nuclear roof.

Under quite different circumstances, during a summit conference for instance, the feeling that the West is growing "soft" and hence needs to be protected from "submitting" to Communism might produce an atmosphere that would lead one of the many people who have access to the more than forty thousand nuclear weapons the United States possesses to decide that he was called upon to deliver the United States from a "soft" President, and provoke a showdown. Psychological tests and watchful eyes can reduce this danger; no precaution known to the social scientist can prevent it in the long run. The not infrequent defection of persons painstakingly selected to handle top-secret information shows the inadequacy of all known screening methods.

In *Red Alert*, a novel that should be required reading for all who doubt the possibility of unauthorized action, Peter Bryant convincingly depicts a general of the Strategic Air Command, afflicted with an incurable disease and hence in no fear of reprimand, who proceeds to bomb Russia, circumventing all the clever devices geared to prevent this. During 1959 the U. S. Air Force alone discharged 4213 men on disability grounds; one fourth of this total were released because of psychotic disorders, psychoneurotic disorders, or

anxiety reactions. Those who conclude that therefore no
psychologically handicapped men remain in the service
should take into account the conclusion of a study of acci-
dental-war possibilities by a group of psychiatrists: "No existing tests will reliably screen out individuals susceptible to
mental breakdowns. The range of potentially serious psychological problems is extremely wide. The possibly harmful
effects of great responsibility, maintained over long time
periods in . . . [a] cold-war time role, are nearly impossible
to predict."[2]

MISCALCULATION

Aware of the feeling of regained potency that many Americans experienced after the show of power that forced the
Russians to withdraw their missiles from Cuba, President
Kennedy warned that we are not to expect frequent repetition
of such acts with impunity. "One major mistake by any one
of the sides," he said, "and there will be 150 million deaths
on both sides, within the first eighteen hours." Can anyone
who has read some history really expect governments to act
year after year without making "one major mistake"? If any
generalization is warranted, I would hazard the opposite one
—that if there is anything stupid that can be done, sooner or
later a government will do it. But past "miscalculations"
differ from future ones in the magnitude of the disaster
courted. Napoleon undertook a "miscalculated" campaign,
but the French people lived to tell about it; Hitler unwisely
attacked the West and Russia at the same time, but the German people lived to prosper. After a major nuclear war, even
if some individuals survive, neither the Russian nor the American nation is likely to.

The only occasion on which an atomic bomb was dropped
on human beings seems to have been the result of a false

[2] Cited in Seymour Melman, *The Peace Race*, (New York: Ballantine
Books, 1961), p. 15.

calculation. An authoritative study by a RAND expert concluded that the bombing of Hiroshima and Nagasaki "made no essential contribution to Japan's surrender without a last battle."[3] The expert, whose conclusions are supported by a U. S. Strategic Bombing survey, adds: "The American government, of course, could not know at the time what we know now, and those who made the decision were convinced that many lives, American as well as Japanese, would be saved by it." But this is precisely the point; Truman was misinformed and gave the wrong order. There is no reason to believe that a much larger strike could not be similarly misdirected.

PROLIFERATION OF NUCLEAR ARMS

When I was writing on this subject a few years ago, this danger was still quite speculative.[4] Since then the French independent striking power has become a reality and the Chinese one is expected to follow soon. Egypt is reported to be able to produce radioactive warheads for its missiles, and Israel can hardly be expected to sit back and watch. It is difficult to predict which country will be the next to build or buy nuclear bombs, but there will undoubtedly be others.[5] The day is fast approaching when leaders much less responsible than those of either the United States or the U.S.S.R. will have access to one or more nuclear triggers. With adventurous inclinations, they might make up for their relatively poor means of delivery. For a while these small nuclear powers may even retain their ability to draw their super-power

[3] Paul Kecskemeti, *Strategic Surrender* (Stanford, Calif.: Stanford University Press, 1958), p. 209.

[4] *The Hard Way to Peace, op. cit.*, pp. 53 ff.

[5] The ability to produce these bombs more cheaply and readily in the future, hence making it possible for many countries to produce them, is discussed by Christoph Hohenemser, "The Nth Country Problem Today," in Seymour Melman (ed.), *Disarmament: Its Politics and Economics* (Boston: American Academy of Arts and Sciences, 1962), pp. 238–76.

allies into a war they have provoked. The day is not too remote when half a score of nations will have fleets of missile-carrying submarines roaming the oceans, and the victim of their attack will not know which state is the aggressor. Nor should the possibilty of a nuclear war between smaller powers, for instance in the Middle East, be taken lightly.

ESCALATION

In the past, confrontations between American and Communist forces have remained limited: in Quemoy and Matsu, to shelling of the islands; in South Vietnam, to guerrilla and counterguerrilla warfare; in Korea, to country-wide conventional war. But the possibility of escalation to nuclear weapons in such engagements is less theoretical than it seems. In South Vietnam, Diem's position was maintained in 1963 with the help of more than fourteen thousand American troops and massive shipments of arms, largely because the Soviets and Chinese did not match the American support. The Chinese had their own reasons for holding back, but should these change, China might well spare two-hundred-thousand volunteers to come to the help of the Vietnamese guerrillas. The United States would then either have to retreat under superior pressure, or, which is more likely, increase its forces. This soon could lead the warfare to the level of a Korean War, to new drafts and taxes, which no American Administration is likely to favor, or to the use of tactical nuclear weapons as the only alternative to retreat.

The plan for the defense of the access routes to West Berlin explicitly calls for the use of tactical nuclear weapons. If the Communists again close the routes that lead to West Berlin from West Germany, NATO is expected to send an armored column to open them. If this column is stopped, NATO forces are to come to its assistance. Since there are about fifty-nine Communist divisions on the Central European front compared to twenty-three and a half NATO divisions (though differences in size and quality favor the West), the NATO forces might have to retreat. If such an eventuality arises, the Russians are to be warned, and then— after a pause—tactical nuclear weapons are to be employed. This is expected to escalate rapidly to a Soviet bombardment of West European ports and airfields that would leave American divisions in Europe without supplies and, militarily speaking, would require American bombardment of Russian supply bases, which in all likelihood would involve the U.S. mainland as the Soviets struck back.

The newest vogue in American strategic thinking is to work out designs and rules for limited nuclear wars. McNamara, for instance, suggested in his Ann Arbor speech in June 1963 that such a war should be focused on military targets and missile bases, to spare the civilian population as much as possible. This is sometimes referred to as a counterforce, rather than a countercity, strategy. But because an attempt to destroy all the enemy's military bases might involve so much destruction of cities that the enemy would be hard put to it to tell which kind of attack he was being exposed to, it has been further suggested that the United States might forego some military targets close to cities. (There are, however, narrow limits within which this can be done without significantly weakening the American strike.)

Even more fanciful is a full theory of *controlled war*, which has an important following in the Defense Department. This advocates preparing weapons that permit the waging of nuclear war on many levels. However, the Russian forces, at least as composed in the early sixties, do not allow the Kremlin to envisage such a "controlled" war. Russia is long on conventional and large nuclear weapons, short on the tactical and middle-size ones of which the United States has an ample supply and which are important for less than all-out war. It is not surprising that the Russians have categorically refused,

in formal and informal contacts, to consider any such limitations.

The lay observer cannot but feel horror of nuclear war of
any size, shape, or level (not that he favors a conventional
one). He cannot but feel that the artificial rules imposed by
strategists in map-filled rooms, based on computer rationality,
will not guide generals in the chaos of a nuclear attack, or
allay the confusion that will follow. Nor can he dismiss the
gnawing feeling that banking on the ability to limit a nuclear
war simply makes such a war more likely.

A TECHNOLOGICAL BREAKTHROUGH

The whole balance-of-terror system is based on the assumption that no effective missile defense can be found. Military
pundits point to the iron laws that "offense develops more
rapidly than defense," and that if one side comes up with a
weapon, so will the other. Actually there are no iron laws of
military strategy, any more than there are iron laws of cook-
ing, and the ability to predict the technology of weapons is
surely less developed than that of weather forecasting. It may
be that by the time the United States or the U.S.S.R. comes
up with an antimissile defense the other side will be close
behind; but if one of the sides succeeds in deploying such a
system a short time before the other, it will be able to strike
first. I do not claim that this will happen or is likely to happen, but anyone who claims that such breakthroughs *cannot*
happen plays God.

HOW LIKELY IS NUCLEAR WAR?

The eminent British scientist and author C. P. Snow, having examined the various possible routes to nuclear war,
stated on December 27, 1960, that as the nuclear arms race
continues and other states develop nuclear weapons, "Within,
at the most, ten years, some of these bombs are going off. I am

saying this as responsibly as I can. *That* is the certainty . . . a certainty of disaster." The temptation to put the danger, which is ominous enough as it is, in this absolute way is great. Once this premise is accepted, it follows that if we are to continue this way we will all be dead, and hence, it is suggested, *any* other course is preferable, because if we are dead nothing at all will be left. In my judgment no such "certainty" can be documented, nor does it help the advocates of disarmament to tie their cause to such an extreme and indefensible argument.

Those who claim that no such accident, unauthorized action, miscalculation, technological breakthrough, etc., could occur are no more rational. Nobody familiar with the nature of machines, men, communications, and government can fail to see that any and all of these possibilities *might* materialize. Half a century ago there were many experts who asserted that the great ocean liner *Titanic* was unsinkable and there were many who, on the eve of the First World War, thought that the very existence of the tremendous military machines ensured peace since "statesmen, as well as nations, shrink from the thought of a conflict so immense."[6] I do not claim that nuclear war is likely, much less that it is a certainty; I rest my case on the claim that I see no reason why one should hold that it *cannot* occur.[7]

This brings us to the more sophisticated argument in favor of deterrence as a way of life. This states that the likelihood of unsettling the balance of terror is small, and sane people do not worry about hypothetical events that have low proba-

[6] Stanley Leathes, as quoted in Lewis F. Richardson, *Arms and Insecurity* (Pittsburgh: Boxwood Press, 1960), p. 1.

[7] The famous Lloyd's insurance company, happy to insure one against practically every risk, is not quite ready to cover nuclear war. World War II was partly insurable for Lloyd's, which sold monthly policies against death or dismemberment caused by buzz bombs after calculating the odds at 1000 to 1. But nuclear war is quite another matter. Lloyd's has added a clause canceling all its maritime policies in event of East-West conflagration "whether there be a declaration of war or not."

bilities. If we are to fear such events, it is said, we had better stop breathing the air because it might be contaminated, and not cross the street because a car might hit us. Let me say first that people do express legitimate concern about both public health and traffic dangers. More important, while we can calculate half accurately the dangers of crossing the street, calculations of the likelihood of a nuclear war are pseudo-scientific, make-believe statistics. No one can calculate the likelihood of an event that has never happened. If I state that a war has a chance of three out of a hundred to occur next year, and you feel it is six out of a hundred, what evidence will support or refute one or the other of us? It can be stated, however, without reservation, that the longer we live in the shadow of the bombs, the more likely a nuclear war becomes.

The most important consideration is not one of probabilities but of utilities, which statistical beginners tend to ignore. Most people would be quite willing to bet ten dollars if the odds were two to one in their favor; they would probably not hesitate much if the bet were, under the same odds, one hundred dollars. Offered a bet, on the *same odds*, of one hundred thousand dollars, most people would not accept; the consideration of what would happen if they lost would prevent them from taking the relatively low risk. The dangers of *such* a loss, even if comparatively unlikely, are felt to be higher than the more likely gains of the same magnitude. In the nuclear arms race, hundreds of millions of lives are hanging in the balance in every interbloc confrontation, during every day scientists spend in laboratories, providing new instruments for the military trade.

Faced with these circumstances, some people panic; they say that they are willing to give up all that is dear to them but life itself, but they fail to respond to the basic human condition. Human life, as distinct from all other forms, derives its meaning from the values man lives for; if these are swept away, life becomes meaningless and worthless. Hence the search for a way out of the nuclear whirlpool should not and cannot be found by asking Americans, Russians, or any other group of human beings to sacrifice their basic values and beliefs. It must be found in the realm of respect for the tenets of our own way of life and those of others. Frills can be trimmed and concessions exchanged, but neither freedom nor social justice can be debased in the search for firmer foundations for peace and human survival than the unstable balance of terror.

DISARMAMENT OR ARMS CONTROL?

As an understanding of the dangers of life on a small world in the age of big bombs has grown, the search for a way out of deterrence has intensified. Some ideas are monopolistic and impractical; some are still duopolistic, and to that extent obsolescent. But most recent developments seem to point to the formulation of a military strategy that is more in accord with the concept of competition under rules.

Complete and general disarmament has such an appeal to human imagination that both the U.S.S.R. and the United States are on record as favoring it. If their offers were completely sincere and their desires half as potent as those expressed in speeches before the United Nations, one could not see what could possibly prevent them from introducing a plan firmly supported by both. Actually, both Russian and American plans for total disarmament are, as J. W. Fulbright, chairman of the Senate Foreign Relations Committee, effectively put it, "an exercise in cold war fantasy, a manifestation of the deception and pretense of the new diplomacy. . . . There is nothing but mischief in negotiations which no statesman seriously expects to succeed. They become a forum for the generation of false hopes and profound disappointment. . . ."[8] Both sides have put forward proposals that, if accepted by the other side, would grant them important strategic advantages as disarmament is carried out.[9] The U.S.S.R., which is believed to have an important advantage in conventional weapons, has suggested eliminating all nuclear bombs and means of delivery first. The United States has suggested, as a first step, a 30 per cent across-the-board cut of all weapons, and inspection of the weapons systems that remain, a proposal that would give the United States access to the Russian missile sites, whose power, unlike the protected American sites, rests on secrecy. Both plans include a number of what the negotiators call "jokers," that is, measures that are known to be utterly unacceptable to the other side.

Total disarmament is impossible in the foreseeable future. The fear that a nation would conceal nuclear bombs and then threaten to drop them from commercial airliners or send them by parcel post (assuming all military planes and missiles have been scrapped) is so great that nationalism will have to end, a strong sense of world community evolve, a powerful international police force be organized, and global government be established (to formulate and execute universally binding laws) before such disarmament will be possible. The difficulties of reaching a consensus on even comparatively minor matters in the United Nations shows how remote such a day is. Deep differences of belief, interest, and outlook bar for the near future the development of the global institutions necessary for total disarmament. The blocs are once again like the giant firms in our car-market analogue; they could solve their

[8] Clayton Lectures, given at Tufts University, April 29, 1963. Senator John F. Kennedy said in 1959: "Disarmament remains a pious phrase which both sides invoke—but which they will not invoke together." Quoted in Lapp, *op. cit.*, p. 142. This seems still to be the prevailing attitude.

[9] This and the following statements are based on discussion with officials of the U. S. State and Defense departments and with the U.S. and U.S.S.R. representatives at the disarmament negotiations in Geneva.

problems by forming one united firm, but their inability to agree on such an extensive merger leads them to consider less complete but more feasible measures to avoid cutthroat competition.

ARMS CONTROL

Many highly varied measures have been suggested under the heading of arms control, a term widely used to refer to limited projects directed toward curbing the danger of war. Some are useful, but their scope is limited. For instance, the United States has installed various electronic locks on its Minuteman missiles to reduce the danger of unauthorized firing (the locks are electronically released from a small number of central command posts). The Russians, it is hoped, have taken similar steps. This kind of precaution has some value but hardly touches the heart of the matter. Other arms-control measures (such as withdrawing tanks one mile from the East-West border in Berlin rather than stationing them on the line itself) reduce international tensions but have little value if not followed up—that is, if whatever relaxation is produced is not used to work out more extensive controls.

By far the most extensive arms-control plans discussed and favored in Washington still seek to perfect rather than to supersede the military duopoly. Even these "far-reaching" plans assume that there are two and only two tightly integrated military super-blocs, both armed with nuclear weapons; that these blocs would agree to limit the number of nuclear weapons and missiles they retain and stop production of other means of strategic warfare; and that the cessation of such production as well as the limitation of weapons retained could be verified through inspection. The number of weapons retained would, it is said, have to be large, so that the few weapons that could be hidden or secretly produced, even under inspection, would not allow the violator to gain a critical advantage.

An extensive inspection would be necessary to make unde-
tected large-scale violations unlikely.

Although these plans differ significantly in detail, all are
duopolistic, not only in that they assume two well-integrated
super-blocs, but also because they seek to perfect containment.
If the arms of both sides were balanced, it is believed, deterrence would be stabilized, neither side could penetrate the
other's sphere of influence, and all expansion would be check-
mated. These arms-control schemes require the Communist
camp (and commit the West) to accept a global stalemate
with no legitimate outlet for either side's ambitions, and they
do not take into account the tempo and temperament of the
world-wide revolution in third countries. Could a *status quo*
be imposed on these countries? Would it be maintained if
both sides stalemated each other's arms? Or would third states
be exempted from the *status quo* arrangement and local conflicts be "allowed"? What would then guard against escalation? Arms-control advocates often do not deal with these
questions; they focus exclusively on American-Soviet relations. But the world is not bipolar, and arms control does
not remove the instabilities inherent in the deterrence system.

Arms control offers little if any arms reduction, but requires
extensive inspection, which is another way of saying that arms-
control plans approach the problem in a way unacceptable to
the Soviets. The Soviets object to inspection, especially an inspection scheme that covers not what has been disarmed, but
the forces the sides are allowed to retain. The Soviet Union,
it must be remembered, is a closed society (even under the
Czars, Russia was a closed society), and although, as the
standard of living has risen and de-Stalinization progressed,
the Soviets have opened their society somewhat, they still
have a long way to go before they will feel ready to allow
thousands of foreign inspectors to move freely within the
country. Also, Soviet armed forces, unlike the American military, draw heavily on secrecy for protection. In 1963 American

missiles were rapidly being guarded from attack by their positioning on submarines and in concrete silos. Soviet long-range missiles were fewer in number and believed to be standing exposed on launching pads. Their main defense was that their locations were unknown.[10]

Finally, the Soviets invest almost twice as much in defense, percentagewise, as the Americans. While the United States spends less than 10 per cent of its gross national product for defense purposes, Russia allocates between 15 and 20 per cent of a much smaller gross national product to defense. Arms control based on balancing high piles of arms would entail few savings and would allow for little increase in the Russian standard of living. So it is small wonder that the Soviets are much more interested in disarmament than in arms control.

ARMS REDUCTION—A THIRD ALTERNATIVE

If arms control were the only alternative to total disarmament, which is impossible for the near future, the West would have to stick to it as the best offer it could make to the Soviets, although whether or not the Russians would ever make such a high degree of accommodation on their side is anyone's guess. But there is another possible approach that would satisfy legitimate Western needs and demands, and also be more responsive to Soviet needs, to the global trend away from bipolarity, and to the underdeveloped countries' revolution of rising expectations and their demand for freedom to modify their relations to both blocs. This is arms reduction.

The major characteristics of arms reduction are:

(a) It seeks to *reduce* the armed capabilities of both sides *without* allowing either side to gain a *strategic advantage* at any stage of the process.

(b) *No assumption of bipolarity* is made.

(c) Arms reductions are to be *effectively verified*, but in-

[10] This point was emphasized by P. M. S. Blackett in his *Studies of War* (New York: Hill and Wang, 1962), pp. 128 ff.

spection is viewed as only one, and the least desirable, means of verification; the plan answers the Soviet demand for *tying inspection* to disarmament, and Western demands for effective verification that commitments to reduce arms are carried out.

(d) The process is expected to be *gradual*, that is, no jump toward total disarmament is expected, but neither is a freeze of high piles of arms, except as a transitional state in the shift from upward spiraling to arms reduction; it provides for the saving of resources now used to build and maintain means of destruction.[11]

No First Use[12]

Arms reduction might start, much like arms control, by trying to build on the present situation. As a first step the United States might declare that under no circumstances would it be the first to use nuclear or atomic weapons, calling on Russia to make the same commitment.[13] Such a declaration would have to be preceded by preparations. At the moment, various Western defense plans, especially for West Berlin, envisage the use of nuclear weapons after a conventional round. Some increase in conventional forces might be necessary before the United States could forego reliance on nuclear arms.[14] Several U.S. allies are likely to object to

[11] For a different line of reasoning, which reaches a similar conclusion, see J. David Singer, *Deterrence, Arms Control, and Disarmament* (Columbus, Ohio: Ohio State University Press, 1962).

[12] I am indebted to Dr. Freeman J. Dyson of the Institute for Advanced Study at Princeton and Dr. Donald G. Brennan, president of the Hudson Institute, for a discussion of this policy.

[13] Soviet willingness to make such a commitment was reaffirmed by Khrushchev during the July 1963 test-ban negotiations. See the *New York Times*, July 20, 1963, p. 2.

[14] How many additional troops are needed depends in part on an evaluation of Soviet intentions and the relative quality of their conventional forces. Many European observers belittle the danger of a Soviet invasion of Europe and point to the fact that Russian soldiers rarely fought well in other people's countries, e.g., Finland in 1939, and that several of their divisions are those of "satellite" countries, which might well be less than completely reliable.

such a step. Having experienced a conventional war and believing in the absolute deterring power of nuclear weapons, they tend to favor continued reliance on nuclear bombs. But the sooner the United States compels its allies to recognize the facts of nuclear life, the better for all concerned.[15] Nuclear deterrence will become less and less credible over the years; as the Russian second-strike forces become less vulnerable (the U.S.S.R. is believed to be currently engaged in building a major missile-carrying submarine fleet), it becomes even more irrational for the United States or Europe to strike first. The sooner the Europeans face up to these facts and make the necessary adjustments, the less likely they are to be left (or to feel) exposed, or for the United States to become involved in a nuclear war that could have been avoided.

It is correctly pointed out that West Berlin is one point that would be particularly difficult to defend without nuclear arms, even with massive conventional forces. The West could, however, make it explicit that it would not consider an attack on West Berlin as an isolated event and that such a challenge would be countered on the entire central front. It should also be made clear ahead of time that pressure on West Berlin would be countered by acts such as cutting off European trade with the East and, if necessary, supporting an uprising in East Germany. Practically any other response to attack—however potentially volatile—would be preferable to the present plan calling for the United States to be the first to pull the nuclear trigger.

If the United States had information that a major nuclear attack was in preparation, would it still, it is asked, be bound to hold its fire? The possibility of such a report being inaccurate is one of the major reasons a no-first-use policy is needed. It is widely agreed that unless the information is very

[15] Dr. Donald G. Brennan has made some ingenious suggestions along this line in an unpublished report, "Toward a Consensus in the Alliance: A Proposal for a Staff Integration Program."

reliable, it would pay the United States to sit out a strike (once it was prepared for it) rather than to take the enormous risk of striking first.

An important result of a no-first-use declaration, and of the correlative adjustments that would lend it considerable credibility, would be a major reduction of international tensions; it would remove from interbloc verbal exchanges the all-too-dangerous practice of missile rattling. There is also the advantage that, once its preparations were completed, the United States could make this declaration unilaterally and safely wait for the Russians to reciprocate, rather than tediously seeking to negotiate a joint declaration. And this measure does not require any inspection.

Arresting the Arms Race

The United States might complete its 1963 plans, which provide for increasing the number of nuclear submarines to at least thirty, carrying 656 Polaris missiles, and bringing the total number of Minuteman missiles up to 950 by 1968; and, once these are available and well protected, it could stop the production of more missiles and nuclear bombs. At the same time, strategic bombers, which are rapidly becoming obsolete, could be phased out. This would amount to a one-sided halting of the upward spiral of the nuclear arms race; the Russians would then be expected to stop their production after building a force that gave them a comparable sense of a secure *retaliatory* capacity.

Those who do not follow developments in the field of arms limitations closely may see in this plan the dubious fantasy of a "peacemonger." Let me therefore hasten to state that the plan was, in effect, suggested by Secretary of Defense McNamara in 1963; the figures cited are taken from his statement.[16] Actually, there are indications that the United States

---

[16] Statement of Secretary of Defense Robert S. McNamara before the House Armed Services Committee, January 30, 1963.

is moving toward such a *finite* (as against growing) deterrent. No new strategic bombers are to be ordered; and in mid-1963 the production of nuclear bombs was cut back. A further slowdown in the production of atomic weapons was ordered by President Johnson in January 1964.

The basic assumption behind the plan is that "enough is enough." Once the United States is equipped with enough nuclear fire power to hit every important target in enemy territory; once its missiles are protected; once a safety margin is allowed for (i.e., a certain number of missiles might malfunction, others would miss their targets, etc.) and some extra margin is included for unknown factors, production can be cut off with considerable impunity. This approach is in contrast to the earlier one, in which the number of bombs produced was determined by the amount American plants could furnish, regardless of whether or not they were necessary for security purposes.[17] For a long period, the general tendency— to the degree that funds could be obtained from Congress— was to order every weapon and weapons system for which some use could be conceived. As one general put it, "You never can buy too much *over*-insurance." More crudely, this approach became labeled one of "overkill," that is, the ability to destroy over again a target that has already been devastated. Actually, many statements about overkill are wildly exaggerated; it has been repeatedly suggested—by those who do not take into account the fact that some missiles and arsenals would be destroyed by an enemy strike and some would malfunction, etc.—that the United States has three times as many bombs as would be necessary to kill every man, woman, and child alive. Those claims might be true for bombs in arsenals in peacetime, but it is not true for those the United States would be able to deliver on enemy targets after it had absorbed a first strike.

[17] Earl H. Voss in the Washington *Star*, June 26, 1963.

But this does not mean that there is no validity in the over-kill argument. Somewhere, at some level, enough must be enough. Then, within broad limits, whatever the Communist countries build—and they are believed to have only a fraction of U.S. capacities and capabilities—the United States can rest assured that its deterrent force will suffice. McNamara has suggested that the United States is approaching such a state, and that it should, at least tentatively, refrain from further production once this has been reached. Thus the Administration is pointing to a plateau on which the arms race could rest. This policy (yet to be approved and implemented) is no minor achievement, but it will still leave both sides armed to the teeth, trying to check each other with the terror of nuclear threats. Can we reduce the arms once this plateau has been reached? Or are we really to be *indefinitely* in that state of suspended horror, as Eisenhower suggested in 1953, of "two atomic colossi . . . doomed malevolently to eye each other indefinitely across a trembling world"?

A "Pure" Retaliatory Position

What McNamara did not suggest, but what would follow, if halting the arms race were combined with a no-first-use commitment and arms reduction, would be the bringing of nuclear forces closer to a purely retaliatory or second-strike position. This would require modification of present American plans, but a modification very much in line with other elements of the emerging strategy of peaceful competition.

The problem is to decide the level of armaments at which to bring the nuclear arms race to a halt. McNamara's plans so far call for a very high cut-off point,[18] but include no commitment to no first use. The Defense Department is try-

[18] This is likely to be pushed upward as each service insists that it needs more arms for a safe posture, and a compromise that "mixes" the demands rather than allocates responsibilities will be worked out. On this procedure, see Arthur I. Waskow, *The Limits of Defense* (Garden City: Doubleday, 1962).

ing to combine a halt in the production of nuclear weapons with preparations for a counterforce war which calls for a strike at the enemy's missiles and bases in case a nuclear war erupts. Since the other side's missiles are increasingly protected, it is necessary to aim *three to five* missiles at each to have a reasonable chance to destroy them (probably leaving his submarines intact).[19]

The net effect of American counterforce strategy might, however, be quite different from the one expected, as is often the case with strategies. The Secretary of Defense might see counterforce as a fairer way to fight a nuclear war (if one is to be fought). But to the Russians—with one fifth to one third as many missiles as the United States has—it might well seem (at least so they say) like preparing for a first strike! The fact that some Air Force generals and senators publicly favor such a strike further fires Russian apprehensions. The "humane" nature of the posture adds to their worries; they are probably aware that the United States would be extremely reluctant to hit Russian cities first, unless extremely provoked, but might well be less hesitant about striking at Russian military bases. The Russian response to the counterforce plans, speeches, and postures has been to accelerate production of missiles and protective devices, to prevent the gap between their and the American capabilities from reaching a critical point. This, in turn, pushes the counterforce strategists to heighten the level at which they are willing to cut off the production of nuclear weapons.

If this were all there was to the present U.S.-U.S.S.R. nuclear arms race, we could expect, as happened in the past, each side to respond to the other, raising the levels of its armaments, and we might never reach a plateau to arrest this

[19] Since Polaris-type missiles carry only comparatively small warheads and their range is short and aim inaccurate, there is a tendency to "absorb" the loss they would inflict. The American submarines nevertheless carry sixteen bombs larger than the Hiroshima type. Also, range and payloads are continuously improved.

perilous race. However, a different result might be obtained, and we should make the best of it. The Russians seem set on not just increasing their forces, but making them as invulnerable as possible—not just by putting them in concrete silos (where they can be dug out by three to five American shots), but by putting them on moving platforms and submarines. The Russians may make their force so invulnerable that by 1965–67 the counterforce strategy—about to be fully implemented—will be obsolete; no American superiority will then be able to reduce that force to an "acceptable" level (i.e., of a second strike that the United States would be willing to "absorb"); after all, it takes only several scores of missiles to lay waste to most American cities. Then the production of missiles, now ordered for counterforces, could be frozen; much smaller forces than now planned would suffice for second-strike purposes, and no practically attainable increase would do for a first strike. The point at which both sides have quite invulnerable second-strike but no hope of gaining "acceptable" first-strike forces would be the most likely moment to stop the present upward spiraling of nuclear weapons, accept the second-strike-only position, and move toward multilateral arms reduction.

The earlier the United States takes fully into account the emerging trend the balance of nuclear forces is taking, the sooner it can remove those of its forces that cannot be used except for a first strike and the lower it can set the cutoff point of its production of long-range missiles and bombs. The sooner this occurs, the sooner the Russians will lose their fear of a first strike and conceivably cut off the production of their forces (which for economic as well as other reasons they are under some pressure to do).

One rather important "technical" difficulty must be faced here: it is difficult to distinguish a first- from a second-strike force. A missile is a missile; it might be used for first- *and* second-strike purposes. The question is partly one of intentions, which are always hard to fathom, especially when international tensions distort perception and interpretation. A madman could strike first if he had only one bomb and no missiles. On the other hand, the United States, even in the days when it enjoyed nuclear monopoly, did not bomb Russia. But the amounts and kinds of capabilities the sides build up and the way they position their weapons serve as important clues to the posture they are seeking. When a side that has a clear superiority in number of missiles attempts to increase it, the other side is likely to suspect an effort at attaining a force that would make a first strike "acceptable" to leaders affected by fears, hate, and tensions provoked by half a generation of interbloc conflict. But if the absolute number of missiles and bombs is held stable or reduced, and, in particular, if the gap between the forces of both sides is declining rather than growing, and if vulnerable missiles (usable only in a first strike) are replaced by "invulnerable" ones, we are closer to a purely retaliatory position.

Several limited measures have been suggested that could indicate that a side was taking a purely retaliatory position. For the United States, this would involve removing tactical nuclear weapons, now under the control of low-ranking officers on the front line in Germany, which could hardly be used for a second strike (i.e., following an attack). Removing them would significantly reduce the danger of war by accident or unauthorized action and would lend credibility to a declaration that the United States would not be the first to use nuclear weapons. Another step with the same effect would be the removal of missiles from bases close to the Soviet Union, where they are too exposed to survive a Russian first strike and hence could serve only an American first but not second strike. Similarly, Professor David Frish, of the Massachusetts Institute of Technology, has suggested that Polaris-carrying submarines be positioned on our side of the ocean, from which their intermediate-range missiles could not reach

Russia, to show that they are held for second-strike purposes only (that is, they would move into striking positions only if the United States were attacked). At the moment these submarines are reported to be within range, i.e., in potential first-strike position.[20]

Each of these plans needs further study; some may prove unfeasible or unwise, and others may be preferable. The principle, however, seems sound and clear: the United States should take a "pure" second-strike position and *show* its skeptical adversary that it does not have first-strike intentions. Again, the plan calls for no negotiations, no inspections, and no weakening of the American position. Even if the Russians do not reciprocate, the West will suffer no loss.[21] If U.S. security is based on an effective second-strike force that can fully retaliate after it absorbs a first strike, why should the United States and the world not have the benefits of the tension relaxation and security that would be gained from showing, through steps like those suggested above, that this is indeed its stand?

As efforts to reach first-strike positions (or those that seem such to the other side) are given up, many interbloc arms-limiting measures, such as advance registering of missile launchings, inspection of their payloads (to show that they are civilian), early-warning satellites to be operated by the United Nations, and the like, will be possible, to provide both further protection against first strikes and precedents, experi-

---

[20] Showing the other side that the submarines are on our, and not their, side of the ocean, without endangering them, is a highly complicated technical matter that need not be discussed here. Details are provided in an unpublished study prepared by Professor Frish for the Institute of Defense Analysis.

[21] If the Russians were to increase their nuclear force by as much as 50 per cent, or even 100 per cent, which could hardly escape the notice of American intelligence, their force would still be at least half the size of the American one, i.e., it would provide no credible first-strike force. If the Russians still continued to produce more and more long-range missiles, there would eventually come a point at which the United States might have to resume its production of such missiles.

ence, and a growing international machinery to enforce the rules agreed upon by the sides.

It has been suggested that the resulting relaxation is undesirable, that we should keep the Russians on their toes since this entails a certain cost to them (which they would escape if we shifted to a pure second-strike position). But this is one of those curious arguments that is based, in the ultimate analysis, on the assumption that what is bad for them must be good for us. The fact is that these costs (even if not symmetrical) are imposed on both sides; both share the danger and hence the benefit of removing it.

It is also suggested that the United States' allies might see in the repositioning of forces into a second-strike posture a weakening of the American commitment to their defense. Again, it might be necessary to take the risk of ruffling their feathers to make their and our lives safer.

ARMS REDUCTION

The United States can initiate the McNamara plan to halt the arms race any time it is ready, since it is free to stop production and positioning of missiles when it has enough. It makes, however, a very great difference whether this plan is seen as one step in the process of a *reversal* of the arms race leading toward arms reduction, or is viewed as a more or less *terminal* state at which armaments will be frozen, that is, as an arms-control measure. The Defense Department seems to think of halting the upward spiraling of strategic weapons as a measure complete unto itself, the "finite" implementation of a duopolistic division of the world, "stabilizing" the deterrence system.

Stopping the upward spiraling would in itself be a revolutionary achievement after almost two decades of an open arms race. But it has yet to gain the support of the armed services (which would be greatly reduced, especially the Air Force) and to win the support of Congress (which already has tried to get the Defense Department to order Skybolt missiles and RS-70 bombers which McNamara considers unnecessary); and the public at large, which can defeat it at the polls, has yet to be convinced. Thus, it would take considerable leadership and effort by the Administration to gain acceptance of this plan. On the other hand, it would not be enough, and, in a way, it would even be impossible to stop on this high plateau. Whether a resting place will be found at all depends in part on whether these measures are presented to the Russians as a means of stabilizing high weapons piles, or as a step in the direction of arms reduction.

Most of the dangers of the balance of terror would still exist at the high level of arms where McNamara hopes to freeze the process. Danger of war by accident, unauthorized action, miscalculation, and other contingencies would continue to exist, slightly higher or somewhat lower (depending on what assumptions are made about other factors) than before. (To illustrate, there is no plan to suspend the development of antimissile missiles. A major breakthrough in this area could readily upset the whole system, *after* it had been, otherwise, frozen.) The United States can put a ceiling on nuclear forces, of which it has a large surplus, but not on its conventional and subconventional forces, which are believed to be inferior in quantity. Thus the danger of armed conflicts will not be averted, and actually might be increased, if the nuclear forces are firmly frozen, and no other measures taken. Continuation of conflicts on this "low level" spells the danger of escalation unless more fundamental changes are made.

Finally, it is of much interest to ask what the Soviet position toward McNamara's plan is, and what modification the plan could bear, both to counter intrinsic weaknesses and to be more responsive to legitimate Soviet fears.

The Soviets initially objected to any plan that would leave any nuclear weapons and means of delivery in the hands of any party to a disarmament treaty. They suggested complete elimination of these weapons as the first step of a rapid four-year total disarmament. They continuously stressed their categorical opposition to arms control. The Americans, in many formal and numerous informal meetings (such as the Pugwash conferences in which American and Soviet scientists met for off-the-record talks) repeatedly explained to the Soviets that no nation could be expected to risk its fate to such a degree that it would suddenly be left with no nuclear forces whatsoever to answer a threat by a country that had violated the treaty. The Soviets seem finally to have taken cognizance of this point. They are, it is reported, now willing to consider leaving some nuclear weapons and means of delivery for later stages of disarmament, as long as they are eliminated at some point. It is thus crucial from their viewpoint whether a U.S. proposal to stop the increase in American nuclear forces is advanced as a terminal (arms-control) stage or a phase in the transition toward arms reduction.

The Russians have many reasons for their position. Their economic interest in arms reduction is great, because of their much higher (percentagewise) investment in arms, and because their economy, being fully employed, has no resources to spare. For them arms control means maintaining a high-cost military establishment; arms reduction would mean substantial savings. They also seem to feel that the arms race will continue in different areas if only the production of long-range missiles and nuclear bombs is stopped.

Cultural factors also seem to be operative. Americans are used to a pragmatic approach of "let's avoid the worst and not aim at the best possible world" and to progressing step by step without necessarily having an over-all master plan at the start. This approach clashes with the outlook of a society that is used to thinking in terms of master plans, in which planning ahead for five and ten years is a matter of routine, and that does not hesitate to aim at utopias.

Between the American arms control and the Russian disarmament plans lies arms reduction, to follow the attainment of a pure second-strike position. A meeting ground might be found in first halting the upward spiral, then reversing it. The balance of nuclear power would move from a high to a lower level, still relying on mutual deterrence but working toward the political and security arrangements that would allow it to be superseded. This still leaves open the pace and sequence of arms reduction, and the all-important question of inspection.

PARITY AND TRADE-OFFS

During the initial and rather limited discussions of McNamara's 1963 testimony, several congressional leaders reacted uneasily to the basic conception of parity it implies. While parity has long been implied under duopoly, it was never made as visible and explicit as it would become under "finite deterrence" (which is likely to emerge in the near future, despite efforts to develop a different posture, because of Russian countermoves). As long as the Defense Department bought more and more missiles, bombers, and nuclear weapons, the question of parity could be avoided and the quest for superiority maintained; the debate centered largely around what hardware would be best to add. But if it is suggested that we stop, that we have enough, the question arises: enough for what? The answer is, enough to deter an attacker, by making sure that we can fully retaliate if the enemy strikes first. But since the other side is expected to have a similar capacity by 1965–67, and we cannot gain incontestable superiority before then, we cannot expect to "win" militarily. When improvements in the protection of nuclear forces have rendered any dream of a first strike an illusion, what will remain is a situation wherein neither side can, by definition, "win." It will be a stable and well-protected stalemate. Many congressional leaders—even some who have no first-strike illusions—have not quite accepted this and still hold out for American superiority. They seem to be particularly concerned about the United States deliberately giving up an "advantage" by allowing the Russians to "catch up" numerically in nuclear weapons, though the fact cannot be repeated often enough that enough (including a heavy safety margin for all kinds of known and unknown mishaps) is enough. Strategic parity does not result from equality in numbers of bombers and missiles, as many Americans seem to fear, but has in effect existed ever since both sides developed second-strike forces large enough to devastate each other.

The McNamara plan calls for recognizing and accepting strategic parity and using it to hold the upward spiraling of arms, whatever happens to the numbers game. I believe that such a halt needs to be followed by and tied to arms reduction, in the process of which strategic parity will be maintained so as not to give any side an advantage.

The American proposal for general and complete disarmament, presented before the United Nations in September 1961, avoids such a parity-while-reducing approach (unfortunately this plan still is, as these lines are written, the basis of the various specific proposals the United States advances in negotiations with the U.S.S.R.). The proposal calls, in the first stage, for a 30 per cent across-the-board reduction of strategic weapons.[22] The Russian proposal, on the other

[22] A member of the U.N. staff of Polish nationality suggested to the author that a 30 per cent cut of the much smaller Russian nuclear forces would bring them below the level at which they would constitute a credible second-strike force. I do not have the necessary information to check this severe criticism of the American plan, but if the figures usually quoted in this context are correct, there seems to be substance in the implied Russian concern, which for obvious reasons the U.S.S.R. cannot state publicly.

hand calls for the complete elimination of nuclear weapons in the first round, bringing the United States and the U.S.S.R. to complete strategic parity, while leaving the U.S.S.R. a large conventional advantage which, under these circumstances, would become critical. Both sides are forwarding disarmament proposals that will improve their relative strategic positions rather than maintain parity as arms are reduced.[23]

The situation has led various experts who are less committed to the politics of any bloc and more to arms reduction, to suggest various plans that could bring the sides toward numerical parity and keep strategic parity *as they reduce their arms* so as to bring them to rest on as low a level of arms as possible.

Admiral Sir Anthony Bussard, of the Institute of Strategic Studies in London, has suggested a trade-off of some reduction of Western nuclear forces against Russian conventional ones to bring the two types of forces closer to numerical parity.[24] In effect, he is suggesting matching cuts rather than build-ups. McNamara ties his parity to freezing on high levels, or arms control; Bussard, to arms reduction.

Professor Louis Sohn of Harvard, participating in a study group set up by the U. S. Institute of Defense Analysis and the Arms Control and Disarmament Agency, has suggested a different approach: not abolishing the differences in capabilities all at once, and not maintaining them all the way to the end of arms reduction, but both sides diminishing their capabilities at a different pace, so as to bring them closer and closer to conventional and nuclear numerical parity as they approach disarmament.

Surely other plans could be designed; the essence, whatever the details, is reduction of the level of armaments of

---

[23] This point was made by L. P. Bloomfield, *The United Nations and United States Foreign Policy* (Boston: Little, Brown, 1960), pp. 93, 95.
[24] Private communication.

all major categories and the addition of numerical and conventional parity to the existing strategic nuclear parity, to remove fear of a first strike and reduce the dangers of unintentional war in general and escalation in particular.

The ultimate reduction that the sides will tolerate depends largely on one controversial item: inspection. To put it crudely, the more inspection allowed, it is said, the fewer arms needed (because the surer we are that the other side also has cut its forces, the less deterrent force we need). The less inspection, the more deterring power we shall have to retain. Most observers conclude from this equation that we will not travel very far on the road of arms reduction, since the Russians are so adamantly opposed to inspection. Yet this conclusion might be somewhat hasty.

VERIFICATION VERSUS INSPECTION

Significant arms reductions can be safely carried out without the necessity for reductions by the other side. Here inspection is desirable but not essential. If, for instance, the United States has a large surplus of nuclear arms, it can substantially cut back. If the other side reduces its pile too, well and good; if not, U.S. security is not weakened since there was a surplus to begin with. In June 1963 the United States slowed down the production of nuclear bombs, since it believed that its arsenals were overstocked, but this did not endanger American security. The same holds for obsolete military bases, obsolescent bombers, and other weapons. The Russians follow the same logic; on January 14, 1960, Khrushchev announced that in view of Soviet missile progress the armed forces would be reduced from 3.6 to 2.4 million men without demanding, not to mention "inspecting," similar American cuts.[25]

[25] There is some reason to believe that this reduction was not completed, because of later changes in Russian posture and strategy, resulting in part from the build-up of American conventional forces.

Both sides have so far taken such steps independently of any arms-reduction agreement; they could readily be taken as part of one. They would be particularly useful in the first round when mutual suspicion would still be high and the difficulties of agreeing on "reduction rates" (how many missiles do we have to dismantle for every ten you dismantle?) and on inspection methods would be considerable. Such reductions obviously could not be relied upon to result in extensive arms reductions by both sides, but some additional cuts could be carried out without introducing any new instruments of verification. The closing of bases and the dismantling of installations, for instance, could be effectively verified by photographic and electronic surveillance.

A recent study prepared for the U. S. Arms Control and Disarmament Agency lists a great number of measures that could be verified through intelligence, open sources, voluntary self-disclosure, and "common knowledge"—without inspection on a country's home territory.[26] These include testing of warheads in the atmosphere, underwater, and in outer space; the testing and transfer of large missiles; the closing of foreign military bases; the removal of troops stationed outside the national boundaries; and cessation of extraterritorial deployment of aircraft and warships.

Among the examples of verification that could be achieved without entering the side's territory is *destruction inspection* of an agreed-upon number of weapons carried out in neutral territory. Here the U. S. Arms Control and Disarmament Agency has suggested a very worthwhile idea—a bomber bonfire. Both blocs are faced with a large number of obsolescent bombers that cannot be readily absorbed into civilian transportation and that might, even if turned to civilian use, be reconverted to military use. Both sides have sold some of

[26] *Verification and Response in Disarmament Agreements*, Woods Hole Summer Study, 1962. Institute for Defense Analysis, Washington, D.C.

these bombers at part of their cost to various underdeveloped countries where they drain resources that could otherwise be constructively used and serve to intensify local arms races, e.g., between Egypt and Israel. It has therefore been suggested that both sides contribute these bombers to a big fire, where they would be destroyed.[27] This would hardly solve all East-West problems, but surely many would sigh in relief on the day that American and Russian bombers were burned together rather than being placed in less responsible hands for less worthy purposes. Such a bonfire might well be a symbolic opening for the period of arms reduction.

Verification through *electronic and photographic* devices also seems promising. Free overflight by inspection satellites (of the Samos type) and by reconnaissance planes (of the U-2 type) could verify a great deal of arms reduction. The closing of military bases in third countries, for example, could be effectively checked in this way.

One area in which the United States and the U.S.S.R. have, at least tentatively and tacitly, "agreed" to arms limitation, verified without inspection, is outer space. Extension of the arms race into space could tremendously increase the present upward spiraling of arms. Various Air Force-financed studies talk about thousand-megaton bombs in orbit that could set fire to half a continent ("if the cloud cover is not too thick"); orbital bases, space-bombers, space interceptors dubbed BAMBY, and the like. The number of resources that could be invested in this way is practically endless. It is also especially dangerous since starting a war in outer space, e.g., by shooting down the other side's reconnaissance satellites or orbital bombs, would be relatively painless, with no loss of life involved; but the prospect that such a conflict, once started, would remain limited to outer space seems slim. For all these reasons, despite mounting pressures, the United

[27] *New York Times*, April 3, 1963.

States and the U.S.S.R. have so far not orbited any bombs, though both have developed such capacities, and if one side did deploy such weapons, the other would soon follow. Both are practicing self-restraint, while they carefully check to see, through various surveillance devices, whether the other side is orbiting such weapons.[28]

How long this tacit arrangement will stay in force depends greatly on general developments in the field of armaments. It seems to me that if the arms race continues unchecked, sooner or later one side will orbit weapons (probably blaming the other for the move). But if arms reduction were initiated, it would be possible to fortify the present self-restraint by an explicit agreement not to deploy weapons in space. One way to verify this effectively would be to have all launchings registered with the United Nations before they take place and to allow an observer to check that the payload is strictly "civilian." A monitoring of launching could continue to check to make sure no unregistered orbiting takes place. (Putting all space research, flights, etc., in the hands of an international agency would provide an even more radical solution of the problem, but this is more difficult to attain at this stage of interbloc relations).

Although these various plans allow for more arms reduction and limitation without undue risk than is generally realized, they would still sooner or later be exhausted. It is then that both sides will face the question of inspection. In a sense, it must be faced earlier, because unless there is some understanding about how to proceed at this later stage, at least one of the sides might be reluctant to engage in the earlier rounds. A vital distinction that must be noted here is the difference between inspection and verification. The central point, overlooked surprisingly often, is that what is necessary is to

[28] For a discussion of the whole arms-in-space issue, see D. G. Brennan, "Arms and Arms Control in Outer Space," in L. P. Bloomfield (ed.), *Outer Space* (Englewood Cliffs, N.J.: Prentice-Hall, 1962).

verify that the other side has carried out its commitment to reduce arms, but that inspection is just one of many means of verification. Contrary to widely held beliefs, the Russians have agreed to various modes of rather extensive verification of arms reduction and, recently, even to some limited inspection. They have rejected plans that require extensive inspection, especially in the initial stages.

The Russians themselves suggested the positioning of verification instruments ("black boxes") in their territory to verify compliance with an agreement to cease the testing of nuclear weapons. The "black box" is a package of automatic instruments that record changes in the atmosphere that would be effected by nuclear testing. It also includes instruments to verify that it has been placed in the agreed-upon position, and it is sealed in a way that precludes tampering. The West feels that these instruments would help the verification effort but believes that some on-site inspection is also necessary. A deadlock developed over the number of inspections to be allowed annually. In early 1963 the Russians were willing to allow three and the West demanded seven.

One could spend many pages exploring the technical and statistical details that might be important for a ban on underground testing but that are not necessary for the present discussion. One might ask how effective these "boxes" are; if they can or cannot distinguish between earthquakes and nuclear tests; if they can or cannot detect explosions under a certain size; and how tamperproof they can be made, etc. The main points for our discussion are: (a) that the Russians agreed in principle to the need for international *verification* of commitments to be undertaken and that they offered, on their initiative, an instrument to enhance such verification; (b) that they did agree to some *inspection* (though rather limited) to plug loopholes that mechanical verification instruments might leave open. One may still feel that the Russians did not agree to "enough" inspection (especially not to the

amount the West defined as sufficient), but it is not valid
to claim that they object to verification in principle or that
they will accept no inspection.

One exercise in verification has already been carried out.
When Kennedy and Khrushchev concurred that the Russians
would withdraw their offensive missiles from Cuba in 1962,
certain methods of verification were agreed upon and implemented. Russian ships carrying missiles out of Cuba stopped
next to American ships, the crates containing the missiles
were opened, and the Americans were allowed to review their
contents. The Soviets did not object to American reconnaissance flights over Cuba to observe the demolition of launching pads. Only on-site inspection could not be agreed upon,
though even this was not rejected in principle. Castro agreed
to U.N. inspection of Cuba if it also covered Cuban exiles'
bases in Florida. Although he probably made the offer tongue-
in-cheek, sure that it would be rejected, he did, by this very
offer, recognize the validity of inspection.

It surely does not follow that the United States should not
seek, or that the Soviets will never agree to, verification
through personal inspection inside Russia; it does follow that
the West should seek to construct as many instruments of
verification as possible that do not involve personal inspection, and that several arms-reduction rounds—especially the
first ones—should be designed, if possible, in such a way as
to require no, or at least not extensive, inspection.

The verification methods already suggested could be coupled with those of "open sources" and covert intelligence to
verify considerable reductions of arms. It might well be that
up to two thirds of present strategic and conventional forces
could be so reduced, without much possibility that a violation large enough to be significant could escape attention. Additional arms reduction, in particular the last round, however, seems to require a great deal of inspection. Fortunately,
if we ever reach this stage, inspection will in all likelihood be

much more acceptable. The Russians are expected to make their forces much less vulnerable by 1965–67, which would greatly reduce their military need for secrecy. At the same time there should be continued liberalization of their society, which will increase Soviet willingness to see thousands of foreign inspectors inside the U.S.S.R. It is very difficult to predict how fast this process of liberalization will be, but it can be safely stated that one important factor that will determine its scope is the nature of the international environment. The less "hostile" this seems to the Soviet Union, the more congenial it will be to liberalization, other things being equal. Thus the early rounds of arms reduction can ease the way for later ones requiring on-site inspections.

THE LAST ROUNDS

It is extremely difficult at this stage to depict these later, especially last, phases of arms reduction. At present, both sides are still pointed toward a possible nuclear showdown, charged with fear and mutual suspicion. To suggest stopping production of unnecessary weapons, or to accept the fact that there can be no victory in a nuclear war, still seem heretical and revolutionary even when they come from the Secretary of Defense. Extensive arms reduction seems an illusory goal to most people. To try at this stage to depict in any detail plans for the completion of the process will inevitably smack of daydreaming. It should be noted, though, that at these later stages the opposite atmosphere from the one we live in now is likely to prevail. Once two thirds of the existing military forces have been phased out, two thirds of the arms demolished or altered for peaceful uses, and both sides have demonstrated their adherence to arms-reduction agreements, we will be pointing toward a world of disarmament and stable peace. Many steps now considered impossible will then seem obvious.

Such shifts in mood are by no means unprecedented; military cooperation with Germany would have seemed high treason in 1944 but became quite acceptable by 1950; Japan, a much hated enemy, became a trusted ally in less than a decade. Once more we have to fall back on the principle that specific measures look different, and are different, as the context in which they are advanced changes. Arms reduction, if carried out, will provide a new context for its own completion and for other revisions in political outlook and the attitudes toward bloc solidarity, third countries, and the United Nations.

One approach to the last phase of arms reduction is *zonal disarmament*, that is, requiring each nation to divide its territory into an equal number of fairly large zones, let us say ten. The zones would be opened for inspection, one by one, at time intervals agreed upon by both sides—for example, one every three months. Which zone is to be disarmed at each stage would be determined by lot. Provisions would be made to prevent the transferring of arms, especially of missiles and nuclear weapons, from zone to zone. (This could be achieved by grounding all flights and stopping all ships and other transportation between the particular zone and others for a day or so until the newly disarmed area is inspected.) In this way the strategic force would be reduced gradually and equally for all sides, since as long as it is not known until the lot is drawn which area will be the next to be disarmed, the sides will in all likelihood distribute their forces about equally among the zones.

The disarming of the last zone,[29] the complete removal of the nuclear forces, might have to wait until the people of the respective countries felt that adequate alternative arrangements had been made to protect them from significant violations of the arms-reduction agreement—probably until a strong

[29] This might be that of nuclear submarines, to be verified through port control and sonar systems.

international police force had evolved, or at least until violations seemed so unlikely that no protection was felt necessary. (The Canadians, for instance, have long trusted the Americans to that degree.)

At least a score of other schemes for disarmament have been devised. They all seem rather farfetched and artificially contrived at the moment. Even limited plans for arms reduction, even halting the upward spiraling of arms, still elude us, though the latter is by now supported by members of the Administration itself. The purpose of outlining some of these ideas here is not to claim that this or that plan constitutes the magic key that will unlock the door to the shop where blacksmiths turn swords into plowshares, or that one specific arms-reduction plan is superior to the many others not reviewed here. The plans serve only to illustrate a line of thought, a general approach, that has begun to gain some following in Washington, hopefully in Moscow, and in other capitals as well. The details remain to be worked out by teams of experts as the basic decision to move in this direction gains support.

The border line between the former duopolistic approach and the new approach—that is, moving toward interbloc security arrangements—is not sharp. Many initial measures can serve both. To an American politician, not yet fully successful in winning support for the duopolistic approach against that of all-out cutthroat competition, interpreting these new measures as related to the stabilization of high-level parity seems expedient. To the State Department official talking to the Russians (especially off the record), interpreting the same measures as steps toward arms reduction and peaceful competition is much more relevant. Sooner or later, and the sooner the better, the two lines will have to meet. The American public will have to be made much more aware of the dangers of the tenuous balance of terror, the hopelessness armed-stalemate duopoly offers, and the value of a strategy directed toward a world of genuinely, and effectively guarded, disarmed competition.

The leadership for such shifts in strategy will not readily be followed, because of the deep commitments to the old approach entrenched over the years in the public mind. But, this task will be assisted by the nature of the arms-reduction schemes. Arms reduction might well be gradual, that is, broken into stages and phases, with the transition from phase to phase as slow or rapid as the sides wish. The European Common Market treaty provides an interesting precedent. When it was signed, in order not to arouse potential and actual opponents, it was agreed to space out tariff reductions as well as the formation of supranational authority into numerous steps. But as economic integration proceeded to the satisfaction of most and the great enthusiasm of many, including those who earlier were expected to oppose it, the process was accelerated again and again, by the simple device of implementing the planned phases at a more rapid pace. For example, quota restrictions on trade were removed in four years instead of twelve to fifteen as initially planned.[30]

The first steps toward arms reduction might be undertaken unilaterally, without negotiations and agreements, though a reasonable degree of reciprocation by the other side should be expected. The next rounds would therefore be critical, because they would require verification measures on which the sides would have to agree—for instance, allowing uninhibited overflight by inspection planes. These rounds would be a "mix" between the two approaches; they would still rely on nuclear deterrence, but would introduce some interbloc agreements—to limit the size of the deterrence forces and to reduce military capabilities. This would at the same time increase the importance of nonarmed capacities and competition governed by

[30] This method is examined in some detail in my "Political Unification— A Successful Strategy," World Politics, October 1963, pp. 32–51.

rules. Even at a later stage, as inspection is introduced, we would be combining a world of deterrence, of our-weapons-check-your-weapons, with the new one, of we-reduce-our-arms and you-reduce-yours, under agreed-upon rules and verification according to instruments that we approve together. Only in the last stage will global institutions be the predominant source of security.

A major new insight suggests that we can proceed, without requiring a world authority, further than was long believed possible. We now have reason to believe that much more can be achieved through interbloc agreements and *adversary* inspection (each side inspects the other) and that *impartial* inspection (a neutral, international agency inspects us all) can be considerably delayed.[31] Disarmament is widely associated with the formation of an international inspection agency, an international police force, and hence a world government. The experience of the League of Nations and the United Nations has made abundantly clear the limits of impartial institutions in the present world. Many observers, noting the difficulty in reaching consensus in these institutions, even on minor matters, have concluded that disarmament is impossible. Hence the importance of the new insight that a great deal can be accomplished *without* much strengthening of global institutions. This is not to suggest that the author would not like to see impartial procedures introduced as early as possible, but that he recognizes the need to find measures that are politically as "inexpensive" as possible; to wait for the more demanding solutions might be to delay too long.

Taking a hard new look at all the arms-reduction plans suggested above, including zonal disarmament, we see that they could be carried out by means of adversary and not impartial machinery of verification and inspection. When we arrive at

[31] For an excellent discussion of these two approaches, see Lawrence S. Finkelstein, "The Uses of Reciprocal Inspection," in Melman, *op. cit.*, pp. 82–98.

the inspection phase, American personnel could inspect Russian disarmed zones and Russians, American ones. Each side might wish to call in representatives of its allies; the Russians might want to include Poles and Czechs in their inspection teams in the United States, and the United States might include Canadians and the British in theirs. Both sides might also invite some neutral and U.N. observers, but the main direction and responsibility could belong to the participating governments.

I do not imply that international institutions should not be given more power or that the United Nations and the International Court need not be strengthened. Opportunities and institutions for peaceful settlement of conflicts formerly settled by the use of force must be provided; the more effective this machinery is, the less formidable the resistance to arms reduction and the lower the pressure to rearm when differences of interest and opinion arise between nations. A disarmed world will not be one without tensions and conflict; if it is to stay disarmed, more effective peaceful outlets for tension and for resolution of conflict must be provided.

However, the evolution of international institutions seems to depend in part on some arms reduction, and not the other way around, as has often been suggested. Arms, it is often stated, are just symptoms of deeper ideological, political, and economic conflicts. As long as no solution is found for these problems, there will be armies and arms. Disarmament, it is said, is a treatment of the symptoms instead of the illness. It may well be that a basic treatment for our international disease requires such a fundamental change in the nature of political life as the shift from nation-state to world community. But we would be ill-advised to postpone the treatment of the arms spiral, symptom though it may be, until it is possible for this shift to take place. Like a high fever raging uncontrolled, it might kill the patient before a "basic" treatment could be administered.

Moreover, reducing the fever seems necessary not just to keep the patient alive, but to gain access to his "deeper" problems. Nothing seems more conducive to the growth of international institutions than the initiation and advancing of some phased arms reduction; nothing would serve to build up mutual confidence among nations more than carrying out, as agreed, step by step, several arms-reduction measures. The halting and reversing of the arms spiral, more than anything else, will alter our outlook from the barren radioactive deserts we often seem pointed toward now, to the promise of self-fulfilling prophecy contained in arms reduction, of deserts watered by atoms-for-peace, and joint Soviet-American exploration of space.

It is not a question of having or not having international institutions. We already have elementary frameworks in the United Nations, its specialized agencies, and other international organizations. Those are likely to grow in power and importance as the level of armaments declines. The question is one of sequence and emphasis. First, it seems to me, arms reduction and adversary inspection will be stressed, while international institutions and community consciousness gradually unfold in the background. Later, their growth might accelerate; if all goes well they will eventually make complete and general disarmament possible.

ARMS REDUCTION—AN ELEMENT OF A STRATEGY

The gradual evolution of international institutions and a global community, and the Western strategies that would be best geared to these developments, are the subject of the next chapter, where the relationship between reduction of arms, the efforts to supersede deterrence, and the decline of bipolarity to the emergence of nonaligned countries, and remote deterrence—in short, to other elements of the competition strategy—are explored. My main thesis, as throughout this book, is that the various elements are closely connected. While they can be independently discussed, they cannot be independently implemented. They all form part of one global, strategic approach.[32]

In this chapter the reduction of nuclear forces has been discussed in terms of two powers, the United States and the U.S.S.R., despite the earlier emphasis upon the growing political importance and independence of other countries, in particular China and the European nations. This seems justified, since for at least the next five years the nuclear forces of countries other than the two super-powers will remain, in comparison, highly limited. If the super-powers reduced their arms to as much as one tenth of their present strength, they would still have many times the number of nuclear weapons all the other powers combined will have in the near future. For instance, if the United States cuts its forty thousand weapons to four thousand, it would still possess fifty times more than China and France are likely to have for quite a number of years. (If the size as well as number of the weapons is taken into account, the difference would be much greater. The same holds for means of delivery.) It is surely desirable to include all other major powers in a ban on nuclear weapons as soon as possible; but to claim that the two super-powers cannot make important progress unless this is done is a common, but not a valid, argument against disarmament. The more the two super-powers cooperate in reducing their forces, and the more they learn to work with each other for global security arrangements, the more ready and willing they will be to ap-

---

[32] I pointed to this "system" quality or interdependence of the various international problems we now face in an earlier publication. This caused a reviewer to complain that one should not expect *all* one's suggestions to be accepted or rejected and offer a package proposal on a take-it-or-leave-it basis. Actually, all I wish to stress is the necessity to treat all the major elements of the situation in a coordinated fashion. This by no means implies that any particular set of suggestions for such a treatment is the only valid or feasible one or that because piecemeal treatment is less effective, no treatment is preferable.

ply pressure on their allies to participate in the arms-reduction scheme.

If nuclear disarmament of other countries is not immediately indispensable, what about reduction of their conventional forces? Would the United States and the U.S.S.R. agree to disarm if other countries refused? Here again a careful distinction must be made between the process of arms reduction and the prospect of general and complete disarmament. No one could expect any country to agree to total disarmament unless the others complied. This at first seems a staggering demand, since the "others" include a large number of countries. Actually many of them, especially African ones, are not armed much above their internal security needs. Other powers, particularly rim-land countries, keep their arms up only under the pressure and with the financing of the superpowers and would cut them if the United States and the U.S.S.R. so desired. Still other countries might readily accept disarmament if both blocs or an international police force guaranteed their present borders. A few countries might have to be disarmed by the blocs or the international police. (A small international police force, enough to protect smaller nations from each other and to disarm them if necessary, might well be operative long before there is one able to impose its will on the super-powers, as the U.N. operation in the Congo suggests.) For the first rounds of arms reduction even these measures are unnecessary since the superiority of the super-powers is so vast that they could readily reduce their arms nine tenths without worrying about whether a Cambodia or even a Brazil fully retained its forces.

Major reductions of conventional forces of both the super-powers and their allies will become possible as remote deterrence is implemented. Initially, removing troops from third countries to centrally located bases or nearby seaborne fleets might cut down few if any forces. (It would, however, reduce the arms available to the third countries, which would later alleviate problems of disarmament.) But as both super-powers become more internally geared to nonarmed competition, as U.N. observer forces are deployed at border tension points, as tyrannical regimes are replaced by governments more responsive to their people and hence less susceptible to subversion and less in need of arms, and as general socio-economic conditions in these countries improve, the need for holding outside forces to protect them will decline. Cuts in Russian and Chinese conventional forces would indicate reduced ability to intervene in the third area, and hence the Western need to hold forces to counter such interference would decline. Here, however, China, France, and other large powers would have to participate in reduction of forces, or the United States and the U.S.S.R. could not be expected to reduce their own until an international force, with their support, became strong enough not just to counter an invasion of India into Goa or Egypt into Yemen, but of China into India, which is a long way off.

In sum, the rise of pluralism does not hamper arms reduction, which can be initiated and advanced largely as a scheme of the two super-powers. If they can win or gain the cooperation of their allies, the cooperation of other powers can be left, if necessary, to a much later stage, one in which an international police force will enter the picture. This is not to suggest that arms reduction of third powers should or will be delayed, but it might be, without preventing the initiation and progress of the plans discussed above.

Arms reduction is, of course, significantly tied to limiting the interbloc competition to nonarmed means. Any institutional arrangement that helps to safeguard nonarmed competition, e.g., limited U.N. observer forces, would allow *some* reduction of conventional arms by both camps. At the same time, reduction of the conventional capabilities of the major powers increases the stability of nonarmed competition and frees some resources for the build-up of nonarmed capacities. At least one of the major potential instabilities of the strategic deterrence system, escalation of local wars in third countries, is also diminished as nonarmed competition is more firmly established. In principle, progress on these two fronts is mutually supportive.

There is, of course, not always a perfect balance among these spheres. By 1963 considerable imbalance had developed, in part because the interdependence of these different issues was not fully recognized and even less fully taken into account. The West in 1963 adhered, almost without exception, to a duopolistic approach in the general field of armaments, especially in regard to nuclear forces. Although it gradually recognized, it by no means became fully adapted to, the decline of bipolarity, and it has yet to augment its ability to act in a plural world. It has progressed furthest toward a world of peaceful competition in its increased tolerance of nonalignment and its intervention for progress in third countries. But the West's ability to implement and benefit from these policy innovations was hampered because it did not adequately match them with adjustments in the military sphere. The increase of conventional and subconventional forces did not go well with an attempt to provide leadership to the progressive forces in the underdeveloped continents and to stabilize the nonarmed competition. Ordering more missiles, advancing the counterforce strategy, and refusing to be committed to no first use of nuclear bombs—which the other side seemed to fear as pointing toward a first-strike posture—did not help the efforts to arrest the nuclear arms race.

The slowly growing interest in interbloc security arrangements clashes with the still ambivalent attitude toward arms control and reluctance to accept arms reduction as a primary policy goal. Since it is in the area of armed capacities that Western strategy is still the most duopolistic, it is here that the largest adjustments will have to be made if the West is to benefit from those steps taken in the nonarmed sphere, and if it is to move farther from the gates of nuclear hell toward a safer, and hopefully better, world.

Chapter VI

INTERNATIONAL RELATIONS
IN THE NUCLEAR AGE

Conflicts among nations or blocs have often occurred before, though never has their scope been as global and their potential destructiveness as great as today's East-West conflict. There are many views about how such a conflict is to be resolved, ranging all the way from those who seek to wipe out the other side to those who would rather surrender. Opinions in the West have focused upon two less extreme positions: one held by those who believe that the conflict cannot be peacefully resolved, and another followed by those who believe in and work for its resolution. After briefly reviewing these two alternatives, let us consider a third possibility.

Duopoly is a strategy supported by advocates of both positions. Those who are pessimistic about Communism, expecting its adherents neither to mellow nor to be estranged, favor duopoly as the best way to counter the continuous challenges of international Communism. The Communists, according to this approach, will continue to prod the West in countless ways; and the West has to counter each new onslaught with a well-armed holding operation. The result will not be "conflict resolution" but a protracted conflict.[1] This, it is emphasized, is a strategy in itself. To seek resolution with such an opponent, it is said, is not only naïve but downright dangerous.

While the supporters of "protracted conflict" are in substantial agreement about the near future, they differ in their long-run projections. "Sophisticated" protractionists expect

[1] Robert Strausz-Hupé *et al.*, *Protracted Conflict* (New York: Harper, 1959).

the conflict to continue as long as can be foreseen and question in principle the wisdom of trying to explore and prepare for the distant future. Agressive protractionists seek to prepare continuously for a "break" that will enable the United States to gain a strategic advantage over the enemy sufficient to compel his surrender. They neither heed the experts' judgment that such an advantage is extremely unlikely nor do they face the question of their (and our) fate if the other side is the first to gain such an advantage. Optimistic protractionists expect the Communist regime to disintegrate at some future date. They see in any riot in the East, crop failure, or defection to the West, a sign that the day of reckoning is closer.

Duopoly is also the strategy most favored by those who anticipate a resolution of the conflict. The Communists, at least the Soviet-led ones, it is said, are increasingly accepting the division of the world into two spheres of influence and are mitigating their prodding of the West. According to this view, we are about to enter a period of peaceful coexistence based on the freezing of a global *status quo*. Even today it is largely the Chinese, and to a degree the Communist parties in some underdeveloped countries, that are still actively expansionist. Once duopoly is fully accepted by both camps, it is argued, each will respect the territorial integrity and boundaries of the other, and the conflict will be resolved.

Other plans for conflict resolution are far less popular. One of the better known might be called the lawyers' solution, because it is favored largely by those who are legally oriented. This proposes that representatives of all the nations meet to draft a constitution for a world government, to which all nations would then transfer their ultimate sovereignty, especially the control of the major means of violence. The world government would set up an international police force to prevent nations from rearming. There are a great variety of schemes for the possible make-up of a world government and its rights and powers, but there has been comparatively little analysis of how such a government could be brought about and little careful study of what has so far prevented its establishment.

Both the protractionist and the resolutionist positions are unsatisfactory. The protactionists seem not to recognize the changes in the international situation. They underestimate the urgency of curbing the interbloc conflict and the readiness of the other side for far-reaching accommodations. Those in search of a full resolution of the conflict seem to expect the Russians to accept, without major modifications, a mode of resolution worked out in the West and often quite unresponsive to the basic values and interests of the East. It is not reasonable to assume the Communists are becoming ready to accept either the global allocation of spheres of influence or a world state democratically ruled (as this term is used in the West) which would be respectful of private property and would follow a policy of minimal interference in the world economy, in short, a laissez-faire state spelled large.

The essence of our argument in this book has been that a third alternative is emerging, less difficult to attain than complete conflict resolution but offering much more than even the optimistic protractionist hopes for. Out of the Communist expansionist efforts and the duopolistic responses of the West a pattern of competition under rules is gradually evolving. If this competition were fully established, what would its characteristics be? Conflict would be combined with its "resolution" in the sense that, on the one hand, conflict would be continued, even intensified, while on the other, certain modes and means of conflict would be eliminated. Armed conflicts would be "resolved," nonarmed conflicts intensified.

The world of peaceful competition would not be without conflict, but without international violence. The participants might well continue to feel and express hostility, have and admit to differences of faith and interest, and use their re-

sources to advance values they wish others to follow. In this
sense nonarmed competition is much less demanding than
all-inclusive resolution of conflict, which assumes that the
differences will somehow be settled.

This point should be emphasized. The question is often
raised: if the Communists seek to bring their way of life to
all people, how can there be peace, disarmament, or mutual
accommodation unless they give up their expansionist goal?
Left-leaning authors tend to answer that the Soviet-led camp
has already given up expansionism. One analyst even went so
far as to call the U.S.S.R. "conservative."[2] Duopolists more
cautiously talk about the Soviets' increased concern with
standard of living and the internal liberalization of the
U.S.S.R. as sublimating its foreign ambitions. While there is
little question that some such changes have occurred (though
their extent and stability are less clear), my main thesis is that
an abandonment of the central foreign-policy goal of the Communist camp, which would require a deep change in its
ideological-messianic nature, is not necessary for a major
accommodation of interbloc relations and the advent of an
international system adapted to the nuclear age. *Ex* *Detente*

The crucial question is not whether the Soviets seek to extend their way of life to other people, but what means they
use for this purpose. The distinction is not between expansion
and freezing, but between armed and peaceful promotion of
values. The Communists, I have suggested, especially the
Soviet-led group, have moved increasingly toward reliance on
peaceful means, even though this may be merely an expedient
adaptation to transient circumstances, to be reversed without
notice. The question, however, is not so much what the Soviets did in the past, faced with a Western duopolistic strategy,
but how they will respond now to an approach that seeks to
stabilize peaceful competition. Their initial commitment to

[2] Erich Fromm, *May Man Prevail?* (Garden City, N.Y.: Doubleday, 1961),
Ch. II *passim*. For my view of changes in Soviet policy, see Chapter I above.

peaceful competition may have been limited in time and in scope; still, as the West encourages peaceful engagement, and as interbloc arrangements are set up to stabilize disarmed competition, the Soviet bloc's commitment to peaceful competition might deepen. Testifying before the Senate Foreign Relations Committee, leading Sovietologist Marshall D. Shulman, of Harvard University, stated in the fall of 1963: "The most striking characteristic of recent Soviet foreign policy has been the way in which policies undertaken for short-time expediential purposes have tended to elongate in time and become imbedded in doctrine and political strategy."

The West does not have to "trust" the East or vice versa, to lay down arms. The strategy of competition combines remote deterrence in third countries and a pure retaliatory posture (second-strike) in bloc countries, with inspection and observer forces. Its limitation to peaceful means is not based on trust, but on interest; it is not a question of giving or breaking one's word, but of setting up the necessary machinery to verify and enforce commitments.

The most satisfactory way to complete the shift to peaceful competition is by what has become known as the gradualist approach. This combines a set of principles for the transformation from one mode of operation to a quite different one, and applies to such divergent developments as the formation of the European Common Market and the gradual growth of African political unity, as well as to the change in interbloc relations.

The essence of the gradualist approach is to break the transition into numerous limited steps. This has many advantages: psychologically, both political leaders and voters are reluctant (unless a major crisis occurs) to support drastic changes. Breaking the transition into many steps permits, at each point, only a minimal departure from the safety of the known.

Taking a small step at a time also allows for experimentation. Does the other side adhere to its commitment? Does it, too, reduce arms? Do the verification procedures work as expected? The small steps provide a sense of reversibility, which can be further strengthened by making special provisions, for instance, holding forces in a high degree of readiness when remote deterrence is first introduced. All this makes for a minimum-regret strategy, in which the cumulative gains can be large but both real risks and unreal fears are minimized.

Since each existing system builds up vested interests, patterns of thought, and emotional commitments, another advantage of gradual transition is that it allows time for these to become adjusted, while a direct, all-out attempt to change is likely to provoke active resistance. This problem often comes up when the effect of industrial interest in arms production on disarmament is discussed. The issue is a complex one, but it should suffice to say that there is a big difference between a proposal to cut the annual production of arms by 10 per cent and a suggestion to reduce the U.S. defense budget by more than \$23 billion (i.e., 50 per cent) in one year.[3]

Since the gradualist approach is partially a psychological one that seeks to overcome irrational fears, it stresses symbolic steps that create an atmosphere that will support its general purpose, especially in the first stage. The negotiation of the partial nuclear test-ban treaty in mid-1963 was preceded by such psychological groundwork. It began with a hint from the White House that the President was about to make a major foreign-policy address, which attracted the public to television and radio sets. Then, on June 10, 1963, at the American University in Washington, President Kennedy made what has since become known as the "Strategy for Peace" speech.

[3] Seymour Melman (ed.), *Strategy for American Security* (privately published, April 30, 1963). Emile Benoit and Kenneth E. Boulding (eds.), *Disarmament and the Economy* (New York: Harper & Row, 1963).

The speech, which came only eight months after the Cuban blockade, called attention to the dangers of nuclear war and took a reconciliatory tone toward the Soviet Union. President Kennedy said "constructive changes" had taken place, which "might bring within reach solutions which now seem beyond us." He was carefully optimistic about the prospect of peace: "Our problems are man-made . . . and can be solved by man." But the President's concern was not limited to changes in the other camp; the speech was directed as much to the American people as it was to the Russian government. U.S. policies, declared the President, must be so constructed "that it becomes in the Communist interest to agree to a genuine peace"; and he explicitly called on the American people to "re-examine," i.e., modify, their attitudes toward the U.S.S.R. and the Cold War. He also informed his listeners that the United States had halted all nuclear tests in the atmosphere and would not resume them unless another country did so.

The U.S.S.R. reciprocated immediately. Kennedy's speech was published in full in the government newspaper *Izvestia*, an opportunity for communication with the Russian government rarely accorded to a Western leader. The next day the Soviets reversed their earlier objection to a Western-favored proposal that the United Nations send observers to war-torn Yemen. The United States then removed, for the first time since 1956, its objection to the restoration of full status to the Hungarian delegation to the United Nations. Premier Khrushchev announced that he had ordered production of strategic bombers halted.

A brief study of the headlines these speeches, announcements, moves, and steps generated around the world, and a limited review of the millions of words of interpretation they inspired, shows that they indeed had a "relaxing" effect. Newspapers told their readers about a "thaw" in the Cold War; a "pause"; the beginning of an East-West *détente*; a renewal of "the Camp David atmosphere." While many commentators warned their readers not to expect too much, most hastened to affirm their support of the "liquidation of the Cold War." In short, an atmosphere cogenial to negotiation and, even more important, to public acceptance of the results of negotiation was created.

From mid-1963 on, the psychological atmosphere was reinforced by such steps as the actual ratification of the limited nuclear test-ban treaty by the original signatories, discussions of joint Russian-American exploration of space, the sale of American wheat surpluses to the Soviets, consideration of a new American consulate in Leningrad and a Russian one in Chicago, and, not least, continuous press reports on meetings among the sides and new plans they were rumored to be considering. The door was opened for an accelerated transition from duopoly to nonviolent competition, which could proceed on many fronts. Some steps might be military (e.g., reduction of arms); others, political (e.g., settlement of the Berlin dispute); and still others, economic (e.g., increased East-West trade). There is no one route, no single sequence, and progress on each front would support progress on others, by increasing the psychological momentum and providing the necessary instruments. There is a close relationship between settlement of the Berlin question and the reduction of armed forces in Europe; between an increase in interbloc trade and the reduction of international tensions. It is part and parcel of the gradualist approach not to be confined to any one avenue but systematically to seek advances on many fronts; to coordinate progress in one area with beneficial steps elsewhere, because of the close relationship between military, economic, political, and psychological factors.

There is, of course, no assurance that once the process has been initiated it would continue automatically. Any major change—such as a reconciliation between China and Russia, the election of a political extremist to the U.S. presidency, or a major technological breakthrough in defense weaponry —may halt the process long before it is completed or has progressed very far. While the problems are man-made, and man can presumably solve them, no one man—not even the head of the mightiest nation on earth—has full control of the process.

Modern civilization in general, and Western thought in particular, view man as largely a rational creature in command of his fate. Each individual, it is conceded, might be only a unit in a large societal and international complex; but the leaders of the super-powers are often believed to be free to direct their nations and blocs as they see fit. Even a cursory examination of recent history shows how much these leaders, too, are governed by forces over which they have but limited control. Each one is faced by the limitations imposed by nature, his opponents, his allies, third countries, and domestic politics, in addition to the limitations of resources and knowledge, commitments previously made, and others. Only a limited area is left for maneuverability. The fate of the legislative program of the New Frontier readily illustrates this point.

These "uncontrollable" factors have a logic and a dynamic of their own. For instance, the refusal of the leaders of secondary powers within each bloc to perpetuate the dominance of the super-powers will continue, despite the efforts of the bloc leaders to counter this trend and regardless of whatever any one national leader in America, France, Russia, or China does. Similarly, the time required for the modernization of underdeveloped countries will continue to set sharp limits on the effectiveness of the development programs of East, West, and third parties, whatever their efforts.

It is within these limits that men, political leaders of great nations included, can and do act. Mindful of the limits, I suggest that the stream of international relations in the nuclear age flows in the direction of competition under rules. The critical decision of each of the major participants in the next years is whether it wishes to support and accelerate the shift or to block it. In the preceding chapters several shifts that are partially completed, and the direction in which they might be extended, were discussed. Let us now examine the elements of a completed transition and then review some additional, new steps that might be initiated or magnified to accelerate the transformation.

TOWARD A GLOBAL COMMUNITY?

The dictates of realism have, I hope, prevailed in these pages. Strategists, I have stressed, should sweep aside the cobwebs of the past and respond to the ever-changing international situation, free to appreciate historical trends as they unfold. However, no wind is useful to the ship that has no destination; the goal the strategist seeks to bring about must be indicated. Only a sense of the desired goal can command the necessary effort a shift in strategy requires, and efforts are likely to be misguided unless work on all the necessary components progresses in a coordinated fashion.

However, in sketching the world to be achieved, I leave aside much of the moderation and humane skepticism often associated with the gradualist approach. I favor limited adjustment at each stage; but together such adjustments amount to a fundamental change. There is little progress at each turn of the wheel, but in the long run, much ground must and can be covered. The approach is gradualist only as far as the means are concerned; the goal is fundamental and far-reaching.

Drawing on systems analysis as developed by modern political and social sciences, we recognize only a limited number of resting points at which international relations can be stabilized. Traditional balance-of-power politics, such as was practiced in nineteenth-century Europe, was one such resting point. By checking and balancing each other, with Britain acting as the ultimate balancer (and in so doing, serving its own interests), the European nations experienced a century without a general war, between 1815 and 1914. Duopoly is a massive effort to apply this pattern to the twentieth-century world, counting upon the United States and the West to balance the Soviet Union and the East to provide a global balance of power and hence stability and peace. As already suggested, the realistic basis of this approach is eroded, and its dangers are accumulating.

The new mode of international relations that is evolving, unlike the traditional balance-of-power pattern, requires a global regulating agency, already provided in part by the United Nations and other international organizations, and a growing collaboration between the two super-powers, Russia and the United States. Most political scientists, it must be said, do not believe such global regulation of international relations is feasible (or necessary), and look forward to some improved state of balance-of-power politics, such as, say, two nuclear camps (or more), balancing each other, coupled with limited arms-control measures, to trim the system of its more irrational dangers. Pointing to the limited success of existent international organizations, they see little hope for the stabilization of international relations through a world authority.

What they frequently do not take fully into account, however, is the decline of bloc solidarity, the rise of global pluralism and an international floating vote, and, above all, the fact that evolving super-power collaboration tends to present the advance of American and Russian interests as a service to global welfare, including the forwarding of global rules and institutions. A major advance in the efficiency of international institutions may follow, not because of some sudden drastic change in human nature, or the long-awaited elimination of power politics, but because the strengthening of global institutions will serve the deepest national interests of the two super-powers and of many smaller ones. As has been shown, peaceful competition might *initially* rest on bilateral Eastern and Western exchanges of inspection and observer forces, but *stabilization* requires the evolution of impartial institutions for peaceful negotiation of the differences of interest and belief that will continue to exist. This would be best served by neutral parties, especially global institutions.

Having disagreed with the majority of my colleagues, who see hope in the "practical future"[4] for an improved balance-of-power system but not for effective global institutions, I also part company with almost all those who believe that the only "realistic" chance for global institutions is to limit their scope and function. Most writers on the subject favor the formation of world authority that would peacefully settle conflicts and enforce the settlements reached, when necessary, through an international police force, but would leave all other matters to national or state governments, since, it is believed, the more tasks the world authority is expected to carry out, the more difficult it will be for the sides to agree on its structure and policy. All nations might agree to some measures to counter the danger of nuclear war, it is argued, but when it comes to questions of supporting progressive governments, fighting racial discrimination, or enhancing development, consensus would hardly be possible.

An effective world authority, it seems to me, could not be attained, and, if attained, could not be maintained, unless it served the world community more fully than as a law-and-order-enforcement authority. To put it in even more basic terms, a safer world will require a more just one. Governments—whether in a community, state, federation, or larger polity—that preserve only law and order tend to perpetuate a social and political *status quo* and do not provide the machinery through which basic social wrongs can be corrected. It is under such governments that large alienated social

---

[4] Practical future refers to the period for which actual plans and preparations are being made. Its length is determined empirically.

groups are found, groups that—failing to find a peaceful way to redress their grievances—turn to violent means to attain their goals. No police force could arrest five hundred million hungry people, if—armed only with empty soup bowls and wooden forks—they marched toward an affluent society. Nor could so indifferent a government be expected to command the loyalty and support of the majority of the world's people. The world state, like the national one, will have to learn the lesson that stabilization requires some amount of state regulation of the economy so as to redress the more outstanding social grievances. The world authority will have to provide not only a police force and jails, but also a development agency; will have not only to impose taxation to support agencies for law and order, but also to shift resources from the "haves" to the "have nots"; will have to be not only a means of affording security but also of furnishing at least a minimal standard of living and human rights to most people, and the hope of improvement and redress to those who have not yet obtained either.

Here lies the deeper tie between world authority and a global community. A government, however large its forces, will not be stable unless the majority of the politically conscious and active citizens support it. Such support is attained by providing not simply protection against hypothetical and abstract dangers, but the positive and concrete sense of care that attends the promotion of social welfare and human dignity.

Actually, there is already more consensus between East and West on the value of alleviating hunger, dispelling ignorance, and combatting disease than is often recognized. The possibility of working out agreed policies to serve these goals—or an agreement to tolerate a variety of policies—should not be ruled out too quickly, especially if the trend continues toward welfare capitalism in the West and liberalization in the East.

In many ways the ultimate foundation of the global society, and world authority, would be a sense of community coextensive with that of all mankind. While the nation is still the predominant symbol of identification for most men, there is already a growing sense of identification with larger social groupings, such as *Europa* among the citizens of the Common Market countries; Africa or Latin America among the educated elites of the nations of these continents. The universal extension of this community-sense is a slow and difficult process, but deliberate efforts to accelerate it will hasten the day commitment to mankind becomes more than a grammar-school platitude. This sense of community will provide the firmest foundation for the international rules that limit the competition to peaceful means. The ultimate foundation of rules that are voluntarily observed is always a community that formulated them, thus committing itself to follow them.

The stabilization of peaceful competition, of a safer and better world, has thus to include the gradual building up of (a) global machinery for the peaceful settlement of conflict, a global legislature, judiciary, and executive, including a police force; (b) a machinery for global regulation of the economy to encourage economic growth, to avoid mass unemployment, to bring about reallocation in favor of the "have-not" areas; and (c) the growth of a sense of a world community. Peaceful competition was *initiated* when all these developments had hardly begun; it will *progress* as these evolve; its ultimate *stabilization* depends on their maturation.

Many factors affect the evolution of the world community that would stabilize peaceful global competition. The great and indispensable decision is whether actively to support the stabilization process, or to adhere to the illusions of duopoly. In the following pages several key policy decisions are examined in this light. Each one is significantly affected by the angle from which it is regarded. Policy toward the United

Nations, trade among the blocs, international communication, and so on, all look and are different depending upon whether they are viewed in the duopolistic context or that of peaceful competition. Several such subjects are examined here in some detail, but the main principle can readily be applied to others as well.

A NEW UNITED NATIONS

If the shift from a bipolar world to one of competition under rules continues, the much-maligned United Nations will enter a new period in which its roles and importance will gradually grow. However, the day when it will live up to the ideals orators proclaim upon its anniversaries is still very far away.

In its short lifetime, the United Nations has already raised many complex issues and passed through several phases, neither of which can be examined here in any detail.[5] Briefly, in 1945 and 1946, before the advent of duopoly, many Americans expected the United Nations to establish global law and order. This was to be achieved through "collective security," according to which all the U.N. members would confront any potential aggressor with such overwhelming power that aggression would either be deterred or quickly suppressed if it did occur.

When the Cold War broke out and became an acknowledged reality in 1947, the disappointment with the United Nations, especially in the United States, was profound. During the next ten years a mixture of highly duopolistic approaches and some elements of the fair-competition approach governed American behavior toward the United Nations. Duopoly was reflected in an effort to freeze an existing distribution of power in the organization; in the refusal to

[5] See Leland M. Goodrich, *The United Nations* (New York: Crowell, 1959); Arthur N. Holcombe (ed.), *Organizing Peace in the Nuclear Age* (New York: New York University Press, 1959); and Bloomfield, *op. cit.*

seat Communist China in the General Assembly and to replace Nationalist China on the Security Council; and in the
attempt to prevent the East from gaining additional positions
in the civil service of the United Nations. The main expression of duopoly, however, was revealed in a prevailing tendency to use the United Nations in a way consistent with a
narrow interpretation of American interests.

While the United States may initially have been quite willing to allow the United Nations to act as a genuine embryo
world authority (though defined in Western terms, e.g., ruled
democratically) and have felt that it was the Soviet Union
that prevented the United Nations from acquiring such
status, once it gave up this hope, it also largely gave up efforts to use the United Nations to engage the U.S.S.R. in
a growing web of international institutions, and hence increasingly tie the Soviet Union to a global community. Instead, the United States often used the United Nations to
rally public opinion in the West and in nonaligned countries
against the Communist bloc. Western troops fought the
Communist invasion of South Korea under the U.N. flag,
taking a stance as if Russia had violated an acknowledged
law of an already established world government, and the
world police force was putting the aggressor in its place. Using the large Western majority in the General Assembly
—often as great as fifty-five to five—the United States led the
United Nations, with the help of the votes of such countries
as Portugal and Spain, Nicaragua and Haiti, into one resolution after another condemning Russia. The Russians, at the
same time, hampered the work of the United Nations, especially in matter that fell within the jurisdiction of the
Security Council, by frequent use of the veto right. The
United Nations was overwhelmingly Western; the other side,
though participating, was largely frozen out of constructive
sharing of control. No wonder that at the height of the bipolar
period of the late forties and early fifties, the United Nations'

activities, prestige, and interbloc significance were at a low point.

Even in these days the West did not adhere exclusively to a duopolistic approach. The ideal of the United Nations as an institutional framework in which conflicts could be peacefully settled continued to be kept alive, both in the rhetoric used and in the beliefs of many people who refused to give up hope in the ideal. Moreover, limited work took place that was much more in line with peaceful engagement. The United States succeeded in engaging the U.S.S.R. and several other countries in a joint effort to help hungry children, through UNICEF. In 1955 UNICEF Director-General Maurice Pate enlisted Soviet support for this organ in which membership had, as he said, "become sort of a status symbol in international affairs."[6] Russia's first donation was used to buy her own DDT, which in turn served antimalaria campaigns in twenty countries. And by 1960 the Russian contribution had been substantially increased.

In the mid-fifties, and increasingly in the early sixties, the United Nations became a more suitable place for the development of an effective of international machinery. Many factors combined to bring this about, not the least of which were the change of administration in the United States and modifications of Soviet foreign policy; but the key element was the admission of many new members to the United Nations. The original membership of fifty-one signatories of the Charter was expanded to eighty by 1956; by mid-1963 there were 110 members. By the early 1960s the Afro-Asian countries alone could muster enough votes to prevent either East or West from gaining a majority in the General Assembly without their support. Thus the United Nations changed from an organization dominated by the West and obstructed by the Russians to one in which both sides often have to ap-

[6] "Profiles," *The New Yorker*, December 2, 1961, p. 92.

peal to third countries to carry a resolution they favor
(though there are still remnants from the earlier years, such
as the China problem and the overrepresentation of Latin
American countries and underrepresentation of Asian and
African states in the Security Council). Not only has the
floating vote increased many times, but new issues—especially
those of anticolonialism and development—have provided
"universal" causes in terms of which both the United States
and the U.S.S.R. couch their contributions to the general
welfare.

Coming on top of earlier disappointments in the United
Nations, the combination of the loss of Western hegemony
and continued Russian obstructionism created much ill-feel-
ing toward the United Nations among important segments of
the American public. At the same time, the General Assembly's tendency to favor the anticolonial countries angered
the conservatives in France, Britain, Belgium, and other ex-
colonial powers.

Only in the early sixties did the United Nations seem to
begin to outgrow these crises. There is increasing, though far
from complete, acceptance of the fact that neither the United
States nor the U.S.S.R. will dominate the United Nations
(though the United States has fared considerably better than
the U.S.S.R., even in recent years). There is an increasing
though not yet strong tendency in the West to use the United
Nations less as "an organization of the free world" and more
as a place to integrate the Soviet-led camp into the international community.

This raises the questions of whether the Russians are really
willing to be integrated into an international community; and,
if they are "mellowing" anyway, whether such integration is
necessary. The point underlying these questions deserves to
be highlighted because it is at the back of many other questions. The key assumption is that nations are rational beings
possessing full control over their fate. They are free to choose,

it is assumed, between being engaged and staying aloof, and their quality at the beginning and end of such an engagement is essentially the same. Actually, nations, when engaged, find it very difficult to become disengaged. If we treat the Russians as outcasts, with whom we never voluntarily share controls, whom we do not consult, and whom we try to exclude, the evolution of international institutions will make little progress. But if efforts are made to engage the Soviet-led camp peacefully, especially if it is actually mellowing, it will be hard for the Communist bloc to resist integration. The significance of peaceful engagement under these circumstances is to cement the more friendly relations generated in periods of grace, to counter pressures to regress, and gradually to build up a world composed not of blocs, which might become hostile again, but of permanent ties to an international community. This, in turn, is the ultimate foundation of most of the factors that limit the competition to peaceful means.

The United States faces here the difficult problem every participant in a competition faces: it wishes to improve its position without undermining the very framework in which the competition takes place; especially as this framework is just evolving. Thus every time the United States puts before the General Assembly or the Security Council a resolution which it knows the U.S.S.R. will reject, it probably expects to gain the Assembly's approval or force the U.S.S.R. to use the veto in the Security Council, and thus evoke the disapproval of world public opinion. But frequent use of this device alienates the U.S.S.R. from the United Nations and becomes a transient maneuver in the eyes of the new nations. Thus, for instance, while no African or Asian country opposed the resolution to condemn the U.S.S.R. for its intervention in Hungary in 1956 and fifteen supported it, as the United States reintroduced a similar resolution year after year the number of new nations that supported it diminished. One might take a moralist stance that the Soviet intervention in

Hungary deserves to be redenounced indefinitely, but obviously the new nations, which constitute the majority in the United Nations, do not think so, nor does such repeated condemnation, of a sin that cannot be uncommitted, serve to integrate the East into the United Nations.

Another reason why the United Nations of the early sixties, while far from an ideal global organization, is more suited for the task of community building than the United Nations of the late forties or mid-fifties, is that the large number of nonaligned nations, which constitute a floating vote, often encourages moderation and interbloc cooperation, even when they themselves might occasionally lack some of these qualities.[7] Being nonduopolistic is rapidly becoming a strategy requirement for any bloc seeking majority support in the United Nations. (It goes without saying that it will require parallel changes in the foreign policy of the U.S.S.R. and other countries, but the discussion here is focused on American strategy.) This means that the United States will have to be as concerned with building up the framework of the United Nations as with improving its own position within it. Years of "putting the United Nations on ice" with "studied inattention," as one observer put it, will have to be followed by increased interest and investment in the United Nations.

What steps could the United States promote and the United Nations accept if the future were to harbor the kind of evolution outlined here? Once again the gradualist approach may be applied. If any renewed attempts were made in the near future to thrust upon the still weak United Nations such formidable tasks as preventing war, providing global security, or undertaking the development of three continents, little but damaging disappointment could follow. The United Nations is hardly more ready now than it was in 1945 to provide the basis for a world government. The need is for limited actions

[7] See Chapter III, pp. 85–86.

that will gradually extend the United Nations' ability to provide the institutional framework for global security, for the regulation of the world economy, and for the deepening of international community ties.

The specific suggestions most frequently forwarded to extend the United Nations are largely of an institutional nature, but these are sometimes criticized as misunderstanding the way international organizations evolve. The United Nations, it is said, is already institutionally more advanced than the willingness of its members to utilize it. The immediate need is to change the members' attitudes, not the organization. Nothing could be closer to the truth. Only if military, political, socio-economic, and psychological factors become favorable to a stronger United Nations, will a stronger organization result.

Still, the significance of institutional levers should not be underestimated. While a world government cannot be simply legislated into being, if the institutional growth of the United Nations would keep it one step, rather than a hundred, ahead of ongoing socio-political processes, this institutional growth could serve not only to reflect progress already attained in the world community but also to accelerate it. It is in this spirit that the following ideas are reviewed. As these institutional innovations are introduced, and as progress is made on the community level, more far-reaching measures, such as abolishing the veto power in the Security Council and providing for representation in the General Assembly more closely related to the size of the population of a country, might be introduced.[8]

Community-building Activities

The United Nations itself can contribute to psychological disarmament by a host of educational, cultural, and communi-

[8] See Grenville Clark and Louis B. Sohn, *World Peace through World Law* (Cambridge: Harvard University Press, 1958).

cation activities (their financing is discussed below). The formation of a global radio and TV network, to use U.N.-owned satellites and to broadcast programs prepared by UNESCO, would have a desirable effect. Facilitating and significantly increasing exchanges of movies and records is still a valid idea. Exchange visits of students, youth representatives, teachers, and political leaders might be approached on a completely new scale. Mass exchanges should be organized between the blocs, and between the "have" and the "have-not" countries. The need for written and verbal translation is so great that only a major improvement in the now experimental translation machines can provide genuine hope for overcoming this hurdle. The United Nations might encourage the development of these machines, if only by indicating increased interest and appreciation.

The value of projects such as American-Russian exploration of space, and joint geographical, weather, and medical research has often been suggested because these both provide great economies, accelerate progress, and increase global bonds. Whether such joint projects are extended, under the United Nations or some other international agency, depends on the state of interbloc relations and the level of international tensions. But, once initiated, they would further and cement progressive trends. Since there are no magic keys, a more acceptable international system will have to be pieced together from such small and in themselves limited measures. Their accumulation might not bring a major change in interbloc relations, but it would support the evolution of an international community that was initiated by technological, political, and other developments.

One significant area of a quite different nature where East and West might cooperate is that of human rights. The day is, of course, remote when the Soviet Union will tolerate the investigation within its borders of a violation of the right of religious freedom, or the United States of race relations in the American South. But there is no acute demand for such investigation. There is, however, a distinct world public opinion and an overwhelming majority in the United Nations for sanctions against extreme violations of human rights by such a country as South Africa. The United States, together with the nonaligned nations and the U.S.S.R., might more actively condemn the very small group of nations that attempt to hide inhuman autocracies behind the rationale of nonintervention. I favor neither the use of force (even by the United Nations) against such countries nor their expulsion from the organization, since it would be beneficial if all countries were members, and expulsion would isolate them from the world community when what is necessary is their further integration. But other sanctions, such as cutting off trade, terminating aid, leveling strong moral denunciations, and imposing a total arms embargo, might serve to express effectively common sentiments of the growing world community.

Building the international community forces re-examination of the China question. Membership in the United Nations is not in itself a sign of moral approval (otherwise, most countries could allege causes for the exclusion of some others). Nor does membership in any way assure the continuation of any particular regime. The isolation of the government of a sixth of the world's population does not promise a smooth future for the United Nations, which is to serve as a *global* institutional framework and to be charged with supervising various arms-reduction measures, in which China will sooner or later have to be included if they are to have any lasting validity.

The objections to the seating of Communist China in the United Nations might be greater now than they were. In 1963, for the first time, the U.S.S.R. did not initiate a motion for the seating of Communist China. United States policy is to differentiate as much as possible between Moscow and Peking by relative receptiveness to the one coupled with a complete ostracism of the other. But this policy has already become too inflexible, and numerous advantages could be gained, without harm to U.S. interests, if it were revised. China should be treated with the same limited courtesy that Stalin's Russia was after the advent of the Cold War, which would still allow the United States to show differences in attitude toward China and the U.S.S.R. The world of international relations is not limited to friendly or hostile relations. The American attitude toward China should be changed from refusal to acknowledge that it exists, to the cool tolerance that permits membership in the United Nations, diplomatic relations, and freedom to travel, but not much else. Otherwise, not only will the global community remain hopelessly incomplete, but one factor that might contribute to a more reasonable posture on China's part will be neglected.

Gradually Extending the United Nations

As the global community gradually grows, the institutional machinery of the United Nations might be extended and more interbloc negotiations conducted through the United Nations, rather than outside it. Slowly the United Nations might acquire a more active and effective role in settling conflicts between countries other than the super-powers, helping to settle disputes such as those between Pakistan and India, Bolivia and Chile, Indonesia and Malaysia, the Arab countries and Israel, and the like. The more the United Nations is used to settle such conflicts before war erupts and to terminate such wars if they occur, the more likely the United Nations is to be able to extend this mediating function to larger states and eventually even to the super-powers. While the United Nations so far has brought about little reconciliation, such effort is not without precedent. It did, for instance, play a major mediatory role in bringing about a settlement in

West New Guinea, and it did help to achieve a cease fire in Kashmir.

The internationalization of geographical areas of conflict is not a procedure now favored. But once it became more widely practiced it might gain popularity. It provides a way for the sides to maintain face while resolving a conflict and even to gain status as having contributed to the strengthening of the United Nations. Once remote deterrence is established and the embryo of a U.N. police force exists, the internationalization of Berlin might become possible and would surely be a major contribution to peace in Europe. Since both the procedure and the issue are of much importance, a somewhat fuller discussion of this seems warranted.

Among the various plans that have been advanced for the solution of the Berlin dispute, one reasonable proposal suggests turning the entire city (with the exception of a small part of East Berlin that serves as East Germany's capital) over to the United Nations; both sides would guarantee its independence, by treaty and by remote deterrence forces. The access routes from West Germany to Berlin would also be internationalized. All foreign national troops would be withdrawn from the city and their place taken by units under the U.N. command, to be recruited from small powers—Nigeria, India, and Sweden, for instance. Removal of walls that partition the city would be an integral part of its internationalization. While the freedom of transportation on routes between West Germany and Berlin would be guaranteed, both West Germany and East Germany would be free (if they desired) to forbid their people to travel to Berlin, a right all nations reserve. (The United States, for instance, forbids travel to China and Cuba.)

Internationalization of many other areas of contention has been suggested. Among the areas listed—each has yet to be carefully examined—are the Chinese offshore islands, Quemoy and Matsu; the Suez Canal; a route to the sea for Bolivia through Chile; and even the Guantanamo naval base in Cuba. Such ideas may seem unrealistic today, but if the desire to augment accommodation between countries grows, so will interest in this method of settlement. The need to build up the United Nations will provide some additional incentive for internationalization, since such measures would increase the world organization's functions, power, and status. Again, while this practice has far from established itself, the internationalization of either territory or routes is not without precedent. Concerning land areas, by far the most promising (though as yet incomplete) arrangement involves Antarctica. Many countries were staking claims there, including Britain, France, Norway, Chile, New Zealand, Argentina, Belgium, Japan, and South Africa. The United States and the U.S.S.R. rejected all these claims and led the other nations toward a treaty (signed in 1959) that reserved the area for peaceful purposes only and opened it for unrestricted scientific use by all. Even an inspection privilege was set up, to allow each country to inspect at wish the stations of the others to verify their nonmilitary use. The ultimate disposition of the area has yet to be decided; it could make a fine first U.N. territory. The granting of full U.N. status to the Tiran Straits (leading into the Gulf of Aqaba at the south of Israel and Jordan) might be considered next.

Giving the United Nations sovereignty over all waters that are now international, beginning with the high seas, should be relatively easy. Besides increasing the possessions of the United Nations and providing more precedents for U.N. territories, this might also prove an important source of revenue when, for instance, oil or minerals were located and their removal became possible.

Granting the United Nations sovereignty over the moon and other stars on which men might land would surely be a more attractive prospect than extending national jurisdictions and quarrels into outer space. Actually it has been suggested that the "territorial" air space of nations, like their territorial water, will have some defined limit, let us say twenty-five miles high. Higher up, U.N. satellites might orbit in U.N. space, serving global communications and disarmament verification.

Eventually more far-reaching steps might be possible, such as granting a United Nations body automatic jurisdiction and power of compulsory arbitration over all interstate conflicts. One day the United Nations might even promulgate world law, its courts try the violators, and its police force enforce the law. But much can be achieved before the distant day the United Nations acquires global sovereignty, and achieving these more limited goals would bring the day closer.

Global Security—Through the United Nations?

Any discussion of the United Nations' role in preventing wars and advancing disarmament sooner or later leads to the question of an international police force. The question arises because most of those who favor an international police force also believe in total disarmament *now*, and hence need a power to point to as a guarantor of law and order as national ones presumably disappear. This, it has been suggested earlier, may well be a fruitless approach, since the demands of such a force are so high that, far from commanding support, they tend to associate the whole idea with utopian dreams.

But the real question is not whether we should or should not have an international police force. It has become increasingly clear that the more ambitious plans, in the short run, are neither feasible nor necessary for limitation of arms and progress toward interbloc accommodation. Eventually a U.N. peace force might well be "assembled" from a large number of smaller units.

Some ingenious suggestions have been made for the gradual evolution of the central international police force, though even these are not easy to come by. The purpose of this force would eventually be to *protect* disarmed countries from each other; hence it will have to be stronger than their internal security forces (each country is expected to maintain a small force to counter criminals, or to prevent a mass march across the border to attack another country, even with pitchforks and walking sticks). Later, perhaps much later, the U.N. force would also *enforce* disarmament by investigating information about violations, imposing fines for minor violations, and, it has been suggested, destroying—even by bombing if necessary—illicitly constructed military facilities.[9]

Both far-reaching and gradual suggestions to strengthen U.N. operations require increased financial resources for that organization, whose regular budget is still smaller than that of New York City's sanitation department, i.e., about eighty million dollars in 1963. In the past, many U.N. activities, for instance peace-keeping operations in the Congo, suffered from lack of funds. Not all the additional activities suggested require large funds; extension of student exchanges, for one, requires relatively little additional expenditure. Other activities might be expected to pay for themselves, such as the provision of a U.N. communications network, which might charge for commercial use. (Though even this is complicated because of the objections of private companies and the need for initial investments.) A few activities might even be a source of profit, such as the control of some international waterways and mining concessions to be given on U.N.-owned high seas. It has also been suggested that the nations might give the United Nations permanent endowments, the income from which will be used for peace-keeping activities, to avoid the implicit veto in refusing to finance a specific peace-keeping operation as it comes up. Many citizens of different nations have expressed, in public-opinion polls, their willingness to pay a small tax directly to the United Nations, though so far their respective governments have been less favorable to this

9 Arthur I. Waskow (*et. al.*), *Quis Custodiet? Controlling the Police in a Disarmed World* (Washington, D.C.: Peace Research Institute, 1963).

idea, an attitude that might change. Other sources of revenue that have been suggested include increased government allowances and permitting citizens to make direct contributions to specific U.N. agencies (as they now may to UNICEF).[10]

The financing of U.N. activities embraces only one facet of the relationship between the United Nations and the global economy. Many suggestions have been forwarded for global economic rationalization. Since most of them can be carried out either by the United Nations or by independent global organizations, they are discussed separately here, without going into the question of jurisdiction.

TOWARD A WORLD ECONOMY

There are few aspects of East-West relations where the duopolistic approach is more completely intact and fully enforced than in the economic field. The United States has long exerted pressure to divide the world into two trading zones —one Communist and one non-Communist—and to keep trade between them at a minimum. On the face of it, the United States limits only the trading activities of Americans and forbids only the selling to Communist countries of a relatively limited list of strategic materials. In addition, the United States has disallowed practically all trade with Cuba and Communist China. In effect, Americans who seek to trade with a Communist country need an export license, and these, it is known, are difficult to obtain for most products (other than those consumer goods, in which the Communist countries are not interested). The United States also forbids the extension of credit to countries that have not completed the repayment of their war debts to the United States, which the U.S.S.R. has not.[11]

[10] John G. Stoessinger, "Financing the United Nations," *International Conciliation*, November 1961, pp. 50 ff.
[11] The 1934 Johnson Act.

The United States has further induced its NATO allies to curb much of their trade with the East, and put pressure on non-NATO countries, from Brazil to Japan, to refrain from trading with Communist countries. Ships that haul cargo to Cuba have been blacklisted and refused entry into American ports. Several allies broke the line; Canada has traded with China, Cuba, and Russia; Japan increased its trade with China. But the over-all picture shows that trade between Communist and non-Communist countries has remained on a low level; only 4 per cent of the trade of underdeveloped countries was with the Soviet bloc, and an even smaller percentage of the total Communist countries' trade was with the United States.[12]

Two reasons for American efforts to maintain separate trading zones are particularly relevant to the general study of U.S. strategy. One is the assumption that if nonaligned, underdeveloped countries become trade partners of the Communist bloc, this will lead to their subjugation; the other is the belief that Communist trade with the United States and Western Europe strengthens the Communist regimes. Both assumptions fit well into duopoly, but neither is defensible if stabilization of free competition is desired.

The underdeveloped countries are rejecting American pressures against trade with Communist states; many of them have increased their trade with the East. Sometimes this trade has, in effect, been forced by the West, as in 1955 when Egypt suddenly could not find an outlet for cotton, its major export crop, and Russia offered to buy it. In other cases it was a question of finding the additional export markets that most

[12] *New York Times*, September 29, 1963. Many factors other than American pressure account for this low level, including the inferior quality and poor standardization of many Communist products; the conduct of trade through state monopolies, to which Western firms are unaccustomed; and Soviet shortage of hard foreign currency, and the lack of products the West is interested in. Our discussion, however, focuses, as does the rest of this volume, on the aspects of American policy involved.

of these countries seek. In still others, the U.S.S.R. offered better terms and lower prices on products also sold by the West, trying either to attain political advantages or to break into a market, or—which should by no means be excluded— because some products in which it has a relative advantage are more cheaply produced in the U.S.S.R. The most important fact, however, is that even when this trade with Communist countries was at its highest, even when the Soviet-sold machines were accompanied by technicians sent to set them up, and even when the U.S.S.R. held all the spare parts, the trade did not lead in a single case to the subjugation of the trading country. The myth must be laid to rest once and for all: trade—unlike investment—is not an instrument by which a country can be brought to its knees, as long as the West is ready to provide products the East might decide suddenly to cut off.

No less important is the fact that pressure on countries to refrain from trade with the East undermines an important area of peaceful competition. It is quite proper for the West to offer better terms or products; that is competition. But to generate political pressure to forego or sharply limit trade with the East is to block one major mode of peaceful engagement of the East in the world community.

Limitations on trade, it also must be noted, consolidate not only the West, but the Eastern bloc as well. This was shown in the early sixties, as the European Common Market began to erect barriers against trade with East European countries. This forced the Eastern countries to trade more with each other in anticipation of future developments, and brought, for the first time, some life into the Communist countries' economic union.

Above all, it is said, American-Russian trade is curbed in order not to strengthen the Communist regime. In the fall of 1963 the U.S.S.R. bought large amounts of wheat from

Canada and Australia, and offered to buy wheat from the United States. This brought up once more the whole trade debate. Those who opposed the deal stated that the very need for such purchases in the West indicated the failure of the Soviet agricultural system, and, in effect, the whole method of planned economy; that at precisely this point, when the Soviet people have insufficient bread, the West would be aiding the Communist regime, and perhaps even saving it from being overthrown, if it stepped in and provided food. Disintegration from within, accelerated by duopoly from without, is still a potent theme in American strategy toward the U.S.S.R. when trade is concerned.

What are the facts? First, part of the wheat bought is to be allocated to Cuba and some East European countries that are traditional wheat buyers since they specialize in the production of other products. Second, Soviet agricultural planning is indeed faulty, but there was also the factor of unusually bad weather. However, even if the United States did not sell a single bushel of wheat to the Russians, the Soviet masses would not go hungry and the regime would not collapse. Soviet agriculture has passed through much deeper crises in the forty-six years since the Communists gained control—and in periods when the regime was much less popular, and the amount of other produce available much smaller. The simplistic notion that an otherwise firmly established regime, in command of an effective police system, after a generation and a half of educational and propaganda efforts, and followed by a substantial increase in the standard of living and some liberalization, will collapse because of some passing shortage in one, even a basic, product, is naïve indeed.

Other statements against selling wheat to the U.S.S.R. and increased interbloc trade in general, are even less well founded. Professor Strausz-Hupé worried that American wheat sales would enable the Soviets to hide the failure of their agriculture,[13] which would be quite a trick in view of the headlines the offer itself generated, not to mention actual American shipment to the U.S.S.R. and Khrushchev's announcement of the offer to the Russian people. Senator Dodd complained that "every bushel of wheat we ship . . . will divert manpower from the farms into the Soviet military machine."[14] Since the Soviets already have twice as many troops as the West and have not used these forces on any massive scale for at least fifteen years, one wonders what these additional farm hands would do in the army. Moreover, would such a shift not make the U.S.S.R. dependent on extensive U.S. favors every time the weather destroys a crop? Finally, to purchase wheat, corn, and other such products, the U.S.S.R. is using up significant parts of its foreign currency and gold reserves. The Russians have a trade deficit with non-Communist countries as it is. Hence if these resources are spent on buying agricultural products, they cannot be used to buy raw materials and machines, products more directly related to their military potential.

The more generic issue should be faced. The major decision —to trade or not to trade in nonstrategic materials—ought to be an integral part of general strategy; the trade policy must fit into, not contradict, it. If the United States continues to hope for and work toward disintegration of the Soviet system rather than seeking peaceful coexistence, then duopoly in general, including sharp limitation of trade, will be called for. But if the United States wishes to engage the Soviet Union in a peaceful competition and integrate it into one international community, expansion of trade is called for. This in itself will not disrupt blocs or bind nations irrevocably; it will provide for a lowering of bloc barriers, an increase in contacts between East and West, some new interest in the

---

13 *New York Times*, October 6, 1963.
14 *Ibid.* October 4, 1963.

peaceful state of affairs necessary for trade, and an increase in commitment to global machinery to provide the appropriate facilities. One can be for duopoly and against trade, or one can support a strategy of competition and interbloc trade; but favoring a shift to peaceful competition and being against expansion of interbloc trade is a policy whose inconsistency can be explained more readily by the narrow considerations of domestic politics and the specific influence of affected companies that fear increased competition, than by the real interests of the West or the world.

Very much the same considerations apply to sharing, as against dividing, other instruments of economic policy. Several examples might be briefly touched upon. In 1963 the Kennedy Administration initiated various negotiations to reduce tariffs and quotas that stand in the way of free trade among nations. While some of these were oriented toward easing trade in general, by far the most important were between the United States and its European allies. To some degree the African associates of the European Common Market were to benefit, and some effort was made not to penalize other countries, such as Japan and the Latin American states, but the Communist countries were largely omitted. The consequence, it has already been suggested, has been to increase the dependence of Eastern European countries on Moscow and on their economic integration with each other, thus consolidating Eastern-bloc relations. This is not a policy conducive to the building of a world community. Soviet proposals for a world-trade conference, supported by many nonaligned nations in the United Nations, were first ignored and then evaded by the West.

The United States, in order to help the developing countries, has recently supported various agreements to protect the prices of major items these countries export, to prevent high fluctuations and to prevent a further decline. The mechanisms used are complex, since there are several products (coffee, cacao, tin, and others) and a large variety of schemes is employed to protect their prices. In some of the products the U.S.S.R. is neither a major consumer nor a major producer, e.g., coffee; in others, it is a more important factor, e.g., tin. The question is, whether the U.S.S.R. is to be included in such arrangements or to be excluded.

The general tendency in the past has been to exclude the Communist countries. But if the strategy of competition is to be more earnestly pursued, the East should be asked to participate in these regulatory bodies set up to guide the world economy; and for two reasons. Generally, the more global institutions the Soviet-led camp is involved in, the more integrated the world community and the more stabilized peaceful competition become. Specifically, many of these regulations cannot, in the long run, be adequately implemented if the East does not cooperate. Recent Soviet pressure on Western regulation of the markets and prices of oil is one example, its effect on the prices of tin, another.

Other matters of economic regulation in which the East should be included if the competition strategy is followed concern the monetary system of the world. Here differences in the structure of the economies and governments often pose serious technical difficulties, but learning to overcome them is essential if the road toward world economic authorities is to be opened.

A recent study of the world economy by a leading Dutch economist, published by the American Twentieth Century Fund, goes much further and lists the following new sets of tasks the United Nations should carry out:[15] "The United Nations could formulate the *main aims* of world economic policy and prepare, at regular intervals, five- or ten-year fore-

[15] Jan Tinbergen, *Shaping the World Economy* (New York: Twentieth Century Fund, 1963).

casts of economic development. On the basis of these studies, the *annual discussion* in the Economic and Social Council of the United Nations could be given more operative importance. Following the example of OEEC, *national policies* may be discussed with a view to convincing governments of the overriding importance of world aims." This would amount to world planning by the United Nations, since modern practice is not to issue a master plan, which the economic enterprises are then expected to follow, but the more gentle art of indicating the economy's needs, pointing out the production plans of other units, and persuading rather than ordering harmonization. In the near future such planning (or programming, as it is often called) by the United Nations seems unlikely; most countries have not yet succeeded in introducing it on the national level and quite a few still object to it in principle, as excessive government interference. But this is not to imply that one day the world economy will not be programmed from one global center.

One item, frequently discussed by those who favor building up global economic ties, is the administration of foreign aid through the United Nations (or some other universal organization) rather than by individual states. The recipient countries in particular are anxious to rid themselves of the political strings implicitly or explicitly attached to bloc-country aid. They also hope to gain a larger say in the allocation of funds. Some aid is already given through the United Nations, but this is only 1 per cent of the total granted. (Part of it is dispersed through organizations with titles and charters that make them look as if they were universal but that are actually under Western influence; the World Bank, for instance.) Any increase in the amount of aid channeled through genuine global organizations will have many of the benefits the recipient countries expect, and will also increase the significance of the global organization. But there are two major disadvantages that, at least for the near future, seem to me to outweigh all expected benefits.

First of all, the amount of aid given by both camps stopped growing in 1962–63. The major reason is that the dominant motivations for granting aid have been national and bloc interests, and, even as things are, both the U. S. Congress and the Soviet leadership seem to feel increasingly that the relation between aid given and political yields obtained is vague, and the yields that can be established are not big enough. If the aid were taken out of the interbloc competition, it is doubtful that either the United States or the U.S.S.R. would have sufficient motivation to provide more than a fraction of the sums granted so far. If the aid were given by the United Nations, it would have to be based largely on humanitarian considerations and the general benefit to be gained from the strengthening of the world community which would hopefully ensue. Surely the recipient countries would prefer to receive U.N. aid rather than American or Russian aid, but that might entail sacrificing most of what they now get.

Secondly, unlike opening the routes for trade, regulating primary commodity prices, and building world monetary facilities—all of which provide rules or institutions *in which* the competition is to be conducted—aid is a major *means* by which that competition is waged. Turning it into a means provided by the community, rather than an instrument the sides use individually to advance their causes peacefully, might, at this stage at least, make the means of peaceful competition dangerously meager and increase the pressure to employ more lethal means. There are many other areas in which economic cooperation can be advanced on the global level. Perhaps when those are more nearly exhausted, the world community will be strong enough for the sides to provide substantial aid on a joint, noncompetitive basis, and the conflict will have subsided enough not to require even this outlet. Meanwhile, it probably would be best if, while some additional aid were channeled through the United Nations, the sides continued to compete vigorously over who gives more, on better terms, to more "have-not" nations.

REGIONAL UNIFICATION AND SECURITY

The success of the European Common Market has generated new interest in regional organizations and is a source of concern to those who seek a global community and fear that regional communities will become only nations writ large. The tendency of some regional organizations to be exclusive clubs that turn down new applicants and pursue a narrow economic policy of forwarding their community while refusing to cooperate with others adds worry to concern.

I believe, on the other hand, that regional unification is generally beneficial to the growth of the world community. For such a community to be formed, people have to be able to reach agreements on what form it is to take and what course it is to follow. Experience suggests that the diversity of approaches and interests of 120 nations is so large as to make agreement next to impossible. The reduction of the number of nations acting independently might eventually lead to twenty-odd regional units instead of the present 120 national ones. Even some tensions between the emerging regional groupings are not necessarily a detrimental factor, as these accelerate their internal consolidation. The fact that nations first integrate to counter and to compete with each other will not necessarily prevent their later cooperation on a global level.[16] In short, I see the development of most regional (and subregional) unifications as a stepping stone toward the world community.

There are several criteria by which the variety of emerging unification movements—from the Organization of African

[16] These processes are explored in my *Political Unification: A Comparative Study of Leaders and Forces* (forthcoming).

States to the Central American Common Market to the Federation of Malaysia—can be judged in regard to their potential effect on the world community: (a) Organizations that cut across the Eastern and Western blocs' boundaries and include countries of both camps are more conducive to global community than those that consolidate within the blocs. Unfortunately none of the existing regional organizations has yet satisfied this criterion. (b) Open organizations, willing to accept new members, are preferable to closed groupings, though there is a limit beyond which further increases in membership impair effective operation. (c) Economic and political unions are preferable to purely military alliances, since the latter tend to disintegrate as the external danger passes and only rarely serve as the foundation on which economic and political cooperation can be firmly established. (Hence the limited success of NATO, a military organization, in serving as a community builder, as compared to the European Coal and Steel Community, the forerunner of the European Economic Community.) (d) Of great importance are provisions for keeping the external barriers of the new unions as low as possible to make it as easy as possible for them, at a later stage, to integrate with each other and, most important, to increase their cooperation with international organizations, especially the United Nations, to serve as building stones of a world community and not as obstacles to its growth.

The formation of regional communities and organizations is no longer an empty dream but a growing reality. There have been many failures, as too-ambitious plans were launched or inexperience impaired early efforts, but the general trend is unmistakably toward more regional unification. The early sixties have witnessed the emergence of many new nations, and the impression was created that this stream would continue. Actually the pattern is almost at an end, and in the late sixties unifications might well exceed secessions and the formation of new nations. New regional organizations, mainly of the economic type, have already been formed in Asia, Africa, and Latin America, while the development of the Eastern European economic organization slowly gains in importance.

One of the most promising ideas concerning regional organizations is that of regional arms reduction and regional security forces. The most widely discussed plan is for denuclearized zones, that is, groups of countries that commit themselves not to produce or possess, nor allow other countries to place, nuclear weapons in their territory. Several leading Latin American countries have declared their eagerness to form a non-nuclear club; so have several African states. The U.S.S.R. has suggested a non-nuclear zone in the Far East and Central Europe. Such clubs would be of special value if the formation of regional non-nuclear groupings were to be accompanied by the foundation of some, however limited, regional inspection machinery, staffed jointly by the countries of the region. The machinery could later be extended to serve more ambitious arms-control or reduction programs.

Much depends, of course, on present conditions within the various regions. African countries, with some notable exceptions, have only small military forces. Here the main function of regional security would be to prevent local arms races and the investment of scarce resources in oversized military establishments. In other areas, such as Latin America, arms reduction is called for.

Following in the footsteps of an agreement between outside powers not to ship arms into a region (or a commitment by the region's countries not to accept them), to be verified by regional patrols, the countries of a region might engage in multilateral arms reduction. Argentina and Brazil, for instance, are carefully keeping an eye on each other's armed forces, each increasing its own forces relative to increases by the other. Under such a plan, these nations would instead reduce their arms in some coordinated fashion, without disturbing the relative balance. (This would require these countries to be in the hands of civilian governments, both strong enough to carry out such a plan and interested in weakening their respective military establishments. The likelihood of a stable domestic situation would be enhanced if regional security demonstrates that no national dangers are involved in cutting down the military establishments.)

The formation of a regional police force would be an even more advanced arrangement; it would allow either the complete elimination of national military and police forces or at least their reduction to limited small internal-security forces. The regional force would be in charge of protecting the existing borders (which might require a prior settling of border disputes), enforcing arms-reduction measures, and possibly contributing to internal security. These forces could later serve as units of the U.N. peace force and be integrated into its command as it evolved. It has even been suggested, somewhat on the imaginary side, that the forces of one region, let us say Africa, might be used to maintain the security of another, for example, Latin America, in exchange for Latin American units guarding Africa. All these plans could be implemented long before there was a U.N. peace force large enough to check the major blocs.

Regional forces would have many advantages. They would supplement the remote deterrence forces and make armed invasion or subversion of any one country much more difficult. At a later stage, the fact that the smaller powers had already reduced their arms would facilitate big-power conventional arms reductions,[17] assuming, of course, that the regional forces are integrated into a U.N. force. No less important is that regional security arrangements would make

[17] See Chapter V, above.

wars between the countries of the region practically impossible (and hence should be accompanied by regional machinery for the peaceful settlement of conflicts) and would enhance democratic, or at least civilian, governments, by weakening if not abolishing national military establishments.

WINNING WITHOUT WAR

Many plans have been sketched in this book; many others are circulated in governmental circles and in formal as well as informal contacts between East and West. Still others could and will be devised. The significance of each plan in itself is small; what are important are the ideas behind it, and the principles it illustrates. Given a Cold War, arms-race context, the details of our optimistic scenario are but words written on the stale air of duopoly; given a different context, they might become part of the wind of change, introducing a fresher atmosphere. The context, though, is not arbitrarily set. It is determined in part by governments, political leaders, voters, and strategists; in part, it is the total result of a variety of interacting trends, which no one group controls.

The rise of global pluralism, reflected in the rebellion of the bloc lieutenants and in the increased size and weight of the nonaligned camp; the increasing danger of nuclear weapons in general and nuclear anarchy in particular; the changed nature of the Soviet-led camp and its foreign policy, as limited, tentative, and expedient as it initially may have been; and the determination of the Kennedy and Johnson Administrations to increase U.S. capacity to compete peacefully with the Communist movement for the leadership of the progressive forces in the underdeveloped continents and to initiate the reversal of the nuclear arms race, all point in one direction. The conditions are ripe and the context has been provided for the stabilization of peaceful competition. The Western attempt to freeze the division of the world into two spheres of influence, with the many specific policy conclusions that followed, has already been in part discarded. New steps to rule out the use of arms in the global contest are at hand, and the instruments necessary to enforce commitments to compete without arms are increasingly available.

Still, much of the transformation has yet to take place. The world is still poised uneasily on the nuclear brink. Any major mistake, as President Kennedy often pointed out, might take the lives of hundreds of millions of people on both sides, if not put an abrupt end to human life on this planet. There will be no safe world until nuclear bombs yield their deadly contents to atoms-for-peace, and long-range missiles serve for the delivery of mail, scientific explorations, and the launching of communications satellites. Arms have often provided a stalemate, never a lasting peace. Collisions have been delayed, but sooner or later there has always been a government that tried to win a war. The age of nuclear weapons has not brought sudden maturity to man or turned governments into wise and restrained repositories of power. Until peaceful competition between the powers of the earth is stabilized, peace will be tenuous and nuclear war will lurk in the shadows. The road is long, and the labor monumental; but because the world is driven by the fear of mushroom clouds drifting over radioactive continents, and attracted by the prospects of a world without war, the transition has been initiated and might be completed.

Victory is not in sight, but there are growing signs that it is no longer beyond our reach. When the trumpets are sounded next time, it could be a new kind of victory; not of nation over nation, men over men, but of Man over fear and bombs, over starvation and epidemics, over tyrannies and police terror. Competition, Americans have known for generations, is not an instrument for one participant to subjugate the other, but a challenge to all. Ultimately, competition advances values which benefit all competitors more than it enriches any one of them. The victory of peaceful competition will not be the triumph of a nation or a bloc, but of stable peace, social justice, and freedom; these can win without war.

INDEX

Accident, war by, 167–68, 175 ff
Adenauer, Konrad, 59, 61
Afghanistan, 104, 109, 149
Africa, 24, 78–82, 100–1, 119, 123, 219, 254; Communist broadcasts to, 21; and denuclearized zone, 87; foreign aid to, 56 (see also specific countries); and large social groupings, 228; Soviet air routes denied, 158; and U.N., 80, 87, 121–22, 123, 231, 255. See also specific countries
Agrarian reform, 120. See also Intervention for progress; specific countries
Aid, foreign, 83, 115–44 passim, 145–46, 151, 152, 160, 251–52; European, 56; Soviet, 149, 157, 251. See also Technical assistance; specific countries
Airlines, commercial, 158, 178
Airman (publication), 98
Air power. See specific countries, planes
Albania, 29, 37, 89 n, 109
Alexander, Robert J., 143 n
Algeria, 82, 90, 154–55; aid to, 99; Ben Bella's program for, 130; F.L.N. in, 39; war in, 40, 69, 116–17, 122
Alliance for Progress, 120, 127–28, 146
Allies and nonallies, differences between, 105
Almond, Gabriel A., 9 n
America. See United States
Analogue of automotive industry, 24–27, 71–72, 178–79
Anglo-Saxon countries, 24, 41, 46. See also West, the; specific countries
Angola, 121–22, 123
Ann Arbor, Mich., 173
Antarctica, 240
Anti-Americanism. See United States; specific anti-American countries, groups

Anticolonialism, 24, 116 ff, 120, 124; record of U.S., 120–24. See also Alliance for Progress; etc.; specific colonies, countries
Antimissile missiles, 174, 192
Antisubversion networks, Western, 90
APRA, 119, 133
Arab countries, 238. See also Egypt; etc.
Argentina, 111, 135; and Antarctica, 240
Armed invasion: Soviet use of, 14 ff. See also specific invasions
Armed subversion: Soviet use of, 14 ff. See also specific countries
Arms, 164–214, 215 ff, 254–55; control, 179–81, 193, 194, 196, 254; duopoly and (see Duopoly); embargoes on (see Remote deterrence); providing of (see Remote deterrence; specific countries); reduction, 181–214, 254–55; for Soviet expansion, 14–18. See also Bombers; Defense; Deterrence; Disarmament; NATO; Nuclear weapons; etc.; specific countries, wars
Arms Control and Disarmament Agency, 196
Arnold, H. J. P., 19–20 n
Arosemena, Juan Demóstenes, 111
Asia, 24, 56, 95–96, 119, 146; regional organizations in, 254; and remote deterrence, 100, 104; voting in U.N., 80, 231. See also specific countries
Aspaturian, Vernon V., 16 n, 77 n
Associated Press, 120
Aswan Dam, 79
Atlantic Assembly of Parliamentarians, 44
Atlantic partnership, proposals and plans for, 42–63
Atomic weapons. See Nuclear weapons
Australia, 246
Austria, 91–94, 100, 109